I won't give you a leg up, Mr Death

Arunabha Sengupta

Vitastaa
Let Knowledge Spread

Published by
Renu Kaul Verma
Vitastaa Publishing Pvt Ltd
2/15, Ansari Road, Daryaganj
New Delhi - 110 002
info@vitastapublishing.com

ISBN 978-93-82711-89-6

Cover and layout by Vits Press
Printed by Vikas Computer and Printers

Dedication

To

My family, own and

extended through my patients

Two roads diverged in a wood, and I—
I took the one less traveled by,
And that has made all the difference.

Robert Frost
The Road Not Taken

Some days later, he became aware of a sky lighting up gradually and the light passing through his closed eyelids. He was crossing the westward rays of a rising sun during his eastward flight, and if there could be a precise moment when a new day could be said to have begun, it was now. The dark sky turned crimson at first. Soon the light of the sky would spread to the earth and the sleepy towns and villages would wake up one after another. The next town to cross would have woken up earlier than the town already passed because the sun rises in the east. It would still be a long flight that would cross over continents, over mountains, and over deserts and seas, to finally reach the land, which has thousand-year-old shrines and temples and a tradition old enough not to begrudge his homecoming, after a mere forty years of absence.

Author's Note

'Those who are diseased and down, they are also fighting.' A poet, himself a cancer patient, told me once. 'It is also wrong to assume that the patients think of their diseases only. They think of many other things,' he said. Many of them remain alive to their aspirations and dreams, respond to tenderness, fall in love; a few resolve not to allow the disease to dominate their lives.

This story is a fictionalised account of one such person, who was determined not to let the fear of death make him beg to persist at any cost. About the place, time, and characters of the story —the places described are all real, only blurred to some extent to keep them free from the vulgarities of a memoir. The time is the transition time in India, in late nineties, when internet and cellular phones were things of everyday use for some people, while for some others they were still distant dreams; when new dynamics were emerging in political and social fields, health care was transforming itself from a service to an industry, and Calcutta was yet to become Kolkata. The characters are mostly imaginary barring a few who have barged in from real life with so much authority that the descriptions of incidents concerning them had to be true to the minutest details as they had happened. To tell their parts of the story, in fact, there was no need to invent much.

There was, of course, need to borrow, for literature's sake, and to glean facts from different sources to adhere to the specifics as truly as possible. The borrowings have all been acknowledged in the story, in some way or the other. For the sources, even a very short list must include: *Kochbeharer Itihas* (In Bengali) by Bhagavati Charan Banerjee; *Bhawaia* (in Bengali) by Dr Sukha Bilas Burman; *Uttarbange Rajbanshi Samajer Debdebi O Puja-parban* (in Bengali), a PhD thesis by Shri Girijashankar Roy; *Teesta Parer Birtanta* and *Teesta Puran* (Bengali novels) by Shri Debesh Roy; *West Bengal District Gazeteer, Jalpaiguri*, published by Shri Barun De, 1981; *Koch Rajbanshi and Kamtapuri the truth unveiled* , by Nalini Ranjan Ray, a PDF publication by Centre for Koch Rajbanshi Studies and Development (CKRSD), Guwahati, 2013; *Kamtapur and The Koch Rajbanshi Imagination* by Arupjyoti Das. I also made free use of various websites and information available on the net. For spelling of Bengali words and proper nouns I have used the older and more commonly used spellings, thus preferring Serampore over Srirampur or Srirampore , Rajbanshi over Rajbongshi, and likewise.

And lastly, the title of the book comes from slight alteration of a line from the poem *Conscientious Objector* by Edna St Vincent Millay, published in *Wine from These Grapes* by Harper Brothers, 1934.

I owe huge debts of gratitude to the families whose private stories I have appropriated and adapted, to Renu Kaul Verma for putting her head and heart behind the publication, to Veena Batra for painstakingly editing the manuscript, to some friends who read the draft and nodded encouragement, to my cousins whom I quizzed to ascertain various details without telling them why, to my niece for presenting me that thingamabob that I used less as a phone but more as a dictionary, and to my wife, who did not read the book but was still able to comment.

One

The vision he saw was that of a turbulent river whooshing through, foaming and rustling around large rocks and boulders, along a deep chasm between two ledges of a hill. Much above the water, slanting sunrays were passing through the slim tendrils of a cement and concrete latticework that bridged the land on both sides of the arroyo. Before he could trudge down a bushy path and go nearer, he heard a voice. The sounds of a person calling out, faint and distant at first and then louder and nearer, entered into his ears, followed by a jolt and then there was a sense of motion. He woke up just in time to see the wide door of a well-lit room sliding open for his trolley-bed and then shutting itself tight. Inside the room, robot arms dropped down from the ceiling and devices all around him came alive one by one with blinks and beeps. Outside, the April morning had started cold and somehow a chill crept in from there. As he waited on the operation table for his biopsy procedure to begin, he felt cold and uncomfortable.

2

He tried to blanket out the chill by thinking about a sunlit valley with a clear blue sky where butterfly gliders were setting off from green-blue ledges. He, though, thought about his wrangling friends, about his red spits that looked so vulgar in the washbasins against the white of the porcelain. A monitor started to beep near his head to report every time his heart pumped blood through him and his thoughts raced back to an evening seven years ago when he, drunk and befuddled, had thrown up and passed out in a hospital cubicle at the bedside of his comatose wife, with machines beeping around her, just hours before she died.

Dr Lammertt removed the prop he had inserted between his teeth and mumbled to the nurse. He simultaneously closed his mouth and opened his eyes and blinked immediately, blinded by the bright light focused on his face. He turned his face sideways and, through a misty haze covering his eyes, saw the nurse tossing a bit of tissue from his tongue into a small blue plastic container.

'It will be three days before we know what is what so I'm fixing a consultation for you on Thursday,' Dr Lammertt said when he discharged his patient later in the evening. The aged doctor, himself looking somewhat out of place in this steel and glass futuristic University Hospital, appeared irritated that this man had no one to accompany him to the clinic. The burly middle-aged man simply shrugged. He, Kanu Chatterjee, an old hand in the advertising business in Amsterdam, could not possibly ask his partners Godlef or Rykaard to accompany him. Not when they were about to split their advertising business after twenty-five years.

Outside, the sky was dark but lights blazed in and around the stout square buildings. Beyond them were the city lights, blinkers on taller buildings. The old city of Amsterdam, the moods and bearings of which he had been photographing for thirty years now, was livening up to another night of revelries but it all appeared strangely unfamiliar to

Kanu this evening. As he sauntered to the parking lot, a distinct feeling of brittleness accompanied him, as if some one had punched a hole in his body and his vitals were seeping through. A group of workmen in blue overalls passing by seemed to watch him. Two elderly women looking confused were about to ask him for directions but then they did not. People moving on the road appeared strange, distanced, as if they were observing him from the other side of a divide.

A leaflet fluttered under one wiper of the windshield of his car. The heading in large bold types read. 'Jesus is great: Two years of penance for all your sins.'

Penance! Kanu stared at the word for a full minute. It looked like a bomb with a burning fuse, about to explode on him.

'God dammit,' he cried. Three men casually crossing the outbound lane jumped and cursed as his car pulled out abruptly from the parking lot. The car began to wander through the back streets of Amstelveen. It slowed in front of a small house fronted by a lawn with a thinly laid gravelled walk leading up to its ill painted, drab door. That door once had a bad lock that often refused to open. Kanu, when he stayed as a paying guest in that house years ago, had suffered many anxious moments to get it right. The car turned right and Kanu remembered there had been a laundromat once. Opposite to that, there used to be a small eatery. Farther down the street, there would be the house, the only all-white house with hollyhocks in the garden in that street. Once his home, now sold.

Verdic greeted Kanu in the foyer of their apartment building where every floor was the same as the others above or below it, and the staircases were wide so the furniture did not require to be hoisted up through the windows. Verdic, now employed as their caretaker, had been one of the squatters who once occupied these apartment houses and had fought with the police. He lived alone but always talked about some family in

Utrecht. Verdic extended a hand. 'That is lot of grocery you got there. Do you want me to help with them?' He looked very displeased though. 'It's bad news again about my brother. They are going to cut him up again,' he complained shaking his head.

There was mild pain at the biopsy site now and Kanu did not want to talk but with Verdic there was no need to talk back to keep a conversation going. Verdic believed in telling stories in full, morals and all. His narrations, therefore, would include many other smaller stories, amazing facts about life and of course his personal opinions. All that was required to make him continue was to raise half an eyebrow or stretch a lip.

Verdic spat in a nearby bin, emitting thick brown globs of tobacco stained saliva and resumed. 'He can't keep down the food he takes, throws it up again. The operation did him no good. He should've tried other measures. I asked him to go to a doctor in Utrecht and all he had to do was to take some tea potions. Who cares if you have got cancer or whatever so long you can hold your drink and manage some mouthfuls?' He took a few packets from Kanu's hand and began to clamber up the stairs behind him. Kanu walked up slowly. There was no hurry to open the door to his apartment — the rooms behind which would be dark, unoccupied, and unkempt like a cave. Without any flowers, fresh from the garden and fragrant. He had shifted to this apartment two years before. After his wife Ludwina's death, he and Nanu, their son, did try to keep a household going for sometime but gradually it became impossible.

Then one evening, 'Dad, do you remember my telling you about the job in USA I applied for? To the Excel Bridge company?'

They were setting the table for dinner. Kanu had cooked rice and chicken. Ludwina used to cook Indian dishes often enough and Nanu liked them.

'Well, they mailed today. I've two weeks to join their office in New

Jersey. Do you think you'll be all right here alone?'

'Of course son, whatever is good for you.' They had sat side by side, eating slowly. Kanu had poured himself a large drink and listened to Nanu revealing a few details about the bridge construction company he would join. He looked happy. After Nanu had migrated, the decision to sell their house and moving to an apartment was almost predetermined.

Kanu heard Verdic slapping the door, 'The book of future has seven locks but these people know.' He was concluding his story about a healer he knew. That healer was a member of a secret cult, repository of much ancient wisdom, Verdic whispered before he left.

There was no need to cook. No solid food for two days, the doctor had advised. The magazine, which Kanu bought with the groceries at the provision store because of the headlines it flaunted, had two stories on persons battling fatal diseases. One was by a young woman, who felt that inside her there was a real person and it was important for that person to enjoy life. What good are those years, which one spends only in bed just for treatment? she had wondered.

'You got an argument there, lady,' Kanu smiled and with a red pen circled the name of the writer. An environmentalist had told the other story. It was about his hopping about from one hospital to another or at times between the beds of different departments of the same hospital. Yet, two years down that path, he still did not know if he was going to live or not. Kanu hastily put the magazine away; his ulcer might still turn out to be a simple ulcer. He had never been ill in his life. This was just a bad dream; by Thursday, he would laugh about it. He sat on the sofa and switched on the television. An advertisement jingled through, 'Your money makes money for you while you sleep.'

'Your money makes money for us. That's what you mean; don't you?' Kanu switched the television off. Through the door, his work desk in the side room was visible. Stacks of papers piled on it waited for attention.

Mostly computer printouts about the new business he was planning to set up. There would be mails to check. Kanu sighed. Had he not lost money in the stock market, he could do things he wanted to do. Now he would have to plan again. The thought terrified him. He had seldom planned. Life had not granted him that opportunity; almost always his fate had outwitted him to push him on unplanned journeys. At some point of time in his life, he began to distrust his own fate, began to think of going odd ways to get around it. His friends thought he was nuts, slapped the nickname 'fantast' on him. Ludwina often called him a woolgatherer, while he wished to be just another regular guy who brought the milk, helped with the laundry, and mowed the lawn.

A salty taste filled his mouth. Kanu went into the bathroom, spat, and then examined his spittle with a clinical eye. It was all red, looking dangerously more dense and bright. Kanu hastily opened the tap to wash away the stain and rinsed his mouth. After a thorough rinsing with an antiseptic gargle and cold water, the wash became clear. He felt better.

He had to call Nanu and tell him. That task worried him. Nanu had grown up grieving a mother squashed on a highway on her way home and then dying bit by bit in a hospital, but Kanu had never told him what had actually happened in the night she died. He had kept it a secret but that secret kept following him like a hound, always at his heels, to stalk him as a ghoul in every dark alley since that night.

Amsterdam at that time was passing through some bitterly cold days without any sun and Ludwina had been in the ICU for twenty-nine days, on ventilator support. She never did come round fully after her operation that went on through the entire night of the accident to mend her broken bones and torn viscera. All through that night, Kanu and Nanu had sat together shocked but hopeful, as everybody said they should be, because Ludwina did not die on the spot even after a heavy truck had hit her car. All hopes, with each passing day, though froze one after another and had to be put away. For twenty-nine days and nights, for them it was only a fearful gawking at a swathed heap buried among machines in a green-walled small cubicle. Then the doctors had started to talk in uncertain terms. They began to say that even if she survived, she would mostly be dead, without any speech, and without any movement. They could not say how long she might survive in that condition – for a few weeks or some months. The prospect scared Kanu. If one month had passed in this manner, then there could be another month, then another, and then gradually it might become a part of their life, his life, and then a routine ultimately. People had lived for years as mere vegetables before. A particular doctor was sympathetic. To help a patient to die, in such cases, he explained, was an honourable thing to do, infinitely kinder than to let one languish in a life that was no life at all. He had said to Kanu that Dutch laws took a lenient or even supportive view of such acts, done with compassion in one's heart for the final emancipation of a loved one, but still going through the legal route would be a long one. On the thirtieth day, Kanu had made a formal request to the doctor to find a way and then had gone to a bar near the hospital, a bar he had been frequenting for the past one month to cut short the endless inactive hours. There, sitting in a corner alone, after a while Kanu thought he had heard Ludwina speaking.

'I wouldn't have done this to you,' she was saying.

'I know,' Kanu had groaned. 'You and your Christian beliefs! All your saints and gospels, your stupid notions about preservation of life, salvation. Yes, you would've dragged me on, for years if necessary, even if I had no vanity left. What good would've that done to me? Or to you or to Nanu?'

The voice persisted. 'No one has the power to take another person's life.'

'You call that life? You would've been a pitiable heap, like a bag of sand.'

'Still it's killing a life. I'm worried about your soul Kanu, worried what this will make of you. What you're going to do is …'

'No. It isn't.' Kanu had cried out before Ludwina could utter the word Kanu thought she was about to say.

The waitress who had been serving Kanu throughout the afternoon had dashed to his table and leaned on it. 'What is it that isn't?' she had asked.

Kanu looked at her. She knew about the accident. They all knew about the accident — in that bar just a block away from the hospital, in the florist's shop from where he bought flowers for Ludwina everyday, in the hospital cafeteria where he used to sneak in for a bite — they all knew. The accident was in the news. The waitress had become familiar enough to start a conversation. They had talked before but that afternoon her query unsettled him. What was she suspecting Kanu to have done? As she leaned on his table and waited for an answer, Kanu felt all eyes in the bar were looking at him.

Were they accusing him? Could they not see that what he had done was in fact an act of mercy? He had ordered another double to get the girl off his back but then gulped it down quickly as he felt edgy and nervous every time someone looked at him. With a large bouquet in his hand, he had then gone straight to Ludwina's cabin to sit beside her and argue his case. Then the bile that was retching up through his gullet had begun to escape through his mouth and he vomited in that bouquet still clutched in his hand. A nurse found him sleeping with his head resting on the foot end of the bed, the white and purple carnations smeared with his vomit pressed under his face.

The hospital called him just before daybreak next morning and by the time he and Nanu entered Ludwina's by then silent cabin, she had developed a dusky blue colour. Her bed looked austere without all those machines crowding around her.

Nanu must not know about that secret and about the stories

that Godlef and Rykaard had spread about his losing money through speculations and gambling and then trying to make it up by brokering deals behind them. They even talked of a secret affair that they thought had made Kanu desperate. Kanu connected to his mail account and took sometime to draft a mail to Nanu. It would be easier to do so than calling him and running the risk of getting emotional. His homepage opened a search engine. Diffidently he typed, 'Miracle cures for cancer'.

***

First, it was a sense of suffocation and then an uncanny feeling. The feeling of some soft alien beings moving over his face disturbed him. Kanu tried to raise his head but could not. He tried to move his legs but they seemed to have become heavy, powerless to make any movement. There were movements on his legs. Some creatures crept down them and tugged at his toes. A terrible fright choked him. There were rats all over his body! Big furry rats were eating him alive. Why then did he not feel any pain? Was he dead? The soft bodies over his face began to smother him. He could not breathe. He fought to move his muscles, move his limbs, and finally with a great effort jerked his head away. Some broken and muffled guttural sounds entered his ears and slowly brought him back to a state of half wakefulness. He lay panting, exhausted. Then the thumping in his chest slowed down and his head cleared enough to realise that the sounds had emerged from his own throat; he had been sleeping with a pillow over his face. In the soft blue night-light, the rug covering his legs seemed to have mysteriously heaped up at places. He tried to get up but slumped back, shocked and terrified. He had been dreaming about being dead, alone in this room, big rats scurrying over his desolate body, biting off his toes.

He scurried to the bathroom. The wash from his mouth returned clear. At least the ulcer had not bled. This could well be a false alarm; the doctors might be wrong and they would admit that on Thursday.

He cocked a finger at his own reflection in the mirror in the closet. It still showed a man who looked younger than his fifty-eight years, without wrinkles or bags under the eyes, hair graying at the temples but not yet receding.

In the living room, Ludwina stared at him from the top of a cabinet. She was smiling with Kanu on her right and Nanu on her left. 'Ludwina Ludwig,' he whispered to the photograph, 'I came to this country following you from Norfolk to live a life and be happy. Look where I'm now, all twisted up like a misplaced knot. You're gone, Nanu is in another country, and Godlef and Rykaard are ganging up to squeeze me out.' He tapped on her lips. 'What should I do if on Thursday they say it is cancer? Must I be a burden to your dear boy?' He ran his fingers over her face, her forehead, her nose, and her mouth. He remembered an old wives' tale. If three people are in a photograph together then the one in the middle will die first.

It was now his turn to face death. Kanu stepped back and sat on a sofa. Who was that old gentleman pensively observing him from the other sofa? 'Is it you, Mr Death?' he asked softly. 'Not so soon, perhaps? People in this city easily live to be ninety years old. Besides, even if I have cancer, surely I can still have a few more years to live!' The figure on the other sofa continued to smile. It did not talk back.

Kanu felt annoyed. 'Don't threaten me,' he cried. He looked around his apartment. Every morning he would wake up alone in this apartment with a salty taste in his mouth and then would plod to the bathroom listening to the sounds of his own movements in the empty rooms. He would check his spittle, check his urine and feces, do a few exercises, and remember to take the pills to get him through another day that would inevitably end with a dinner with the *News at Nine*. News every hour, on the hour — the world appearing and disappearing via small windows and then being quickly translated into currency values — but with each passing day he knew less people to talk to. Now this gentleman would come to keep him company and he would have to pass wistful nights with more macabre dreams. How dreary it would be to worry all the time about what might happen in the days before he died.

'Okay, take me when you will,' he said to the apparition on the other sofa, 'but never in that manner.' He pointed his finger to Ludwina's photograph. 'What you did to her was awful.'

As he stood up and turned to go back to his bedroom, his throat constricted and tears welling up in his eyes made his vision unclear. His head reeled forcing him to lean back on the sofa and close his eyes to steady himself. As his hands gripped the arm of the sofa, his fingers clawed the fabric, gathering it in his clenched fists. After some moments, he raised his head, looked with a vague comprehension at the other sofa, and muttered with all the force he could muster, 'I won't give you a leg up, Mr Death. In no way.'

Two

'Dr Snow will see you now.' The words startled Kanu. He saw the lady assistant standing in front of him, waiting for him to get up. The way she pronounced the word 'now' seized him. The word seemed to echo, enlarging upon itself. *Now*! Kanu ruminated. Thursday, sixth April, 12.30 pm at a hospital in central Amsterdam, a girl in a deep blue blouse with white polka dots waiting to escort him to a judgment that would make him change track one more time in the course of his life. What was in this moment that he had to be here, in this moment that perhaps might be the two billionth one in his fifty-eighth blessed year — a moment that he could have passed in any other way, in any of the million different ways that a human being passes his life, like, say, buying a newspaper from an old lady at a small railway station while waiting for the train to come?

'Shall we go?' the lady asked again smiling but her smile seemed to be lost amidst the vast colourful area of the reception for outpatients. The light, coming through the large tinted windows and from the artfully hidden interior sources, matched the eerie silence of that huge hall.

'Good day. Please sit on that stool,' Dr Snow said with his thumb pointing backwards over his shoulder. Dr Snow sat with his back towards a very complicated looking steel cabinet, which held several instruments of glinting steel; thumb-thick black cables coiled around hooks dangled within the cabinet. A revolving stool meekly waited in front of that.

Kanu sat on the stool. With a deft push of his long legs, the doctor turned and propelled his chair to position himself in front of Kanu, and began to examine him. 'Wider, wider, lemmesee,' he purred and Kanu felt the touch of cold steel in his mouth as the doctor introduced an L-shaped instrument in his mouth. 'That looks fine, nothing more except that ulcer,' he said withdrawing the instrument.

The nurse, hovering near his side, quickly sprayed a medicine down Kanu's throat.

'Easy, easy, lemmesee,' Dr Snow purred again introducing one end of a black cable in his mouth and looking down an eyepiece. He looked grave when he withdrew this instrument. 'Your ulcer has extended posteriorly, that's more towards your throat than to the front of your mouth.'

'Does that make a difference?'

'A great deal, a great deal indeed, if we're going to operate.' The doctor discussed briefly his biopsy results and then began a commentary, 'Difficult to operate, to obtain negative margins all around... if your ulcer was a centimeter more to the front.' He snapped his fingers, '... would've been a happier story.'

'Is an operation a must? Is that the only way?'

'Why don't we ask Dr Seth, our radiotherapist about it? He is from India as you are. Let him see you and opine if radiation can help!' With another deft push he propelled himself to the table in the center and began to punch numbers on the telephone.

Dr Seth had calm eyes, an easy laugh, and fat fingers full of rings with large stones. Three days in a week, he spent in Brussels where he had family business of precious stones and diamonds. 'Where are you from?' he asked. 'I mean where from in India? We are from Varanasi. Not from Ahmedabad.'

Kanu could have said he was from Calcutta. That is what people usually do; when one's birthplace is rather obscure, they usually mention the big city nearby. Kanu however said, 'Serampore', his hometown, a small place on the same holy river as Dr Seth's birthplace. For some reason, the mere mention of his birthplace to this unknown man set him off on an impulsive blabbering about his life, about Ludwina and Nanu, about his leaving India. 'It's almost a lifetime ago that I left India and have never been back. I don't remember much,' he said at the end. 'Do you go there often?'

Dr Seth nodded. 'I do, to attend conferences but I always spend a night or two at our house in Varanasi, take a dip in the holy water and pour some on Baba Viswanath. This life and the next life both insured in one go.' He laughed and drummed on the table with his fingers. 'I might still go back when I retire. North Europe is too cold for old bones. They have many big hospitals in India now, catering to patients from the Middle East. Why, even patients from Europe go there now, not wanting to wait for a coronary bypass or a hip prosthesis. In fact, I am myself sitting on offers from some Indian hospitals with new machines.' He began to turn the ring with a large stone on the middle finger of his right hand as he read Kanu's file but kept on talking. 'I need to go there soon; the coming year will be bad for me. Moon will be in transition to Capricorn in another few weeks. I'm already feeling the effects. Has Dr Snow advised an operation?' he asked leaning back in his chair.

'Yes. That's what he suggested to me but he wanted your opinion.'

'Radiation can definitely be tried as a first option, along with a few shots of drugs, and perhaps a boost later. There are some initial reports about this new protocol, which are very encouraging. If it works, you retain a normal tongue.'

'Then why don't we do that?'

'That's an option for you but it depends on a lot of other things. You can always have another opinion. Dr Snow is a good man, a wise man, an experienced cancer surgeon but too nice to be a ruthless cutter. For your kind of disease, you would need a dynamic surgeon. You said your son is in USA. I can give you a letter if you want to consult this hospital in New York. They have the best head and neck surgeons in the world.'

Kanu watched as Dr Seth began to write a letter to a particular surgeon in New York in long hand. It seemed to Kanu that he was writing a very important letter, a letter that concerned him a great deal, perhaps even more than his patient. 'In the end it's God's will,' he said almost to himself. 'Pray to God and pray to your ancestors.' Dr Seth folded his hands and looked upwards.

From the parking lot, Kanu called Nanu. Driving back it occurred to him that Thursday was Verdic's off day. He could call him up to his apartment in the evening and offer him a drink.

Later, while waiting for Verdic he looked up through the window of his room. The dark canopy overhead seemed to enlarge and become more inestimable the more he looked at it. It was funny to think that some stars up there had decided his fate. He remembered one more thing. From a drawer he brought out his old cardholder and fished out a card. The name sounded Yiddish. Rykaard had given him this name and address when Ludwina was in hospital. That man, Rykaard had said, could read the future and had the power to change it.

***

The Friday morning was foggy and dull. The city slept late. Kanu drove carefully on roads slippery from an early morning drizzle. Their advertising firm, of which he was a one-fourth partner, had its office in an old building in Amstelveen and had no lift. Kanu set to work in his empty office that was damp and wrapped in a dreary smell from the old furnishings and frazzled draperies.

An old folder with photographs fell out from a bunch of old papers. One of the photographs showed Ludwina with her father in the Dam Square. An art dealer and one of the few men who knew where they hid *The Night Watch* to save it from loot by the Nazis, Victor Ludwig was obviously a large man. Kanu studied the photograph with a professional eye. He loved photography and pursued it with a passion far keener than his job required. Playing with the light and shade, bringing out the obscure lines, isolating a face in a crowd, or capturing a brief passing moment to tell a story, the possibilities fascinated him. It struck him suddenly that there was no photograph from his side of the family, here or at his home — nothing that could tell others if he had grown old after his father or if Nanu had any tiny part of his grandma. His own memories had become vague, lacking in physicality.

Kanu held his head between his two palms and pressed hard. He wanted to visualise a smile on his mother's face that he would have loved to snap up but what came to his mind was the image of a motif. It was a rectangular piece of white cloth with two red 'S' shaped prints, juxtaposed like mirror images, with five oval dots of varying sizes on top of each 'S'. Those were prints of his mother's feet taken after her death, before her body was consigned to the flames, by smearing her feet abundantly with *Alta*, the red water colour that Hindu married women use to decorate their feet. Red is the colour sported by a Hindu wife — red of the vermillion on her forehead, red of the betel leaves on her lips, and red of the *Alta* on her feet. With it, she sends out the message that she has a husband to look after her and a family to grow. Kanu remembered that they had another such motif in their large family room, framed as a photograph and hung on the wall. Buri Thakuma's footprints had always stayed there, high on the wall but never forgotten. Before going out for any important work it was mandatory for each of the family members to bow to that framed print and pray. His mother's footprints though, for some reason, never adorned a wall of their house; it did not even get a frame. Kanu stored that piece of cloth in his mother's steel trunk and would occasionally look at it and try to understand if his mother was really blessed and happy in the other world in the sense Bara Jethima said she should be because she died with *sindoor* on her forehead and a son and a husband to remember her.

In their large family, his mother was just one of the women among many aunts and elder sisters. When she became ill, she had only Kanu to turn to. Often Kanu would find her crouched on the bed with a pillow pressed against her belly and sometimes she would ask Kanu to go secretively to a homeopath she knew and bring her some medicine. Then she became all yellow and used to lie down most of the time with a thread of cotton twine knotted around several small twigs of the size of matchsticks around her neck. That thread was supposed to get longer each day and sop up the yellow vileness from her body. Besides that, all she had for medicine were the few globules Kanu brought from the homeopath. Soon after his mother's death, he was seventeen then, after a brief illness, his unemployed father almost overnight shrank into nothingness.

Kanu phoned Pamela, Godlef's secretary. Godlef was the major partner of their company. He had not come yet. An instinct, honed by years of struggle to stay alive against plentiful odds, began to tick in Kanu. He must carefully choose his stance. He had last met him in the new office Godlef had set up for himself. Every thing there was flamboyant — the carpet thicker, the furniture new and sleek, and the desktop monitor flatter. Godlef was folding a letter held in his hand, making one fold after another and then running his fingers violently along each of the creases he had made. When the letter was reduced to one sixteenth of its original size, he had said, 'Do I have to remind you that the customer is always right!' Rykaard, the fat stooge, had sat by him with a nasty grin.

'To hell with them.' Kanu scribbled a note to Godlef that he would be away for a few days.

He parked his car at a side street near the Rembrandtplein, sat down at a roadside café, and ordered a soup. A mild drizzle started. That brought a Surinamese couple inside the canopy but the man could be an Indian as well. India was not anymore the forgotten land that one had left behind for good. Some Indians now came and went as if they had two homes. Some had become rich enough to recolonise their own native land, to set up hospitals, hotels, resorts, even foundations to give away charity. Kanu's only link with India had been Rajat, a cousin of his own age. They had written to each other at times; he had written to Rajat after Nanu was born and sent him photographs. Last year Rajat wrote again asking for his permission and help, to reconstruct a portion of their ancestral house. Years ago, it was Rajat who showed him the marble sculpture in the garden house of a rich man, a nude statue in polished white stone, pouring water from a pitcher. From their hidden spot though, they could see only her back. The curve that swelled at the hips and sloped down, the pronounced bend in the waist had fascinated him.

One wintry afternoon that kept the elders in the house wrapped under quilts, Kanu had looked at such curves and bends in flesh. He had stood riveted looking at the woman bending on a couch, her clothes tousled. The next thing he remembered was his head pressed against two heavy breasts, an eager voice whispering in his ears, an impatient hand searching out his young tumescent response. A few years older than he was, she was the wife of a cousin working in a sawmill many miles away in some obscure town. Lonely, stifled and uncared in a decrepit portion of their old dwelling, she adopted the carelessness of its existence and when she went crazy, she sought release through him.

The incident repeated a few times and somehow the elders came to know. One day, an uncle who had been abroad came and Kanu had his life changed. He was to board the SS *Marina* to England and to begin to realise, right from the breakfast table next day in the ship, that it was possible to have food in such great quantities in just one place. In seven years in England and thirty-one here, he had lost his country. His father died a year after he left home and when the news had reached him almost a month later, he did not know how to grieve.

His mobile began to ring. Nanu's words came halting as he tried to place them between other sounds, various indefinable noises from the dash and rush of a busy city. The specialist in New York had agreed to see Kanu.

Three

'Take a walk,' the friendly Bangladeshi desk assistant in the hotel told them, 'it's just there.'

The hotel near the famous hospital in New York appeared to be a regular shelter for cancer patients. An ambulance stood in front of the lobby to pick up an elderly woman in a wheelchair. Cancer Patients Aids Society, the words written in black on its side notified and below those letters, in green and red, there was a phone number available toll free, twenty-four hours a day, seven days a week.

The sidewalks were broad and full of people busily trotting to wherever they were going. While one side of the road was under deep shadows of tall densely packed buildings, the other side looked bright and shimmering under the light of a morning sun. Vendors sold bagels and donuts from makeshift kiosks on trolleys. The air smelt fresh and the morning looked joyful; once in a while, the scent of a familiar perfume emitted a welcome note. Last afternoon it was like entering into a maze.

The road from JFK was jammed all the way. Buildings on either side emptied their bowels, sending more and more vehicles to clog up the passages and their cab had crawled behind a long line of cars.

The hospital was as old as the city block itself. Kanu craned his neck to have a full view of the hospital. All he could see was a tall structure tapering upwards into an incomprehensible needle. The foyer after the entrance was surprisingly small for such a big building. As they moved along the artificially lighted corridors and spaces, Kanu noticed that all one could ever see in this building were endless rows of alleys with small offices or information posts at the crossings. Innumerable rooms and offices lined the corridors but much more remained unseen, inside. If he had his camera with him and had started to shoot down the passages, the pictures would all be alike, nothing to tell one from the other. One could live in this building for a good many years and still not know its soul.

Instructions from the secretary of Dr Nolan whom they were to see were, however, very precise. 'Take elevator number 11, go to the 17th floor, turn right, come straight to the area marked as Head and Neck service, report your arrival at the reception and wait.'

A wooden banister partitioned the waiting area into two separate areas for two doctors. An elderly couple sat on one side. A few travelling bags lay scattered on the carpeted floor in front of them. A young man stood nearby, looking aloof. Only the old woman talked. 'Don't you worry my dear; doctors here know their job. This man, they say, is the best in the world.' Kanu heard her saying as he entered the examination cubicle.

As soon as he had examined Kanu, Dr Nolan came straight to the point. He tapped his pen on a printed anatomical diagram of the oral cavity and neck and indicated to Kanu what he would need to cut off. 'That portion definitely and might be that too and these nodes....'

Kanu watched fascinated as he drew a few small circles along the lines depicting structures of the neck, and then filled them up with great care with ink, making them look like marbles scattered over the diagram. The doctor rambled on about reconstructing his tongue with plastic surgery, about his need to tolerate a feeding tube after operation. The tall, thin figure, clad in a white coat swung jocularly on a revolving stool drawing and scribbling on the chart.

'How good are my chances?' He asked simply, trying to keep his tone flat. He had come this far only for an honest answer to that one question.

'Reasonably good,' Dr Nolan said. He started to write and Kanu could see only his profile.

'*How good are my chances*?' Kanu repeated his question, putting emphasis on each word.

Dr Nolan looked sharply at him. 'Depends on those nodes, how bad they are affected.' He scribbled some figures on the notepaper and then scratched them, 'If you want numbers, if hundred persons like you are treated, forty to forty-five people would live for more than five years.'

'You mean then that there's a possibility, a more than one in two chance that I'll die from this disease within five years!'

'If you want to look at it the hard way, yes.'

'And what do I do in these five years?'

'You get checkups from time to time. Like you do for other chronic diseases, diabetes, hypertension, arthritis. Cancer is just like them, a chronic disease, fairly containable with regular checkups. If something goes wrong with you unfortunately, we take care of that as early as possible.'

'Meaning further operations?'

Dr Nolan now swung back to face him directly and leaned back on the table with both his elbows extended backwards as props for support; his white coat parted to expose his knees jutting forward, one crossed over the other. 'Without them you've no chance,' he said.

'So, for any person like me, all these hopes for cure are then purely conjectural?'

'Might be; but only to the degree that we fail to understand the mysteries of human bodies, which make one person different from another.' Dr Nolan stood up from his revolving stool and straightened his white coat, 'If I can, I want to impress upon you that you need that operation real quick.'

'I understand. But tell me about this operation …can anything go wrong?'

'No. Doesn't happen with me usually. Besides, you'll be under constant monitoring in an intensive care unit, one of the best in the world.' Dr Nolan turned to walk out of the cubicle.

'Intensive care unit'…that was one place Kanu did not want to be in. He felt that same sharp tug, inevitably followed by that same unwilling loathsome return to the past, to that wretched evening seven years ago. Before him appeared Ludwina, her face bloated and partially hidden behind a bandage, lying motionless in a cubicle of the ICU. The machines crowding around her beeped and bellowed …shoos… thud ... shoos … thud... as her chest heaved and retreated alternately. At the end, she made a hideous corpse.

Dr Nolan watched Kanu for a while and then said, 'Your son can meet me when you are ready or you can see my secretary. She will help you. Take care.' He walked out breezily. The secretary came in with some papers and quizzed Kanu if his insurance would cover him for treatment in an American hospital.

Outside, Kanu found Nanu conferring quietly with the other young man accompanying the elderly couple. The old man on the other side had also come out after his consultation. He now sat in front of the secretary's table trying to read and make sense of a thick booklet.

His wife stood frowning. Kanu learnt that the other high priest who saw this man had confirmed that the old man's disease was incurable. Nevertheless, his wife had refused to take a 'No' for an answer and created such a fracas that the doctor had asked them to give consent for an experimental therapy.

'But what did they say to you?' Nanu asked when they came down. 'Don't they want to take you in?'

'Very much so.' Kanu laughed and pointed to a window above, 'They'll be damn happy to put me in one of those rooms but that will have to wait. For now, vamoose! I've to see another doctor at two in the afternoon.' Kanu showed an address to Nanu.

Nanu frowned. 'I was told that Dr Nolan is one of the best in the business; why do you need to see another one?'

'Just you call a cab,' Kanu ruffled his son's hair. The day was too beautiful to ride through the dark tunnels.

A husband-wife team ran the clinic he went to in the afternoon. The husband, who was a radiation oncologist but evidently more passionate about advocating alternative therapies, met Kanu. 'In God We Trust', read the inscription on a framed chrome plate standing between two miniature American flags on his wide desk.

'The main thing is to keep control of your own self. There are ways to beat your cancer and you must choose what is least toxic for you.' Behind the wide desk, the doctor sat upright on an unusually high chair and spoke with a clear voice without any accent. He spoke steadily, pausing only to point to some photographs on the walls and atop the sleek cabinets surrounding the desk. 'My blue ribbon winners,' he chuckled. 'They cured themselves because they took control of their lives, consciously created images. Powerful, strong, positive images that can heal any disease.'

Kanu laughed at the good-natured way the doctor spoke those

words. 'Cancer is all about cells. How can my mind cure it?'

'It can. It damn well can. I can show you twenty well documented studies, which show how positive imagery stimulates the natural killer-cell activity better than any drug. It's your own dear immune system working for you. With the right imagery pain is lessened, tumours decrease in size, and digestion improves. These effects have been scientifically measured so there is nothing hypothetical about it.' The doctor glowed with confidence. 'No need for any million dollar surgery. Radiation plus mind-body control, and you are good.'

At the end of the session, the clinic sold him some books and audiotapes to help in his exercises and meditation.

Back in the hotel, Kanu made a few more calls. The last one was to a clinic that had discovered a drug that attacked the root cause of cancer by correcting the elemental defects in the internal chemistry of a cancer patient. The owner of the clinic, a Polish Count estranged from his country but presently a practicing physician in America, had received accolades from many celebrated journals and newspapers. The receptionist in his office asked Kanu many questions and promised to call back.

'Call room service if you need anything,' Nanu said as he went out for dinner.

Kanu began to read the book he had purchased at the airport because of its intriguing title, *The Mystic Masseur*. The author was Indian. It turned out to be a funny book. Although the story was set in an island thousands of miles away from India, reading it oddly sharpened in his mind blurred images of a house located in a muffusil town of Bengal. Images of a U-shaped two-storied house enclosing a small courtyard. Rows of cracked wooden window frames with slim vertical iron bars decorated the mossy walls beneath an unguarded terrace. Many people lived inside that house but the rooms had very little furniture and the walls were mostly bare without any pretty picture or photograph. Photographs that can tell stories and remind how a person used to look, how he or she smiled. Kanu's parents seldom smiled. His father had the eyes of a dead fish; mother's became all yellow at the end. Her face and body shrank, then disappeared steadily to remain in his memory only as a hood with a red border over her faceless head, then a little heap, and then two cracked soles with bent toes smeared red with Alta.

***

It was difficult at first to understand what the men, the three of them in long white coats, standing around him were saying to him as he perched on a stool. One of the men held him down.

'Don't fret; your car is broken and you can't go anywhere. Now be a good boy and open your mouth, wider, wider,' the man shouted. One of the men had a pair of long tongs in his hand. He forced that into Kanu's mouth, and held his tongue in a tight grip. 'It's a juicy one.' The men patted each other.

'It moves too much,' another man said as he put his hand in Kanu's mouth and pulled out a few marbles. 'Look at them, aren't they beautiful?' The third one took the marbles in his hand and examined them closely. 'There must be more. We must persist in our endeavor,' one of them said. They began to pace through a long corridor, going in and coming out of different rooms and shaking their heads. Suddenly from one room Dr Seth peeped out and cried, 'See you in India.' Verdic sneaked in and with a finger on his lips bade Kanu to follow him. They went down a narrow wooden staircase going down to an endless semi-dark passageway with stone walls lined by long rows of tables from where numerous persons began to holler at them. Each of them had a placard in front of him. Kanu read the names displayed on them one by one: Mind- Body Control, Shark Cartilage, Magnet Therapy, Mistletoe… The men held up the placards and began talking to him.

A thin man with a large pair of spectacles began to make a speech. 'Don't fall for all that they claim as scientific. What's the history of science except discarding one sure theory after another?'

A lone man sat on this side of one of the tables. He pulled Kanu closer to him and whispered, 'I'm a Russian but don't tell that to any one. I can tell you that real doctors are up in the mountains and in the deep forests. They know plants that can cure any illness. They know about herbs and birch trees that grow fungus.'

Verdic came back with a flowing orange robe wrapped around him and began to chant some mantras. Suddenly Godlef and Rykaard barged in, threw out the placards, and began to taunt Kanu and Verdic.

'Run, Kanu, run,' someone yelled behind him. Kanu turned and saw Rajat walking up to him. Rajat looked young, his head tonsured, and he had a begging bowl in one hand and a staff in the other. 'We are going to Kashi,' Rajat said, held Kanu's hand in a firm grip, and pulled him. Kanu tried to run with Rajat but could not move.

The pain in his tongue became intense and that broke his dream. Momentarily, he pictured himself lying in the ICU of the hospital he had visited in the morning, with tubes going in and coming out from his body. Things often go wrong after an operation. Stitches give way, the wounds bleed, pneumonia sets in, and emboli get stuck inside the heart or the lungs. Anything can go wrong and then it would be terrible if Nanu had to suffer like him and carry a burden throughout his life.

An idea drifting through his mind for the last few days and crystallising since his visit to the hospital now became solid enough to take shape. He must talk to Nanu about his idea within the next few days and he must not make it sound very serious. 'The time has now come to talk,' he would begin, 'no, not about malfunctioning computers but about human propensities.' Nanu would know that line. He knew that people often work in one place and then find another to die. He had seen people migrating to all sorts of places, people who had gone to Ceylon, to Australia, to South Africa. India, his own country, could easily be Kanu's destination. Or, it could be the location where he would arrive at his final destination, find a place to die, but not before he had made a final journey there, a journey that would be entirely his alone, even if he had to travel through roads that were forlorn. He would go back to India and there he would search out people, people neglected in life like his parents, and discover smiles on their faces and create portraitures, photograph them in their rare happy moments and make lovable images— bright images, images pure and true as sunflowers.

The idea excited him. He would ask Dr Seth and contact Rajat. He would use the few weeks of radiotherapy there to renew his lost relationships, to regain a home, and then would straightaway set out on his quest searching for the small things of a world he had left four decades ago. It would be a kind of pilgrimage, a pilgrimage that Ludwina would have approved of. Besides, there is no mountain higher than The Himalayas.

Nanu was sleeping in the other bed, with a mauve coloured sheet pulled over his head. Kanu bent over to adjust it. After him, the boy would be all alone in this world, without a family, without a faith. His would be a difficult journey through life until the day when he would domesticate himself and establish a home. He hoped Nanu would be able to learn from life before it had bypassed him even though they had failed to give him a faith. With a faith to follow, Nanu could have developed a sense of belonging, to be a part of some great tradition shared by million others and not feel lonely. Ludwina had never insisted on baptising Nanu; Kanu had never felt the need to talk to his son about Hindu practices about which he himself had very little idea except that there were gods to worship and a dip in the holy water of the Ganga would cure all ills.

The pain in his mouth was now spreading to his ear. He debated against taking a painkiller, then took one, and slept through the night.

***

Some days later, he became aware of a sky lighting up gradually and the light passing through his closed eyelids. He was crossing the westward rays of a rising sun during his eastward flight, and if there could be a precise moment when a new day could be said to have begun, it was now. The dark sky turned crimson at first. Soon the light of the sky would spread to the earth and the sleepy towns and villages would wake up one after another. The next town to cross would have woken up earlier than the town already passed because the sun rises in the east. It would still be a long flight that would cross over continents, over mountains, and over deserts and seas, to finally reach the land, which has thousand-year-old shrines and temples and a tradition old enough not to begrudge his homecoming, after a mere forty years of absence.

Four

The din in the waiting hall of the hospital in Calcutta was unbelievable. Kanu sat with a slip of paper in his hand with a hundred other men and women. Rajat stood in front of the reception desk and tried to engage the receptionist. For four days, Kanu had been trying to come to terms with this forgotten world of smelly crowds and sultry weather. The blue of the sky looked less luminous than he thought it would and the air thicker, almost visible. The city itself was more gray than green.

People sat around him with different postures. Each of them had a few thoughts to reveal or to hide, thoughts that were tender or selfish, thoughts about their illnesses, about pain, about what could be ahead, about a possible loss. On his left, an old woman was busy fiddling with a long tube that had come out through her left nostril. A piece of dirty white sticking plaster kept it taped over her nose. Repeatedly she tucked the end of the tube behind her ear but it kept slipping, yet her face was impassive, rigid like a mask. A man, who looked like a farmhand from the country, sitting opposite him attracted Kanu. He had read about faces being described by the year. When men live through hard times, conditions so harsh as to leave behind marks on their faces, then their faces can become as distinctive as to be pinpointed to that terrible period or even to a particular year. This man had a face where many years had frozen together — a short forehead with upward slanting eyebrows and an anxious lugubrious expression made loud by deep creases. This man looked ancient, Kanu thought, and his would be a terrific portrait to shoot. His face looked ancient but he had strong limbs, which were now taut and tense. With heels raised from the ground, he sat on the edge of his chair as if he wanted to levitate. His eyes focused on a door across the hall. Soon that door opened and a woman came out followed by a nurse. The man rushed to meet them. The nurse handed over a sheaf of papers to the man after delivering a few hurried instructions. As they walked back, the man's eyes met Kanu's. Walking up to Kanu he gently asked, 'Er... can you make me understand these papers? We're poor and ignorant, you see.'

His Bengali was of a different dialect that Kanu had not heard before but he could follow the general idea. He looked at their papers. Mrs Keka Burman, 40 years of age, Hindu female. She had been marked as having an advanced disease. As he sorted out the papers and explained the procedures to follow, an uncanny feeling of that man entering his life disturbed Kanu. He craned his neck to find what Rajat was doing. He had been staying in a hotel and though Rajat came to meet him immediately after Kanu had reached Calcutta, he had looked anxious and old with worries.

'You look like a grandfather!' Kanu had said, looking at his cousin's dry wrinkled skin, bent body, with his bald head hedged by a U-shaped growth of gray hair.

'I'm a grandfather,' Rajat had said. 'Besides, life has been hard. It was for me particularly, living a life that I did not want to live. You know I have always wanted to be away, to be in all those mysterious strange places, to do what you have done. Now, look at you, out again on a journey that most people will not undertake. Tell me first, why have you come back in this manner? Are you not on good terms with your son?'

'I was scared,' Kanu had confided.

'Why? You've money!' Rajat had looked surprised.

Kanu had grinned. 'I've consulted many doctors. Some time or the other, this disease is going to kill me, there or here. Until that happens... Oh Rajat, you don't know how I felt every night waking up alone in my apartment and then pinching myself to see if I was still alive. I want to put something else between now and that time, between death and me.'

Rajat was silent for sometime. Then he had looked up and said, 'Can I tell you one thing? You've not done the last rites for Bhalo Kaku. His soul would still be thirsty for an offering of water from his son. Let me take you to the Ganga one day. I know a priest there who can arrange some sort of oblation.'

'Not my fault. Ma died when I was young and had no say about anything; and I still don't know how father died!'

'I can't tell you how and why he died. He just died after a brief mysterious illness that made him lose blood. The actual end came a little after midnight one day. I remember we had dinner early that night and the little ones were all sent to bed.'

Kanu could visualise what it would have been like in that house on that night. Men of the house would have huddled together in the courtyard or on the dark terrace, probably for once feeling sorry for a kin who never mattered much. Women of the house spoke in hushed tones and tiptoed with a discreet hurry to finish their household chores before the last breath was out. Because then the mourning period would begin, they would become unclean, and would have to throw away all unconsumed food. Did anyone remember to offer the last redeeming drink?

Only after some time Kanu could ask Rajat, 'In our parents' room there was a big trunk, where we kept our own personal things. Do you know if it's still there? When I go home I want that one returned to me.'

Rajat's face clouded. He had his gaze fixed on the couch and he picked up a few specks of dirt from there. Without looking up, he had said cautiously, 'You've no idea how poor we are and in what gross conditions we live. You won't like it there. Besides, the house has long been partitioned and we have four separate kitchens going. It's not the house that you remember.'

In the lobby downstairs, just before Rajat had departed, Kanu had put a hand on his shoulder and had uttered with some difficulty, 'I just wanted to be home for a while. I don't claim anything, not for me, not for Nanu.'

Since that talk Rajat had come daily to his hotel, but always alone, and pretending to play a part in a whim of his rich cousin, as in their adolescent days, but had avoided any mention of their home. Today he had escorted Kanu to this hospital.

Kanu saw him now hurrying towards him. 'They are calling you!'

If the din outside was disquieting, inside it was all haphazard. Doctors sitting at a big table attended to more than one patient at a time. A girl in her twenties held center stage. She stood by a woman, who sat meekly on a stool, and pestered the medics. 'Will she be all right? Will she be cured if we do as you say?'

'We'll try,' a doctor said.

The girl would not give up. 'No. Trying is not enough,' she said. 'Consider, we're five sisters and I'm the eldest—I've two young brothers who are going to school. Our father cannot work; It's often touch and go with him, for his asthma. If we do as you say, we'll be selling our land. I've to get my four sisters married.'

Kanu for his part spun a story about being retired and planning to return home and then developing this sudden illness. 'Some recommendations are there, from an oncologist in Amsterdam.' Kanu tapped his fingers on the papers he carried with him and showed them to the doctor who attended to him. Dr Ved Sanyal was young, a junior consultant. 'Would you like to see them?' Kanu asked him.

They discussed arrangements for his treatment and Kanu felt less inhibited to voice his own preferences as somehow this lack of privacy, his talking about himself in a crowd, paradoxically, brought a sense of anonymity. An attendant led in the man who had accosted Kanu earlier, the man with the interesting face. He handed a letter to Dr Sanyal. 'I've been looking for you for the last three days but I couldn't contact you. I'm Mahen Burman from Monabari; the doctor there has remembered you. We're very poor,' the man said.

'Who? Deep?' Dr Sanyal murmured as he began to read the letter and spoke to the man. Kanu learnt that the man had come for his wife's treatment, from a far-off village called Monabari, where Dr Sanyal had once worked. He and his wife had temporarily found shelter in a rented room near this hospital. Rent was fifty rupees per day for staying; food bill excluded.

Outside the main gate of the hospital, most people stood on the opposite side under the shadows of the canopies of shops selling refreshments and drinks. Kanu and Rajat crossed over. A shopkeeper hastily cleared a space for them, used his machete to slice off the tops of two green coconuts and with the pointed end of the machete chiselled out two little neat holes.

From where Kanu sat, exactly opposite to the hospital gate, he could see the insides of the hospital. People strolled out and joined the gradually enlarging crowd waiting for buses or taxis.

'If this heat persists, people will begin to die.' the shopkeeper said, to no one in particular, but everyone nodded. The month of May anywhere in India is hot and sunny except up in the mountains of the far north. Though here in South Bengal the earth is soft and does not crack easily even during the summer, and though eventually it will rain one day and make the air cool, the summer months are often hot enough to make people suffer.

Kanu stepped out of the shade of the shop to throw his empty coconut in a drum kept on one side. Just then, a sudden gust of wind rose and slapped him on the face. His face burned, his head reeled, and all of a sudden, he was back to a world he had left many years ago. In one instant, the memories of harsh cold days and icy winters were wiped out and Kanu felt he was home. He knew the winds here, knew the sky and the earth. Even the hospital buildings looked familiar. Around them, large leafy trees with spread out branches interspersed between tall slender coconut and palm trees. In the heat, through the rarefied air, all objects quivered and looked as if they belonged to a surreal world. Kanu could feel their vibes — where he was born was only fifty miles from here. He was of this soil and this soil was his.

The place looked all right for him.

Five

The back portion of the oldest building in the hospital housing the general wards now looked rundown but that building had memories going back to a winter morning several years ago. On that sunny morning the daughter of the gracious inventor of the magical rays, a Nobel wining scientist herself, and the prime minister of a young nation came down to this city to lay the foundation stone of the first specialised cancer treatment center in this part of the world. Dr Ved Sanyal circled the small garden by its side to reach the front of the old ward and came across Mahen and his wife.

'Are you going to the radiation department?' Ved asked.

Mahen nodded. Pointing at Ved, he nudged his wife, 'Pay regards, woman. This is that *daktarbabu* so fondly remembered in Monabari and whose mercy we have come to seek.'

Ved was not prepared for this unexpected appearance of a poor peasant from that remote village and, through him, the old world of

Monabari reaching out to his present world in this manner. Monabari to him was still a distant land that had mountains within its view and dreamt of rivers in its solitude. A land surrounded by mysterious forests that have indefinable boundaries and lure the innocents to their secrets inside. Villagers, though, know better. If one enters a forest, without knowing how to meander out through the maze, then one is soon lost. The more one thinks one is going back to the periphery, the deeper one goes in. Monabari though was not so remote that one would chance upon a lost tribe there. People like Mahen and his tribe had lived there for ages but had rarely ventured far. However, the last decade had changed much, even in the remotest parts of India.

Mahen's wife bowed and said, 'Miserable us! We've come so far only because we've been told about you.'

Before Ved could respond to her, he heard, 'Every morning I ask myself to be a good boy...' Someone was merrily reciting a little children's rhyme behind him. He turned to see the upright figure of Gola-da coming towards him with his usual long steady strides. Why people called this man 'Gola-da' Ved never knew, but this man, Samar Roy, was a favourite poet of their generation. A lively boy of around twenty accompanied Gola-da but then Gola-da had friends of all ages.

'This is Jafar,' Gola-da said with his eyes twinkling. He took out a small brown packet of paper from his pocket. 'Look at this fool,' he said. 'He had caught the first city local to bring me this charmed talisman from a fakir he knows … for me… to bring about a cure!'

Ved shook hands with Jafar. 'Anything that helps,' he said to Gola-da.

'But look at you,' Jafar said, 'You've become thin as a stick, Gola-da!'

Ved took a closer look at Gola-da. He had a tall straight muscular build but now looked visibly wasted; the pajama and kurta he was wearing flopped loosely over his large frame.

Gola-da's eyes flashed. 'But I am not sick, neither am I petering out. Do I look sick Jafar?' He thumped his chest. 'What a few pounds of flesh could mean?' he asked. 'I lose them because of those poisons they keep injecting in my body here.' He turned to Jafar. 'By the way Jafar, remember to take a poem I wrote last night to hand over at the weekly's office.' He clutched his throat with both hands. Apparently, long exchanges strained his voice.

'A new poem!' Jafar looked excited. 'What's it about?'

'It's a short one, nothing grand. I only say there that the real fight is from us, from the patients. These doctors here, they always trumpet their fight, glorify it, and get fame and awards. The patients themselves fight the fight. From here...' Gola-da's voice choked and he pointed to his heart.

'And that one there knows no fear,' Jafar cried.

Ved felt sorry that Samar Roy was losing his famous voice that had boomed in many meetings and street fights. This hoarseness, a recent development, could only mean an aggravation of the disease. Ved entered the old ward thinking about Gola-da. He had always regarded himself as a fighter. Here, in sickness too.

The old male ward now accommodated free patients. Inside it some living beings squirmed as worms inside a can. Sixteen patients lay in two rows of beds with very little space between them. They had no secrets from one another. They knew the colour of each other's wounds and if those were clean or purulent, and who among them were bilious or incontinent. They shared their halitosis and the effluvium together. They even knew, at times, if a particular one would live through the night or die during it. On those days, the fifteen others would sleep with their faces turned to the opposite side. The one with the most obnoxious wound would usually be in the last bed against the wall. The head count might be sixteen but they lived together as a mass of jelly, its portions inseparable from one another. Within the conundrum, portions of various ingredients would vary. One day it would be made up of two lungs, one kidney, three larynxes, two stomachs, one colon, three oral cavities, one bone and three cancers about which nobody had any idea. Three days later, it would be a little different. Four colons, one stomach, three lungs, five larynxes, two oral cavities, one brain. The numbers would shift, as they do in a game of dice.

One could count them in other ways also, from an epidemiological point of view. How many of them were over sixty or how many were Hindus or Muslims, or a Santal even. The last one created a problem. What was his religion, nobody knew for sure. The medical administrator ruled him as a Hindu; the matron disagreed gravely. They quarrelled for half an hour and then they forgot everything, even the patient. The orderly counted in another way: three soft rice diets, five liquid diets, six full diets and two 'nil by mouth'. It occurs very rarely that someone sits up in the bed and sings a song for others in that ward or tells them a fairy tale. The ward nurses are less discerning — all of them die eventually.

'I won't give him more than two days. It was so difficult to put in an IV line,' said the ward nurse concluding her briefing about a patient to Ved.

The outpatients' clinic was busy. Case-files piled up high on the table. The senior registrar pushed a few files to Ved. And then they came, one after another, like on any other day, in that confounding potpourri. Three women who had progressed too rapidly in their disease, two men with curable disease but no means for treatment, a father who had not yet finished his duties, a young mother who had just known the joys of life, an adolescent son around whom dreams had been built.

There were also other people who had once passed through this way and had grown either confident or careless about their diseases. In between them, there were the anniversaries, of the patients who had crossed milestones in their race for survival, one year, two years ... five years. They caused cheers. Two old patients talked to each other while Ved wrote his notes. They had developed a friendship over the years. 'Everything is God's grace. Only the limitless benevolence of our family deity Shri Gobinda has saved me.' Ved heard one saying.

'Yes, Allah is kind. Praise be to Allah. Everything is due to His benevolence.' The other agreed.

A sixteen year-old boy was next in line. He had a swelling in the upper arm. A bone sarcoma.

'How much time will you require to treat this?' the boy asked.

Ved looked him over and spoke slowly, 'We'll need to do certain tests to find how things are with you, and then I'll be able to tell you.' He allowed his words to create uncertainties where there was none. He could not tell the boy that for him the choice was clear, an immediate amputation or death. Or, to be more correct, a deferment of death.

'Can't those tests wait till I take my examination? If I take your medicines regularly, this thing will become less painful — perhaps?' the boy kept looking at the swelling in his arm.

Ved was tempted to say, 'No Dyoma, bridges aren't built on 'perhaps' but let go.

His father, for some reason appearing more apologetic than anxious or saddened asked, 'Can I have a word with you in private?'

Before Ved could answer him, the registrar called him from the cloistered area curtained around the examination couch for the patients. Ved remembered he had read somewhere about examination couches being covered with horsehair—he had wondered then and wondered now what that 'horsehair' meant. A female patient lay there. Ved had come to know this lady well over the years and they smiled at each other, from a secret bond of affinity. She said, 'If you ask me what is wrong with me, I can't tell you. But if you ask me how I am keeping, "*most unwell*" I'll say.'

Her groan was telltale as Ved palpated her abdomen, right side and up; the liver was enlarged with nodules. The disease had struck her again, and this time probably in a fatal way. 'We need to talk,' he told her.

Before he could turn, she held his stare with her eyes that had become wide, water gradually filling up to their brims. Emotions fleeted through there, one after another. She slowly gathered herself, wrapping the end of her sari around her shoulders. Looking downwards, she arranged the pleats and whispered, 'What's there left to talk about?'

'The real fight is from us,' Ved remembered Gola-da telling him that morning. The power went out before he got back to his chair. He pushed aside the curtain in the window and saw the man from Amsterdam alighting from a taxi. Inside, the room was getting hotter and the patients waiting outside began to jostle. The registrars began to call two or three patients at a time. Ved watched the beads of perspiration appearing on their foreheads. The odour of their sweating bodies mixed with the smell of sickness around them.

Back in his quarters, just after lunch, he received a phone call. Jamaj was on the line. 'Father wanted to see you urgently,' Jamaj said and that was all he said. Jamaj was the younger brother of Manoj, a classmate, who presently worked as a surgeon in England. The well-laid wide lane to his friend's house had changed little. Wealth in these quarters had been amassed over generations and was too solid to be seen being flaunted around, no rush here to wear the new sleek steel and glass look of the city. 'Rajasthan Metals' — the brass letters on a large black marble plaque looked as shiny as it did ten years ago outside the white house on a green lawn. Inside, his friend's father sat on a sprawling white divan. Without any preamble, he said quietly, 'He is coming back from England, on Sunday. He has got cancer.'

'Who?' Ved asked and then he realised.

Manoj had just taken his bath when Ved went to see him three days later. He looked well, even had that old boyish smile and his eyes twinkled.

'Come, I've something to show you,' Manoj said.

Ved followed him down to a large room on the mezzanine floor. Large unopened cardboard boxes lay scattered around the room.

'Look,' Manoj said, 'my tools have reached before me. I shipped them sometime ago in preparation for my coming back. I wanted to set up a practice myself.'

'Yes, of course. Why not?' Ved wanted to appear enthused. 'These things must give you a good start.'

'Yes. That they'll do; I don't know though how long I shall be using them. My boss, who operated on me, was frank and precise. "Whatever there was to do for you, we've done. Now go back to your family".'

'But,' Ved asked the question that had intrigued him since he had learnt about Manoj's disease, 'would not England have been a better place to complete your treatment!'

The smile on Manoj's lips broadened. His eyes shone playfully as if he was ready to catch Ved in committing a faux pas. 'It's malignant melanoma and the nodes are positive,' he grinned.

Malignant melanoma! The fiercest predator!

After a brief pause during which Ved dithered to invent something to speak, Manoj gave further details with deliberate stress on each word, as if he wanted the world to hear those words once and for all. 'After the operation and after we got the pathology reports, my boss and I consulted many specialists in Europe and America but got the same opinion. In my case, the treatment options are limited. And I've come prepared with drugs and appliances that will last me for two years; even the morphine tablets for the terminal pain when that comes.'

They went downstairs. A room was being made ready for Manoj to set up a consultation chamber.

'It looks professional. You'll get busy soon.' Ved said.

Manoj shrugged his shoulders. 'Then there is fate,' he said, his fingers touching his forehead.

Around them craftsmen worked. The room was filled with a mixture of sounds: the back and forth scuffing sound of saws slicing timber, hammers jangling to drive in nails, chisels clamouring on unyielding wood. Manoj and Ved moved in haphazard circles around the craftsmen and spoke with strained voices, shouting over the sounds.

'Tell me Ved, what did I do to deserve this? Have you heard of a place called Erewhon?' Manoj asked.

'No. Where is it?'

'It's in '*Nowhere*'. Erewhon is *nowhere* read backwards. It is a fictional land, where illness is taken as a sin and any new synthesis is hated.'

When Ved started to leave, Manoj called him to his bedroom. 'Ved come here.' Manoj pushed his trousers down and pointed to a place on his groin. 'Feel here,' he said.

Ved made a gentle palpation. The node was easy to find. It was hard. Ved felt horrified. It could not be that his friend had failed to understand its significance. The disease would probably run faster than they had imagined it would.

Six

For the third time since noon, Kanu got up from his bed to wet his dry throat. Four days had passed since his treatment had started in this hospital. He felt hopeful for he was being treated by one of the finest tools of modern medicine, a radiotherapy machine that had the power to harness and kill the renegade cells wantonly proliferating to form the evil ulcer in his mouth. He now looked forward to his daily dose of radiation, a method of treatment that started with an invention inspired by a noble thought. The inventor Maria Sklodowska-Curie's name was inscribed on the wall outside the radiotherapy room. The dedication below mentioned how a poor girl from Warsaw came to Paris to become a scientist, braving years of hunger and penury, but when she and her husband jointly discovered radium, a radioactive material that later facilitated treatment of millions of cancer patients by radiotherapy, she refused to patent her discovery. For the good of million others, she gave up without the slightest hesitation her own claim to limitless wealth.

Kanu looked at his watch – it was 3.30 pm. Dukhiram, the kitchen attendant, would come soon to serve tea for the patients before the visiting hours began. Even though Kanu could not drink tea now, Dukhiram would still come to his cabin and talk. He was from a village only a few miles inland from the deep waters of the Bay of Bengal. Once every month he visited his family there but every winter he would take leave for a few weeks to set up a shop at the annual big religious fair in Gangasagar.

'If you've done Gangasagar once, that's better than doing all other pilgrimages many times over,' he had told Kanu. 'Go there; touch the soil made holy by the dust from the feet of a thousand pious men; dip in the icy cold, holiest of the holy water just before sunrise on the Makar Sankranti Day and all your miseries would be gone. On that day the sun begins its northward journey by entering the Makar Rashi and the gods, that day, keep the doors of heaven open for the pure souls to get in.' Dukhiram never tired of telling stories about that fair and the people who flocked there from all over India. 'Sahibs too,' he would add.

When Kanu came out for a stroll in the lawn downstairs, the daylight was almost gone. Shadows cast by the buildings were not isolated anymore. In the long covered passage downstairs, a ward assistant came along pushing a patient on a wheelchair. An old woman, stooping forward, sat in that chair gripping the arms tightly. Her hair was as white as her over-starched white sari, the hood of which had slipped down and collared a wrinkled face. Her eyes were transfixed reverentially on the radiation room, as if she was approaching a temple. Snapped that moment, her face would be a photographer's delight. Some of the faces he had seen in these few days had already made him keyed up; Mahen's in particular. He should make a separate folio in black and white for some of those faces. That would highlight the tones better and offset the background.

The lawn outside was crowded and patients and their families loitered here and there. Some sat on the wooden benches around the lawn, some sat on the grass. A family sat in one corner with a small girl in its center. 'I want ice cream,' the girl demanded of her parents. She wanted to run and play. She did not know that sick people were around and they were not merry. She did not care that she herself was sick. She only wanted to savour the new things in a world that was only six years old, one that might not grow any older for her.

Kanu passed them. A memory from another place and time and the taste of an ice cream melting in his mouth came back to him at once. One memory slipped into others — children running around on green grass, sliding down the slopes, and the sweet taste of creamed ice on his tongue. A clear open sky, a velvety steppe rolling out to the horizon, the yellow and orange dresses, Ludwina holding two ice creams in her two hands, one for Nanu , one for herself — the memory lilted and once again Kanu became aware that remembering incidents could be as absorbing as living them. Decide on a point of entry and from there take incidents in different directions, through the fantastic labyrinth of endless possibilities.

'There you are!' A benign cry broke into his thoughts. Kanu turned back to see Dr Ved Sanyal smiling at him. Another person, older, wearing a crumpled pair of pajamas and kurta made of coarse cloth accompanied the doctor. Kanu had one look at that man and could immediately see he was sick. He had that typical look: a head with sparse hair, a copper coloured face taut as a tight fitting mask, a hollowed out neck.

'Is everything fine with you?' the doctor asked.

'Yes, thank you,' Kanu said. 'I slept through the afternoon.'

Dr Sanyal was already talking to his companion. 'Gola-da, meet Mr Krishna Mohan Chatterjee. He's an NRI. And, Mr Chatterjee, this is Samar Roy, a famous poet. We call him Gola-da. There was a time when we used to speak quoting his lines.'

'People call me Kanu,' he extended his hand but the poet did not take it. He made a quick symbolic gesture of a salute to Kanu with his right hand as his left forefinger poked the doctor's chest. 'Hey! You're already putting me in the past tense. That's bad. Gola-da isn't finished yet.' The poet turned his attention to Kanu and said, 'An NRI? Here too?' He eyed the violet marks drawn by the radiotherapist on Kanu's face and neck with a puzzled look but did not say anything more.

'I'm in Cabin One, admitted on Thursday,' Kanu said briefly, explaining his presence in the hospital.

'He lives in Amsterdam but he is retired and has no family there at present. So he's come back to India for his treatment.' Dr Sanyal elaborated on his behalf.

'No place like home to die.' Kanu smiled.

The poet raised his hand to stop Kanu from saying more and said, 'No, no, don't tell me. Don't tell me your story. Let me imagine it. A person lives his whole life in a foreign country and then suddenly comes back one day!'

'What can you imagine when you don't know a thing about him?' Dr Sanyal looked amused.

'A lot. An awful lot,' the poet said. 'They might not be true, but that's unimportant; more vital is what's possible to believe about them.'

Kanu could understand what the poet meant but he saw that the doctor did not agree.

'I've to go,' Dr Sanyal said and left them.

The poet wanted to have tea and they crossed over to the teashop across the road where Kanu drank his first coconut the day he first visited this hospital.

'I'd my last smoke here about a week ago, behind that partition there. Are you a smoker?'

'I was till a month ago.'

'Then you know the feeling.'

They were sitting side by side. The poet turned his chair to face Kanu more squarely, and leaned on the table supporting his head on one hand. 'East or West Bengal?' He asked but did not wait for the answer and continued in a casual tone, 'Have you a wish to fulfill? A college perhaps to make the name of your dead father everlasting?'

Kanu laughed and shook his head. 'No. No headlines here. Here is just a man, who prefers to drift and drown than to wither like a poisoned tree. A man who simply wants to be on a journey of his own and do things he wants to do — Isn't that good enough?'

'Okay, I'll buy that.' Samar Roy said. Then he leaned forward further and locked Kanu in his stare. His eyes looked big and round through the thick glasses he was wearing; and his dark, parched skin attained a certain shine. He raised his left hand with the forefinger pointing at Kanu and held it there suspended in the still air between them before he spoke again. 'Even then, even if you have nowhere to reach, even if the path is lonely, and there are only bushes and wild flowers to look at the wayside, the journey itself is terrific at times. Good for you.' As soon as he had spoken those words, the poet relaxed and eased back to his former posture.

Kanu found out that Samar Roy knew about his birthplace. He knew about Father Darren and where he lay buried. The college was still there. Kanu felt ashamed that he had not asked Rajat about Father Darren who would assemble them in the playground and in the semi-darkness of an approaching evening, tell them about unscaled mountains and unfettered rivers, about the bends in history and the people who made great things happen. It was Father Darren who dinned in them the habit of reading and a desire to dream beyond the ordinary.

It was dark when they went back to their respective wards. Most people had already left the compound and in the darkness of the evening the place looked deserted. A stout man stood on the landing in front of the main door of the ward. Kanu saw him bid farewell to the retreating figure of the young boy he had seen being admitted that day. The middle-aged man, with a head full of curly hair and a heavy jaw, turned his face and remained standing there clutching the rail with his strong hands.

'Hello,' Kanu said, out of habit and by way of courtesy.

'Hello.' The man answered and then recognising Kanu as a patient, he turned around to face him.

'Are you in this ward too?' the man asked. 'My son is admitted there. Please keep an eye on him.'

'What is wrong with him? If you don't mind my asking,' Kanu said.

'He is ill, that's all I know. Doctors are saying one thing or the other, sarcoma of the bone or some such thing. His arm might be removed; doctors are discussing drugs that could be very toxic. His hair will fall off. But what can I complain about? He is sick entirely because of my fault. I've made him sick,' the man said the last words whispering, the muscles on his face twitched and his eyes blinked rapidly.

Kanu felt awkward. 'Don't be afraid. Everything is going to be all right,' he patted the man on his shoulder.

'No. You don't understand. It's due to me that his body has become defective. I've harmed him. I've not wished him well. Let me confess to you that when he was conceived, we lived in extreme poverty. I had no job, not enough food. I procured some drugs and tried an abortion. The drug did not work, or at least that was what I thought at that time. But now I know it poisoned his body.'

Kanu knew that kind of reasoning made no sense but could not make himself say anything comforting to stop the man from crying. Clumsily he stepped backwards, discomfited enough to turn his back on a man now openly howling without any hold, and slipped back inside the ward only to face another outlandish incident. The staff had gathered around an old woman unwilling to leave the ward. The ward nurse appeared confused trying to decide on a very difficult legal issue. The woman claimed to be the mother of the patient in bed no 112 and was refusing to go out of the ward on the plea that she herself was a patient in this hospital, and, as a patient, had the right to remain in the ward even after the visiting hours. Kanu watched the taut and tense creases on her face that looked fragile trying to resist a powerful inner turmoil.

'I don't care if you are a patient in another ward. But you are a visitor here,' Kanu heard the nurse saying. The peculiarity of the situation confused her and took some strength away from her ruling for it was against a very simple but irrefutable argument the lady had. 'He is my son,' she kept on saying simply.

'We know that. But don't make that such a big issue; he doesn't care for you.'

'Don't say such a thing. How can I not take care of him, being his mother, when he is so ill? Do you think that actress wife of his will care two hoots now that he can't bring her enough money to blow away?' A little later, when Mina, the staff nurse, came to his cabin Kanu heard from her a bizarre story. The woman who refused to go away was truly the mother of that patient. Kanu had noticed that temperamental, somewhat reclusive man before. He mostly rested facing the wall on his own fancy bed covers, always had flowers on his locker top, and a recorder plugged in his ears. Kanu, though, had never seen his face for a long enough time to think of a photograph. When the cancer of his mother was detected a few months ago, this man, her son, asked his parents to leave his house arguing that she might infect his children. Soon after, doctors detected an angiosarcoma in his pelvic cavity and got him admitted to this same hospital. His parents came to know of his condition only when they spotted his wife visiting the hospital regularly.

'God notices everything. Forsaking one's own mother, *chi, chi*,' Mina sneered as she told Kanu the story.

Kanu looked at her. A young girl with a Julie Andrews face, not very beautiful but instantly endearing. If she and the mother of that angiosarcoma patient were set within a single frame, it would make what they call a blessed picture. He wished he had talked to that woman and knew more about her feelings. Mina stood near the wooden cupboard on top of which Kanu had kept his briefcase. Her eyes glistened as she gently caressed the rich leather.

'Your blood reports have come. I've kept them in your file. The doctor will see them on the evening round,' she said, moving her hands slowly and fondly over the case.

'Oh, thank you. Hope they are all right!' Kanu said.

'They usually become worse once you are started on the treatment,' she volunteered.

Kanu wondered if she wanted to impress him. However, he liked talking to the bright girl. 'Do I have to have those tests very often?' he asked.

'About once a week,' the girl elaborated, 'unless you've real bad counts to start with or if you are undergoing some tough chemotherapy. Then you have them more often.'

'I'm told I am only getting a very mild dose of chemotherapy and only once a week.'

'On Saturdays only for the time being, but later I don't know. Everybody does get lots of chemo, eventually.' She pouted her lips.

Kanu could not understand the reason for the sudden temperance of her voice as she said that. Surely, he would not hold her responsible if events ultimately turned that way!

On her way out, Mina touched the case once more and asked with a certain coyness, 'This is from foreign, No?'

Kanu began to laugh and felt the gloom around him lifting considerably.

Seven

The rectangular ward in front of the cabin allotted to Kanu had twelve beds, six in each row along two sides of the hall. Each day would begin with great chaos. Watching that from his cabin, when he had his Walkman plugged to his ears and his cabin door open, Kanu felt he was watching acts in a pantomime. Though some of the actors, the occupants of those beds themselves, changed from time to time — some went home, a few died, and new entrants filled the void — the chores were similar on all days. Each morning patients would get up from their beds and lumber around the ward as a band of ghouls between overturned beds and soiled sheets and clothes thrown on the floor. The sweepers would draw screens around the patients who used bedpans. The night nurses, with crumpled uniforms and dishevelled hair freed from their caps taken off to steal a nap during the inactive hours of the night, would whirl through the ward, carrying the burden of unfinished work: three enemas, two antiseptic dressings, five shots of antibiotics, four transfers. The nurses, the ward boys, the sweepers, and even the patients who took too long to use the bedpans would get into each others' time and purpose and would fill the ward with cries and spats. Order would be restored only after the trainee nurses had sponged the patients and made the beds, when tea trolleys had arrived and a new set of staff resumed duty. Then the doctors would trickle in one by one and start their rounds. An hour before noon, visitors would come with packets of sweets, fruits, and biscuits but very few flowers. They would come again in the afternoon, this time staying longer, exchanging news, and giving and receiving affection. Someone would take time to tidy a bed, button up a shirt, and steal a moment of holding hands under the bedsheets. The nights were interminably long. There was no air-conditioning in this ward, and every night ward boys would crisscross the ward, with thick nylon cords to hang the mosquito curtains. The nurses would speak in hushed tones and tuck the patients inside mosquito curtains and would administer quick shots to those they knew would moan during the night.

The days remained stifled and hot until one day it rained, just like that, but without the gale of a typical Nor'wester, a Kal Baisakhi that comes thundering and blows away all that is rubbish and old. The trees bathed quietly while the birds folded their wings and hid their heads. Kanu stood at the window of his cabin and watched a dim sky pouring water on the arid thirsty grounds. Towards the afternoon, the rain stopped as suddenly as it had started and the sky cleared. There was still enough daylight and it seemed it might not rain again for a while. Kanu decided he would venture for his afternoon stroll in the hospital lawn.

If it had not rained, the ground would have been full of people, crowded with patients and their visitors— with those who came because they cared and also those who did not care but still had to come.

'Done with your stroll? So soon?' The rasping voice behind him sounded familiar and Kanu turned to find Bose Babu, the occupant of the last bed in the front row of their ward, frowning at him. Bose Babu's wrinkled face showed every bit of the seventy years he had lived. 'My sons came,' he briefly informed Kanu. His tone became intimate and accusing, 'All good for nothing — the reason why I had not wanted to be admitted to this hospital. This place is so far from our home. We live in Nalhati, you know, near the shrine, one of the celebrated fifty-one *peethas*...' He stopped, looking questioningly at Kanu, apparently unsure whether Kanu was familiar with the geography and history of his place.

Kanu parried that unspoken question. 'How long have you been here?' he asked.

'Something wrong with my lungs. This doctor is not telling me anything and I do not know how long I have to be here!' Bose Babu made some calculations with his fingers. 'Twenty thousand spent already. And don't know how much more. I knew I was not keeping well; felt a little tired even after walking a few paces — and this coughing out blood made me scared – but I never expected Maa Nalateswari to allow this to happen to me.' He looked distinctly unhappy.

Kanu wanted to change the topic. 'You possibly have to manage a big estate?'

'Do you think they can make it to the station before it starts raining again?' Bose Babu asked abruptly looking at the sky. Then he turned back to Kanu and shook his head. 'I must leave this hospital soon, or I'll die.'

It was getting darker out in the lawns. The sky remained cloudy, adding to the darkness. It was not raining but the wind carried moisture, suggesting rain somewhere near. Bose Babu halted and said, 'It's time for me to go back. I've to say my evening prayer.'

An elderly person whom everybody called Charu-da joined them.

It was his business to manage the small affairs of the hospital. Charu-da snickered when Bose Babu left. 'He is still dickering for a good bargain; he asked me to find for him some purchasable land here.'

Kanu thought there could be another explanation. Bose Babu was perhaps more naive than cunning, unaware of his fate foreclosing on him. But then again, why should men with cancer be beyond all planning? Does every king, who is infirm, abdicate? 'Why shouldn't he?' Kanu asked Charu-da.

Charu-da thought for a few moments. Obviously, he had not given the matter much thought but he came up with an answer all the same. 'Well, he should think of doing good deeds and not think of money. Before death, one should strive to earn the fare for the boat to cross to the other side; the boatman is very stern.'

At this time of the day, during his stroll, Mahen, that peasant from a far-off place but with an interesting face, would often catch hold of Kanu — usually with some papers, prescriptions, or hospital bills for Kanu to look at and explain to him. For some queer reason Mahen called them *sarkari kagaj*, 'Governmental papers', and was distrustful of them. Within his apparently benign and friendly disposition, somewhere there lurked a rebel who had something to hate and that attracted Kanu more to him. Mahen was nowhere near this evening. At the far end of the lawn Samar Roy who Kanu had heard was in the intensive care unit for a few days for a chest infection, stood motionless looking up at the sky.

'Look,' he said to Kanu pointing to the sky.

Daylight had renewed its stay postponing the descent of darkness, which a little while ago appeared imminent. An incandescent dome created a bluish white backdrop like a glow screen behind herds of thick clouds.

'Look at those clouds. One of my friends has written that they look like gnus grazing in a distant field,' the poet said gripping Kanu's shoulder. The poet's loose clothes fluttered about his lean body, his gaze fixed on the distant sky. Though his eyes still looked bright, his air was that of a tired man. He was now visibly ill. His grip on Kanu's shoulder was weak, his features indistinct in the afternoon light. He appeared to Kanu as a person who was decaying rapidly.

'Tonight we shall stay here, you and me, out here in the open and watch the sky to see if the moon will come up on the tops of those trees. Inside those rooms, you can never be sure if it's night or day and the doctors there lie to you all the time,' the poet whispered to Kanu.

An uneasiness overcame Kanu. The monotony of always seeing the same intensity of light, feeling the same temperature, sniffing the same air, hearing the same background sounds, hour after hour, without distinction between dawn and dusk, at times makes the inmates of an intensive unit lose their minds and become phobic. Was Samar Roy, a victim of it? Kanu felt scared.

In the darkness of his cabin, he lay down with an audiotape plugged to his ears. It played a gentle tune for some time and then slowly it faded out and another tune began to swirl in, and from it emerged a female voice. 'Close your eyes and sit absolutely still. Let only the air move around you and let that air come inside you. Breathe in, breathe in the air through your nose as long as you can, let the air fill your chest and then let it go. Breathe out the air through your mouth slowly, as slow as possible. Do that with me. Breathe in... and now out. Do it again and again. Make no other movement. Breathe in and out. Make your belly soft and limbs limp. Let not any part of your body remain tense. Imagine the breath of life going to all parts of your body and making them soft…' The voice ebbed away as another tune flowed in. Sounds broke in through Kanu's plugged ears and he took the Walkman off. Someone was knocking on the closed door of his cabin.

The rain had held up Rajat, but since he was already on his way, he decided to come anyway. 'I hope you are getting what you need,' Rajat said.

Kanu looked at him. He wanted to talk to him in detail but Rajat would have to go a long way back and Kanu could not detain him. He had hoped that Rajat had talked with other members of the family and they had settled on something. Rajat made a show of looking at his watch. Kanu wondered if his delay was intentional. For some time, the two brothers sat like two poker players. He, not wanting to betray his impatience, and Rajat, not wanting to allow his rich cousin an easy hold on him; van Gogh would have put them on a canvas, in dull brown colour. *The Poker Players*, Kanu imagined.

'I don't need much,' he said simply when his brother did not say anything more. He fished out two photographs from his bag and gave them to Rajat. 'My wife, and my son,' he said. Ludwina had always wanted a picture of her with a happy smile on her face, flanked by Kanu's family.

Rajat remained silent. He looked at the photographs without any apparent enthusiasm. After some time he looked at Kanu and said, 'Do you remember Father Darren?'

'I do. And I want to visit his grave.'

'Then remember what he used to teach us from the gospels and tradition. One saying he was fond of repeating was, "He who troubles his family shall inherit the wind." Do you remember?'

Kanu understood why Rajat was saying this to him. But why was Father Darren fond of saying that particular one; did he feel that he had made his own devout Irish family unhappy in some way!

Rajat returned the photographs. 'No, Kanu, I don't think it would be a good idea for you to stay in Serampore. But please let us know if we can be of any other help. Ranga-da and Moli, Ranga-da's daughter, wanted to come today but I told them that I would ask you first. Others would come also if you want.' Rajat looked at his watch. 'If I hurry I can catch the express bus,' he said but without the self-assurance of one who knew what he was saying.

Kanu accompanied him outside. He stood on the balcony to see the lanky figure of Rajat unhurriedly plodding to the hospital gate. Before turning the corner, Rajat looked back and waved his hand.

Something churned inside Kanu. 'I really wanted to be home, Rajat,' he shouted.

Rajat could not possibly hear him from that distance. Suddenly his movements became brisk. He turned and plunged forward.

Probably the bus had arrived.

Eight

'Fifteen down, ten to go,' said the young technician to Kanu as he came out of the radiation room built with the solidity of a concrete bunker. The young lad, barely past teens and out of college, sat at the console outside the radiation room and he announced the count every day to Kanu with the solemnity of a bailiff. Between them, it had become a regular joke.

Every day, around eleven in the morning, Kanu had been walking up to the department and now, by the beginning of the third week, it all looked familiar and routine. The apprehension and tension he suffered in the first few days were gone, replaced by a sense of inevitability and monotony. Kanu nodded to the next man waiting to get into the radiation room. He was in a wheelchair and stared back at Kanu with a vacant bored look. Kanu had come to know that look. Patients who stayed long enough developed it. Some patients stayed for months. Many others had briefer sojourns, as brief as their illnesses would allow.

Kanu lumbered back to his ward. Some faces in their Cancer Ward had become familiar to him in the few days he had spent there; the inglorious crowd had separated into cognisable visages. There was Pritam Hazra, always looking lost in the busy surroundings for nothing much was happening to him. He had cancer of the food pipe and the doctors had not been able to decide if they would try to cut his tumour out or burn it. They kept hedging about him, never going all the way in any particular direction. The poor farmer went around with a pipe protruding from his nose like a snout. Next to him was a sapient looking man, with a long beard and beaded chains around his neck. He was the only match for Bose Babu's loquacity in this ward. He was a devotee of goddess Kali and an old inmate, admitted many times before. Everybody called him Kaka because he happened to be the uncle of one of the staff of that ward. Opposite his bed, was the bed of the boy with the sarcoma of his arm but as usual, the boy was not in his bed. On the last bed on the far side was the patient with angiosarcoma of the pelvis.

Over the past two weeks, Kanu had watched the handsome face withering into a shrivelled, discoloured mask and the man now looked distinctly unwell. His mother, Kanu had learnt, had been discharged. Opposite him, the last bed on the near side was Bose Babu's. Between him and Kaka were two young men. One was a new admission and the other, Sanjay Bose, had one of his kidneys taken out a week ago and presently was happy at the prospect of an early discharge. He lived in that heady zone where voyagers adrift in high seas find themselves in after sighting land. Then there was the man in bed No110 from whom Kanu's eyes would move away almost always, instinctively. That man's face had lost its wholesomeness. Distorted by the handiwork of the doctors, it looked like a cubic drawing, separated into ill-fitting parts. That man disturbed Kanu, always instilled in him a sense of disquiet about his ending up like that, a disfigured divided personality.

Next to the ward, an unused space was partitioned to house a makeshift cafeteria and a small library for the patients. The patients, who could move out of bed or were admitted only because they had their homes in places far from this hospital, often had their lunch on the large table there, particularly if a relative had brought in an extra dish to add cheer and variety to their dull subsistence. Kanu had almost made it a practice to have his lunch there, to fortify the bland hospital diet with rice noodles or fruit juices from the cafeteria. Besides, he loved to listen quietly to the chitchat of other patients. He looked at their faces, and tried to figure out what years of living and raising families and abiding by the thousand and one customs in an under-resourced society had taught them.

This day Sanjay joined Kanu for lunch in the cafeteria and Bose Babu followed him. 'Are you sure they will let you go home tomorrow?' he questioned Sanjay.

'In a day or two, yes. Though I will come back in two weeks for a checkup.'

'Then they are going to radiate you. They sure will. That would mean your treatment is still not over!' Bose Babu looked at Sanjay, as if to challenge his joyful disposition.

'I guess the kind of disease we have got, that's never finally over,' Sanjay said without losing the cheerfulness in his voice. 'But my doctor tells me that they could take out all the bad tissues there, along with the root. There is not much more to do.'

'Phoo! They would say that, almost always. Worse than the village usurers, these doctors. Never do they give you the full account at one time.' Bose Babu talked almost incessantly but ate very little and his eyes looked dull. His head shook and his hands trembled. After a few feeble efforts, Bose Babu gave up his attempt to eat. He poured water on his hands that dripped down on the almost untouched food on his plate. He stood up and immediately tumbled. Sanjay had to leap up and steady him. They called for a ward boy and wheeled Bose Babu to his bed.

Later, lying in his bed, thinking about Sanjay, Kanu remembered Ugabe, another kidney cancer patient whom he had met years ago. Ugabe had an incurable kidney cancer, which had spread all over his body. His doctors told him that they could offer him no treatment except to try to keep him pain free. It would be better, the doctors had told Ugabe, if he used his time for other things in life. Ugabe took temporary jobs as a courier, often for not very respectable establishments and toured the world with three pins fixing his right arm and a plate fixing his left hipbone. A big mass of the shape of a rugby ball in his left loin was left to follow its own course as he trotted between countries.

Bose Babu died the next day. Towards the afternoon all patients, as if warned by a secret signal, became aware of an anomalous thing, some sort of a commotion, happening at the far end of the ward. It was a commotion that was different from any other commotion of the world, created by a flurry of activities but muted in execution, without making any noise. It, nevertheless, became noisier in its silence. The doctors and the nurses spoke in hushed voices. Ward assistants moved in circles. All moved on toes like pusillanimous cats, nervous to the core, yet putting up a front that told the world that they were engaged in normal and ordinary acts of duty. A patient had unexpectedly died disregarding all due processes and the staff needed a little chicanery to make things up.

The length of the ward and a row of five beds and their occupants separated Kanu from Bose Babu. Eleven men with the same disease, for once, looked oblivious of anything unusual happening around them. They remained engrossed in their little worlds of six feet by three feet of a hospital bed. The one nearest to the dead man was busy looking intently at the fluid bottle emptying into him slowly, drop by drop, through a tube stuck in his hand. Pritam Hajra got down from his bed and sat on a stool to pour milk through his feeding tube. Sanjay pretended to be asleep; the young boy went to sit at the nurses' table. Only a three-fold screen smeared with old stains, hastily drawn around the bed, stood as a signal that all was done with the occupant there.

A bird came and sat on the windowsill. It chirped. The tree branches undulated and caressed the windows from the outside. Two vehicles plied on the road at the backside. One was a load carrier that passed with much noise, heaving and panting, rocking sideways like a fat duck.

It became impossible to stay in the ward, even in the seclusion of his cabin. Kanu dressed to get out. On his way to the medical superintendent's office to ask permission to go to the hotel that held his luggage, Kanu met Ved. Ved was going out on an errand. Samar Roy, the poet, had discharged himself from the hospital but Ved had promised his daughter to meet some of the poet's friends and urge them to raise funds for his treatment.

'Come with me; I will introduce you to an interesting man,' Ved said.

They went first to a newspaper office, in the heart of the city, but to find the person Ved wanted to meet and whom everybody called Kabir-da, easily the most famous poet of his generation, they had to go to a nearby bar. Kanu was surprised to notice how badly the smell of alcohol and smoke disturbed him. Till only a few weeks ago, he himself was a regular addict. The poet sat at a table surrounded by his friends. They were discussing a book about a little-known tribe and the thrills of a primal life. The writer of the book had stayed with them in their remote village, far away from the cities, in terms of both time and distance.

'Do you know what the authoress liked there most?' Kabir-da asked with a smile. 'It was the swing that the tribal boys fixed for her on a fig tree!'

The men drank and laughed about small things. They discussed very little poetry or politics. Kabir-da talked to everyone. He talked to Ved about Samar Roy; he talked with Kanu about photography. 'What'll you photograph in this city,' he asked Kanu, 'unless you want to do old buildings?'

Kanu had already decided, since that night in New York, not to do buildings anymore but to reverse his angle and find only people in his view. Still, he wondered, why should one look away from a world that many men over ages had toiled to build with their labour and wit? Buildings, statues, market squares, railway stations, their cornices and gables, their hidden lines and shifting shadows—was there no poetry in them?

Kabir-da continued to talk about little known exotic places, away from Calcutta— Geonkhali, Saldungri, Garumara, even the little place Monabari where Ved once worked had an old lovely bungalow where one could stay for a few days. 'You can do Dooars from there. But be careful when you are in a forest, for in a forest often the roles are reversed. You are at the same time a spectator and a spectacle. When you look at a forest, it also looks at you with its thousand eyes.' Kabir-da chuckled.

'Do you go to the jungles often?' Kanu asked and watched the gathering become hilarious.

'Well, it is like this,' one of them explained, 'Kabir-da goes to jungles only when he has planned to go to a desert.'

'That's the fun,' Kabir-da said. 'I obey and then I don't obey. I try to discover the thrills in either way.' For a few moments, he inclined his head towards Kanu and looked into his eyes. 'Find that out yourself! Try to walk a path not walked before, don't even bother if you create a trail or not. The images you will collect will still be no less beautiful.' He whispered almost inaudibly.

A middle-aged man breezed in, fully drenched, looking excited. He approached Kabir-da. 'My book has been published! Here is a copy for you.' He began to write a few lines on the title page.

'What an odd quirk!' Kabir-da pushed the copy to Kanu. 'This book is exactly what we were talking about!' Then he began to discuss the book with the others — the book, which told about the songs sung by the people living up in the north, where villages like Monabari still existed, from where Mahen had come. Kanu listened with interest.

There, nobody knows exactly when, but must be a long time ago, much before the forests had moved back to give ground to new tea gardens and the roads had started to go inside the forests, a few lonely men had forayed for their livelihood to the edges of those forests, near the hills. They were the *maishals*, the mahouts, and the *garials*. The local landlords then had vast lands and large herds of buffaloes that needed wide grazing grounds and water bodies to dip in. In fringes, far away from the common dwelling areas, around the forests, the landlords made their animal farms tended by young *maishals*. They took the buffaloes to the fields, fed them, washed them, and when situations required, fought the night stalkers with torches and spears in their hands, riding the head buffalo. It was not always that they won. During the early months of winter, the elephant catchers, the mahouts, would come to catch wild elephants and tame them there in the jungle itself and for many months, they too lived in the boondocks. The *garials* drove caravans to far-off places, driving through paths haunted by dacoits and wild animals, never knowing if they would return alive and unharmed. The women they left behind in their homes and the women they enthralled in the wilderness composed songs for those lonely men. The women sang about their desertions and futile ripening, and the men sang about their loneliness and unfulfilled desires. Together they made lyrics that echoed through vast stretches of lands and rolled down the rivers.

'But it must be a lost world now, has to be in this age!' a glum looking man pointed out.

'Mostly, perhaps,' the writer said. 'But the mountains have not shifted; the rivers continue to flow. The forests through which elephants pass from this side to that side and then return following the same trail years later are still deep enough. In the little villages, in the hamlets deep inside those areas, time still moves slowly and people still sing those songs. One can even today slip back through time in those places.'

Kanu listened. Was this what he had dreamt of when he took the decision to come back to India? To return back to past times that had bypassed him because he was elsewhere!

'For me, more than the time and the indulgence, it is nature,' Kanu heard Kabir-da saying, 'from where we get our elements. It replenishes us.'

'More to the point,' Kanu said to himself. He had not come back to rediscover eternal India. All he had wanted was to be on his own and take photographs that could tell stories. Before that, the possibility of regaining his health by making a brief stopover in an unsullied unpolluted place, where the air was clean and the vegetables fresh from the fields, interested him.

An hour later, when they emerged from the bar, the roads were under knee-deep water. It had rained hard in the meantime. Buses still plied, like launches, sending strong waves towards the sides. Only a few half-naked children looked happy, inventing games in the water-filled road that had suddenly become a river. Kanu watched Kabir-da and his group descending straight into that river with much uproar and delight.

He bent down to take off his shoes like everybody else and felt pleased. He remembered however not to wet his radiated skin.

Nine

A little before midnight the cries started. The patient in bed number hundred and twelve, the one with the angiosarcoma of the pelvis and fancy bedsheets and an estranged mother, became delirious with pain. His unfettered shrieks horrified the somnolent ward that had gone to sleep earlier than other days. Lying behind the closed door of his cabin, through a state of half-wakefulness, Kanu heard the deep moans, which waxed and waned, through the night. In absence of all other sounds, the painful shrieks jarred the silent ward. That patient had been going downhill for the past few days and everybody had heard him moaning now and then but this night, all of a sudden, he seemed to have crossed a line and given up all authority.

Kanu got up from his bed and called the night nurse. 'I need sedation,' he said.

The nurse went back to her station and consulted the order book to see what medications were allowed for Kanu. She came back with a tablet in her hand and proceeded to pour him a glass of water. 'What a ruckus that man is making, won't let anybody sleep tonight,' she said.

'You can give him a shot,' Kanu said. 'Is he refusing medicines?'

'His hip bones are all eaten up. He gets three shots every day. I gave him his ten o'clock dose and another tablet just half an hour ago. He has no SOS order. Besides, he soils his bed if sedated deeply. I told him that but he will not stop howling.'

'That man is in pain,' Kanu thought, and he needed a painkiller. It was immaterial whether he was decent or uncouth in making that demand. But the nurse had her orders and perhaps she was hesitant to wake up the resident doctor for a fresh order; maybe the occasion was not grave enough. 'Please call a doctor,' he implored her in a polite but persuading way.

Kanu woke up late the next morning. The sedative taken late in the night had kept him tranquil through the wee hours of the morning; yet he felt a degree of weariness enveloping him. His limbs felt sluggish, weak enough even to leave the bed. It was Saturday, he remembered. There would be no radiation but he would have to take his weekly dose of chemotherapy, that, a new concept said, would make the radiation work better. The thought made him laze a few extra minutes in the bed. Though he would receive only a small dose, the drug would keep him squeamish and nauseated for the whole weekend and it would still require needle pricks and the pain of a drip running into his veins. He looked at his hands. Already the drugs had smeared them with blackish blue lines branching upwards from his wrists, leaving behind indelible trails of past passages. He wished the residents would come early and start the drip soon and be done with it by lunchtime.

Kanu spent the rest of the day mostly in his bed, which was unusual for him. In the evening, immediately after the visitors had left, Sanjay brought along a new patient, Tamal, a professional football coach, to meet Kanu. Kaka followed with another new patient, a chemist in a private firm, who kept cleaning his fashionable glasses with a scented handkerchief. Kanu sat half-reclined on his bed and tried to take his mind off the gossip around him and do some breathing exercises to ward off the queasiness.

The chemist was eager to relate his own story. 'I had this suspicion myself, kept complaining to my family doctor. Just plain indigestion, he said and put me on a diet. We had three deaths in our family from cancer. My father and two uncles. But they were all old, and I've still eight years to go before my retirement.'

Kanu stopped his exercise and looked at the men sitting around him. It occurred to him that all four were younger to him in age. They looked healthy, some still waiting to peak and they gossiped like any other group of men, like a group of truck drivers meeting at a halt or a bunch of travelling salesmen blathering away an idle evening in some small hotel at a faraway place. Men here, Kanu had noticed, were most voluble just after the visiting hours and tonight they talked freely. None though mentioned Bose Babu, presently struck off from the daily agenda of the cancer ward. It was not customary here to toll the bell.

Sanjay waved his hand. 'Never heard of any cancer occurring in my family. Still, I'm booked!'

Tamal sprang to his feet. He rolled up his shirtsleeves and flexed his arm. 'Look at this, muscles still as tough as steel. Even a month before I worked out daily with boys who have not left school, never smoked in my life, never had anything more vile than a few cups of tea.'

Kaka pulled at his shirtsleeves, 'Be calm; be calm. It is all God's doing. What can you and I make of that? Just continue to pray to him, seek solace and everything will come good at the end.'

'Who had talked about finding any solace?' Tamal fumed. 'Your God is a greedy one, cunning. He puts people in trouble only to earn propitiation. I'm finished anyway. Even if I live, I will have very little money left to take care of my family. I see no God of yours showing his hand there!'

'Oh, he surely will,' Kaka was adamant in his view. 'He surely will. In proper time.'

The chemist intervened. 'But he is right about the money. My God, I have spent nearly ten thousand for the doctors to understand only what is wrong with me. Now there will be more tests, then medicines, and more tests, operations, rays. I've gone that route already, with my father and uncles. It simply goes on and on.'

Kanu listened. Most seemed miffed that this was actually happening to them. Some were angry. They talked about money, about the unfinished education of their children, about the lands they wanted to buy or now would have to sell. They did not discuss death though—too common an affair to discuss—an affair that takes place daily, often without any extraordinary trappings.

What bothered them more were the interruptions in the order of their lives and they remonstrated more against that disorderliness. For a year, when Nanu attended middle school and the school bus picked him up daily in the morning, Kanu used to take him to a small square in front of a large abandoned house that served as a barrack for the allied soldiers after the war. Every morning as they waited for the bus, a number of incidents used to happen, in the same order, every day. First a milk van would cross the square from left to right, then a yellow bus that carried handicapped children would turn at the nearest bend, then a lady with a long coat and a big handbag would trot in and stop at the bus stop and then the school bus would come. Very rarely the order was broken, and on the days it broke, Kanu suffered from uneasiness. Somehow, that order then looked so important. Sanjay and Tamal began to talk about the breaking down of that order in their lives. 'Why me? Why now?'

'You seem to be having an assembly!' Ved said as he and a junior radiotherapist entered his cabin.

When the other patients left, Kanu told Ved about what the men were discussing, about their predicaments and Kaka's persuasions about keeping faith in the divine.

'Being religious helps,' Ved said. 'I've seen Christian nuns and our monks enduring it the best, I mean the physical part of it, the pain and the corporeal sufferings.' Both he and the radiotherapist concurred that Kanu's tumour was responding well to radiotherapy and the pain was now more because of radiation injury to the sensitive oral mucosa.

Kanu told the doctors how his mother had suffered. She was all yellow and had pain. He told Ved how his father died.

'Your mother probably had a cancer that obstructed her flow of bile. Pancreas comes to my mind,' Ved said. 'Your father's mysterious disease could well have been a type of blood cancer. So you were, at least genetically, a high risk person!'

'Is that how I carried my destiny? In my genes? With a cocked gun pointed to my head and then playing Russian roulette?' Kanu asked. 'Then all that guilt I felt about smoking was needless?'

'No, that could have pressed the trigger!' But it's all very complex biology,' Ved decreed with a mock seriousness.

The radiotherapist was enthused. 'Talking of biology, why don't we put Mr Chatterjee on one of these new protocols of chemotherapy? A tumour so radiosensitive must respond well to the drugs,' he said.

'Most certainly not,' Kanu smiled. Drugs he was not going to try. About that he had made up his mind. Doctors try them anyway, one novel drug after another. Kanu asked Ved, 'How do you know that the new protocol would be something better?'

'Through clinical trials, involving real patients. With their informed consents of course.'

Informed consent! The old stolid gentleman he saw in the New York hospital was asked to give one. Kanu still remembered him staring with utmost incomprehension at the thick form in his hand, befuddled with the impossible task of going through the thirty thousand small prints there, making sense of it, and then saying Yes or No.

'But I can see so many poor patients here who have no money, no insurance or financial support from anywhere. Do they benefit ultimately? Is it possible for them to climb up all the rungs of the ladder to reach where they must reach to get away?'

'For a good many, it is not. Many run out of money and leave the battle halfway or drop down back to the pit, to use your analogy. Ved threw back as he closed the door behind him.

After they had left Kanu pulled out the day's newspaper, not to read the news but to do the crosswords, another trick the clinic in New York had taught him. 'Solve a puzzle every day, preferably from a daily paper and save them as cuttings so that you can look at them at a later day. That way, if you have to think back about last Wednesday, you can think of the words you did correctly on that day and forget about other negative things.' Kanu settled on the couch and began to unscramble the words. There was a long word across but the clue was a giveaway. 'Metamorphosis'. It struck him that there were enough imageries involved in doing a crossword puzzle. Each word itself was a cue to the past, or a granary for the future. The 'r' in metamorphosis easily fitted into a four letter vertical word. 'Dark.' That word too had many connotations — without light, without knowledge, without joy of sprouting of new life. It could be a period in time, a place, a small hamlet, a whole continent, or could exist even in the abstractions of one's mind. Most places known for their radiance and shine at present had been dark once. Kanu thought about what Ved had said about the nuns and the monks. Would he have coped better and in a more balanced way if he was religious?

The ward attendant came to fix the mosquito curtain. A nurse came in to remind him about his bedtime medicines. Tonight Kanu allowed her to take the medicines out of his cupboard and pour him a glass of water. The ward attendant waited at the door for Kanu to go back to bed so that he could switch off the light and close the door. Kanu signalled him to go away. He had found interest in the puzzle. He had also found out that it was true that there was a limit to which a man can grieve for himself; eventually most men would begin to think of other things.

Ten

The last few days of radiotherapy were proving to be difficult. Invisible rays daily singed the delicate linings of his oral cavity and gullet making all sensations there vapid except the pain that persisted relentlessly. Kanu pushed his lunch tray away. It was the twenty-sixth day of his radiotherapy and it had become impossible to eat with the pain in his mouth. The food tasted bland and it did not go down easily. Coming back to his cabin, he picked up a hand mirror and looked at himself. The skin below his ears looked dark and dirty. His lips were cracked and bleeding as fissures had appeared there. He could not stretch them enough to take in food or even smile.

The pain in the throat increased. He tried gargling with warm water and aspirin tablets and again with an antacid preparation that had local anesthetics mixed in it. That brought some relief, still sleep was impossible. He picked up the book he had borrowed from the patients' library and went to return it. Kaka and Tamal stood there looking out through the window at the back. Kanu peeped out to see what had interested them. At the backside of the hospital building, two men were cutting down branches of a tree that had broken during the storm last evening. He saw Mahen standing there, hurling suggestions to the men who tried to cut the wood. Apparently, things were not progressing to his satisfaction and soon he took off his shirt and hitching his *dhoti* further up, took the axe in his hand and began to cut and free the entangled brushwood. His strong arm rose and fell with a sure and easy rhythm. With the axe in his hand, Mahen looked changed. The timid callow man, seemingly lost in alien surroundings was gone, and in his place, Kanu saw a man labouring and perspiring with a delight on his face—the delight of a man who had a territory of his own.

'You seem to know that work well!' Kanu said when he met Mahen later, downstairs on the lawn.

'I do,' Mahen said, 'We live in the woodlands. There our land is completely different from what you have here.' He would not accept Kanu's invitation to sit by him on the wooden bench but sat on the grass in front of the bench and began to tell about their land and their lives. He spoke haltingly, often searching for words to put across the right meaning of idioms used in his dialect. Kanu could see that he was speaking from his heart and he listened with attention. Mahen spoke about their lives in a community with its own customs. Kanu watched him anguishing about the new uncertaintities creeping into their community and the fact that they did not have old and wise men chosen by tradition to guide a clan during its troubles, or to negotiate on its behalf when in conflict. In their place, they had village heads elected by clever political duels. They sat in the panchayat offices in nice brick and cement buildings, talked with the officers from the city, and lorded over their lives. But the forest and the nearby mountain where they lived had remained the same. Floods and droughts still harassed them. Elephants still made forages into their neighbourhoods and they still followed their old practice of paying obeisance to their own popular gods, their *gramdevatas.* To Madan Thakurs and Mata Bishaharis. It occurred to Kanu that in the one month they had been together he had not really seen Mahen's wife. Was she too ill to move about? 'How is your wife, Mahen?' Kanu enquired.

Mahen did not answer immediately. He was looking away at some distant object. After some moments, he shook his head and said, 'The doctors looking after her say that either she stays back for another week of rays or we have to come back again in two weeks to take another type of rays. We must hurry home. God knows how our girl is faring all alone.'

'Well, in any case, you always have to come back again for checkups. The doctors will need to know how effective this treatment has been for your wife and decide if she needs further treatment. I am told that they order the first checkup after a month or so.'

'After a month! How can we wait for another month in this unknown city! Not doable! She will die from worries about our daughter.'

'I guess they'll tell you what to do when they release your wife from here. That is how it is, usually. Go back to your place and come again for checkups.'

'But we live so far, and we're so poor,' Mahen said. 'Can we come back again? Isn't it enough that such big men have treated her with such a pricey and fanciful foreign machine? ' He got up and took a few steps towards the ward only to turn back again. 'Please wait a few moments here. I have to show you the papers the doctor has given this morning.'

Kanu remained seated on the wooden bench. Although buildings crowded on three sides of the lawn, a fairly strong breeze flowed. There was moisture in the air. It was raining nearby. Probably it would rain here again today though the monsoon was yet to arrive according to the weathermen. The grass under the benches had somehow grown thicker and greener. Creepers on the back of the benches and on the concrete slabs behind them sported new leaves. One slender branch of the tree under which Kanu sat extended in front of him and it now moved gently up and down under the weight of thick foliage stirred by the breeze. He waited patiently for Mahen to re-emerge. An idea was beginning to form in his mind.

A taxi waited on the thoroughfare between him and the hospital. A woman was wheeled down a short ramp to the taxi. An elderly man stood near it. 'We will be late,' Kanu heard the old man saying. 'Fifty miles to go and all over those ruts and potholes. God only knows when we will be able to make it home.' The man then changed his tone and addressed the driver, 'And you, you better be very careful how you drive. A sick patient will ride in your cab, no jolts to her, by any means.'

A sick patient? Can one be a patient and not be sick? Kanu looked at the fair woman sitting in the taxi. She bore no trace of her sickness. Someone had taken care to comb and tie her hair neatly, put a thick vermilion mark at the parting of her hair and a round large red dot on her forehead. She looked amused and sat quietly with a shy but droll expression on her face, like a teenage girl who had taken an unauthorised vacation. Momentarily, their eyes met and after batting her long eyelashes a few times she looked away. In that fleeting second Kanu got the distinct impression that she was saying something to him, something like, 'I am going home, when are you?'

Serampore, Kanu had hoped before, would provide him a base if required, before he finally moved on. It would take him in its fold, however briefly, and allow him a place that he could call his home. Like the man in a story he had read. That man came back to his family one evening years after he left it as a wild young man. At first, he sat uneasy as an interloper through an unhurried family dinner while others lazily gossiped. Next morning, curiously, it seemed as if the man was never away. As if the long intervening events filled years never existed. As if the blood between him and the other family members had never turned bad. The man somehow seemed to know all the recent jokes about the family members, the likes, and dislikes of the young members he had not seen growing up. The elders seemed to have forgotten and forgiven the man's past mischief as an inconsequential feat of a young man. With temperance and with the promise of no further surprises, all came together. Kanu had hoped that his story would be similar but it now seemed that it would not.

The taxi waited, apparently because some papers were not ready, and the old man got angrier. He chattered continuously and criticised everything. He was particularly severe about the city roads and the dirty conditions where he lived. He wanted to take his wife some place where it was healthy, the air clean, and the water good. Away from this crowded city, its crammed mucky spaces, and dusty rutted roads. 'And the fish!' The man whimpered as if he was about to cry. 'When did we last eat a fresh one, caught live from a pond, a fair sized *Rui* grown in clean sweet water?'

The lady in the taxi looked uneasy, sitting in full view of all others and being subjected to the continuous harangue of her husband. She looked at Kanu again, this time more openly, as if daring him.

'I'm going nowhere,' Kanu murmured his reply to her unvoiced question. 'Or I could go anywhere, without a care.' He only needed, but needed badly, a place to lie back for a few days, to gain back his health after this radiation treatment, and ponder.

Mahen came out. Kanu stood up excited and immediately stepped into a hole and twisted his ankle. Mahen ran to him and helped him to stand up. 'Can you walk?' he asked offering his shoulders. Without hesitation, Kanu leaned on Mahen as easily as he would have done on an old friend. Surprisingly, Mahen's sweaty and smelly body, his worn out clothes and gawky manners did not bother him.

'Do I need to be X-rayed?' Kanu asked when Ved visited him that evening.

'I don't think so,' Ved said, 'it's just a minor sprain.'

While they were talking the resident from the radiotherapy department came. The seniors had discussed Kanu's case, he informed, and had decided to cut short his therapy because of the reactions. So Kanu should prepare for a discharge earlier than the date fixed. Kanu asked Ved to stay back for a few minutes. He could not tell him about his problem with Serampore but he must include the doctor in the plan that was forming in his mind.

'I was thinking about what your Kabir-da said about the forests and hill resorts in North Bengal. About the nice forest bungalows there. What do you say about my spending some time there for my recovery, as a layover to get myself recharged?' Kanu began.

Eleven

On Sundays, senior doctors usually would not come for ward rounds and patients would not be scheduled for any operation or radiation therapy. The campus would lose its daily crowds and all movements inside would become languid. Ved, who stayed in the hospital quarters, dropped in a little before noon. Half-reclined on the bed with pillows to support his aching back Kanu was engrossed in reading a magazine that had a full-length feature on forests. It described with pictures how the poor woodcutters and the honey gatherers in Sundarbans went inside the jungle wearing masks of human faces to the rear of their heads to confuse the tigers, for the tigers always tend to attack human beings from behind.

'Clever, isn't it?' Ved asked glancing at the picture. 'To present two faces to the prowler! But why are you reading about Sundarbans? Those forest bungalows, or the one in Monabari that Kabir-da sold you so well, are exactly in the opposite direction from where these tigers are.'

'Tell me about them then,' Kanu said sitting up but trying to suppress any tension in his voice.

'I can't tell about them all but I can tell you about Monabari.' Ved perched on the lone couch against the opposite wall and took time to make himself comfortable. It was apparent that he was gearing up for a long chat. 'Just a minute dot on the map of India, Monabari is up in the north, near the Himalayas, six hundred miles from the seacoast. It has jungles, rivers, and a primal tribal setting. I have not been there for some time so cannot tell you what all has changed there. I presume it still has more of nature, the way God has created it, and less of man-made masonries. And certainly not crowded bazaars or smoking chimneys. For a person like you, it could still be a kind of time travel, a journey to a different world that you've not known before.'

Kanu smiled but his smile was shortened by a sudden painful tug. Sores had developed around his mouth and whenever he tried to stretch his lips, they were bruised. He took out a tube of Vaseline and smeared some on his lips. His mouth felt dry and the inside of his throat ached. Just two more days to go, he reassured himself, for his radiotherapy to be over. Ironically, that would also be the time for his discharge from this hospital and he would have to find a place to stay. He chose his words carefully. 'For my photography I need to move about, perhaps remain outdoors for long periods but I must get back some strength before that. How long will it take for my strength to come back? Suppose I need a layover for some time — can it be arranged in those places, in a quiet set-up, like a resort or may be in a forest lodge? And when can you give me an okay report?'

'Six months at least. After six months, if you've no recurrence, then it can be said with some certainty that you're cured, for the time being. Plan for a layover of at least four to six weeks, until we give you the first checkup. Before that you should not move about freely.'

'That's too long a period to stay in forest dak bungalows!'

'Yes. Even too long for that dak bungalow in Monabari about which Kabir-da was so passionate. If you really want a quiet solitary place for recuperation in that area,' Ved looked thoughtful, 'I think you will need to stay in a hotel, nearer to a hill station, or in a tourist lodge, which might not be comfortable enough. It would need some real looking up to find and fix the right place. Let me talk to Deep. He manages the health centre in Monabari now, a quite cheeky, feisty fellow. He would come up with something. I will call him and ask.'

Ved was back again late in the night just when Kanu was about to go to bed. The weekend break of radiation for two days had lessened the soreness in his throat and the evening had passed off without much trouble. The magazine had kept him occupied for the better part of the evening, allowing him rest and time to think. On Sundays, visitors for other patients stayed longer, which left Kanu alone in his cabin. Rajat, though, had not come for four days. He was surprised to see the doctor knocking again, that too so late in the night.

Ved smiled, taking in the look of amazement and curiosity in Kanu's face. 'I have news for you. Could not keep it waiting for tomorrow. Deep has proposed something weird. I told him that such a place would not suit you but he insists that it would be habitable enough.'

'A bed and breakfast? In Monabari?' Kanu was incredulous when Ved explained to him what Deep had suggested.

'Not a bed and breakfast, rather a type of paying guest accommodation. It is not unheard of there as people from other states at times come for government projects and stay for a few months. Some of the smaller resorts there offer home stay to tourists. This family, he tells me, is well off, has built a new annexe to their house but will not move in there for sometime for astrological reasons. It might appear stretched a bit but it can work out just fine. We think we'll not disappoint you.'

'We!' Kanu noticed the pronoun but did not ask about that. 'My Lord has many rooms in his mansion. So says the gospel.' He said with a grin.

'Have you converted to Christianity?' Ved asked. The smile on his face had disappeared.

'No, I'm still a Hindu Brahmin, might be without the verve but twice born all right.' Kanu said, 'I said that because I've been thinking about such things recently.'

'Well, in Monabari you'll have the right space and time to think about such matters.' Ved looked relieved. 'Don't worry. Deep is there. He will guide you. You can be one more Bhatia there, if you want.'

'Bhatia?'

'Bhatia is the word they use for the settlers from south Bengal.'

'Who are they?' Kanu asked. He was curious and uncertain, with all sorts of new doubts creeping in. Moreover, Ved's use of pronouns in place of proper names irritated him, 'If you will please!' he added.

'The sons of the soil, the Rajbanshis. People like Mahen Burman. Did you notice he had Mongoloid features?'

'His features certainly look different, as is his dialect. Is there a mystery?'

'Yes, a regular anthropological conundrum. There are many theories about their original tribe, how they came to settle in these areas many hundred years ago, and what happened to their own language. But they sure are different from the rest of the Bengal and later settlers from South Bengal began to call them 'Bahes', to jeer at their foolishness. The natives sneered back by calling the settlers 'Bhatias'. It is sort of mutual respect for each other or lack of it.'

The power went out. They waited for the generator to take over though it would supply only a few essential circuits. Kanu felt thirsty. He opened a can of soft drink for himself and gave one to Ved. With the drink in hand, he went near the window and drew aside the curtain. A diffusion of light coming from inside the buildings had dimly lighted up the lawn. Beyond that, in the foreground in front, around the tall trees and their shaggy branches, darkness reigned. Far away, a timid lamp suspended from the iron arch over the gate humbled itself against the all-pervading duskiness. In the opposite wing, at some distance, white illuminated panes lit up a portion of the top floor. The intensive care unit had full twenty-four hour power backup.

Ved carried his own drink to stand beside Kanu.

Kanu sipped his drink in silence. The bittersweet liquid tasted bland in his mouth but the cold fluid caressed and soothed the dry ache in his throat. Kanu waited for Ved to resume his talk. When he did not, he himself pitched in, adding a laugh to make his words sound lighthearted. 'It's going to happen then, in my real life; it would appear quite fictional though, I suppose.' He stepped back to sit on the bed.

'What would be fictional?' Ved asked without looking back.

'My staying in Monabari— a rank outsider grafting himself on an unknown family living way back in a rural area! Will the story hold?'

Ved gulped down his drink quickly and turned to face Kanu. 'Why do you worry about that? This is not a story; this is real life. Anything can happen here.' He took one last sip and then resumed on a more serious note, 'I am afraid you are imagining Monabari as one remote Shangri-La in a distant Himalayan abode. It is not. Monabari proper is a big village and though it is half a day's journey away from the district town, and areas around it are sparsely populated, it serves as a block headquarters. It has a railway station, a health center, and the gentry there is educated enough to make conversation. Most important, it has electricity where you would stay, a few telephones, though no mobile towers yet. Yes, just beyond that, it is all dark woodlands. There people like Mahen live, in small hamlets, in huts with mud walls and thatched roofs.

These people, the ordinary Rajbanshis, at least a large number of them, have lived there in the same way since way back in time. Not primitive but surely old fashioned. I can tell you what happened one day soon after I first went there. The quack doctor there requested me one evening to attend a call on his behalf. He had fallen down from a cycle that morning and sprained his ankle. Isn't it rather surprising how you remember some wee details even after years?' Ved extended his right hand holding the drink away from his body to suggest the distance in time and brought the thumb and forefinger of the left hand together to indicate the infinitesimal nature of the recollection.

Kanu listened as he watched Ved talking leaning back on the windowsill.

The words from there came slow and resonating. '...already dark after dusk. The younger brother of the patient escorted me into a courtyard full of people surrounding a man prostrate on a porch. The only light came from one or two oil lamps. The family had called a *dhimal* already. You know what a *dhimal* is?'

Kanu shook his head. He was surprised at Ved's enthusiasm to describe Monabari. 'This man has a thing going with that place,' he thought but he did not interrupt the doctor who had a faraway look in his eyes as he relived an incident that took place in a remote locale on a dark night many years before.

'A *dhimal* is a sorcerer but his powers are less than an *ojha's*. This *dhimal*, they told me, was unsure of his diagnosis. Which meant, till then he was unsure of the nature of the spirit bewitching the patient. Was it the most virulent Kali or Chondi or a less virulent Masan? The *dhimal* was busy plucking some basil leaves but he was quick to place me. The man was clever. He immediately made me a confidant in his actions, starting a discussion about the possible diagnosis. The patient was ill in his head, he told me — he was at least right on that score. The question was what had made him ill. If the patient had gone to the northern side of the pond in unclean clothes after dusk, in all probability it was Bisua Masan. But if he had committed some unholy acts there as well, it could be as bad as a Bhutkali seizure, a real trouble. The *dhimal* complained that he was not being given the proper history, resulting in acatelepsia.'

'Meaning?' Kanu asked. He still felt irritated the way Ved talked reclining his head back in the shadows and holding the drink in front of his mouth like a microphone.

'Inability to understand, a failure to diagnose.' Ved explained his Greek. 'Frankly speaking, when I now think of that shadowy night, that half dark house, an ill man, with no support to fall back upon, I feel like a professional kin to that *dhimal*. With so many gadgets, we goof up as often.'

That man is not going to come and sit here, Kanu thought and pulled a chair to where Ved was standing. He straddled the seat in reverse, supporting his chest on the back of the chair. 'Do they still have those medicine men there?' he asked.

'Yes, but they've become rare. Adulteration, as in other spheres of life, has crept in there too. They don't do so well nowadays, not because the secret knowledge is lost. No faults in the techniques either, for there was never a true science. The ojhas themselves have become phony, loosing faith in their own methods. They lack the conviction of their predecessors. They are simply in it for earning their livelihood.'

'You got a point there,' Kanu nodded; the air was humid and he felt warm. He put down his empty can on the floor and rolled back his shirtsleeves. 'As they say, a rainmaker who does not believe in his charms is a bad rainmaker.'

'Do they say that?' Ved chuckled. 'But you are right. They now owe their existence to mostly poverty and lack of access to modern medicine. Funnily, the village quacks, not the organised medical service, are their main enemies in business. These quacks can cure small ailments with a few tablets, which are often cheaper than contracting an *ojha.*'

'Interesting,' Kanu said, 'because of my illness, many people told me about some exotic means of treatment, some of them plain sorcery. But most of those treatments in the West cost you dearly.'

'Really!' Ved seemed to ponder that. 'Why so?' he asked.

Kanu did not come up with an immediate answer to that so Ved went back to his story of that night, how, out of his natural interest, he waited to see what the *dhimal* did next. The *dhimal* carefully selected some basil leaves and holding them over the patient began chanting some mantras. When the recital was complete, he threw the leaves into a pot with water. 'How the leaves float or swirl in the water is important.' Ved put his drink on the cupboard to stretch his left palm and on it drew patterns with his right index finger. 'If correctly deciphered they can point to the offending goblins.' He went on to describe the real show, how the *dhimal* asked for a seine and covered the patient with that and how he went on jumping around the sick man, concocting elaborate liturgies, constantly cajoling and threatening the offending spirit. 'I asked the family to bring the man to the hospital. To that, they were all aghast. How could they take him to the hospital in that terrible condition! To them it was not a disease that could be treated in the isolation of a medical ward.'

These doctors! Always so fond of theorising! 'Cut the crap, focus on putting in the needle properly,' Kanu's tone was sharper than he intended to make it.

'What needle?' Ved appeared nonplussed, unable to follow.

'What happened?' Kanu asked, 'What happened to the patient?'

'Oh that! That I don't know. He was not brought to the hospital. Mumbo jumbo. It is the mumbo jumbo that impresses them most.'

'What were then,' Kanu wanted to ask, 'all those horrendous

machines that spewed out graphs and data when Ludwina died? All those doctors scurrying and twiddling with the numerous tubes dangling about her and pretending to be pulling off mystical feats — was that not mumbo jumbo as well?'

Ved had not noticed Kanu's peevishness. He continued despite Kanu's earlier sarcasm. 'But that day had more surprises for me,' Ved said. 'What happened after that was even crazier. I went straight to the hospital for it was already time for the evening rounds. When I reached the hospital, it was in an uproar. The nurse on duty and other staff were standing on the verandah and yelling at someone hidden behind the bushes at the back of the health center. A woman brought forcibly to the hospital for safe delivery had gone into labour and had fled there to do the job she regarded as entirely her own.' Ved turned and walked the few paces to the couch and sat down.

Everything about them became quiet. Outside, the air was still and the tree leaves did not rustle. Only a cricket sounded, which added to the eerie absence of light and sound.

'But that was nearly a decade ago,' Kanu resumed their talk. 'Surely things have moved from there. You've Mahen, who is reaching forward.'

'That's true,' Ved said. 'I'm surprised and glad that he did. Our country has changed in the last decade, might be Monabari has changed too. The Monabari I talk of now perhaps lives only in my own imagination. Still, I hope you'll find it different.'

'I'm damned to bite this bullet in any case. And who knows, a last surviving good old *dhimal* could still thrill me or I might come across a true mystic in the hills nearby who knows the ways not known to science.'

'At least you will find the weather cooler.' Ved drew up his knees and rested his elbows on them to support his chin. After few moments he said, 'They say, you either believe in God or in Darwin!'

'Right, you either believe in God or in Darwin. The question is if you believe in God, then do you believe in the devil also! But why would that family agree to host me?'

'You have money!'

Later, after talking to Rajat, Kanu made plans to go to the Ganga and perform the rites for the unappeased wandering soul of his father before he left for Monabari. They would then hire a car to go Serampore for just a visit. Unfortunately, on that day, a general strike was called—The World Bank had proposed some new economic policies for India. On such days, Kanu learnt, nothing moves in this city, not even the human drawn carts the city has so obstinately preserved to serve its gentle citizens.

Twelve

The humid evening gradually transformed into a cool lethargic night as the train to Monabari jingled through the flat terrain of Bengal a week later. Kanu tried to read a book. A full night had to pass before he would finally dock at his new port and he welcomed that intervention. Mahen and Keka had tucked themselves in their berths, in unaccustomed comforts that Kanu insisted on buying for them. He could feel their eagerness for the daylight to break with which this ride would end. Then it would be another hour by a connecting train through the backwoods before they were home.

Kanu read the book and thought about the place and the people he was about to stay with, trying to form a picture from what he was reading and what Ved had told him. The word 'Rajbanshi', he read on, literally means 'the royal race or clan of the king' but as a tribe they bear, as some pundits feel, legacies from the waves of mongoloid tribes that through the ages had wandered into the flat land guarded on the north by the steep Bhutan hills. For a long time though they did not settle here for the forests were wild, the weather cold and damp, and the soil full of sand and rocks. Much later, when some wandering tribes and the land did grow into each other, men began to settle down here in small groups, and when they had grown to a sufficiently large number, they had a king of their own, a man from their Koch tribe.

Teesta is the name of the river they began to live by. There are six other rivers but Teesta spreads the most. For ages, it had brought the Rajbanshis joy and sorrow, hope and despair. Teesta to them is like a mellowed woman that at times turns into an aged gorgon. It is an idol turned into a fetish. Every few years, the water from melted ice in the hills and the rain swell it up enough to cause floods. Some years it rains less and theTeesta dries up. That is even worse for the locals, particularly if it has been preceded by a bad year. Then the rainmakers come. It must be a night without a moon. The women gather in some lonely field to perform secret rites abandoning all their reticence and sing ribald songs while marrying off frogs. The men folk must be far away during this time. The natives live mostly off the land, and except a few landholders, most of them live in extreme hardship. Floods and droughts have repeatedly decimated them, have kept them unsettled and poor. Women and children die more easily, along with the cattle, from poverty and illness.

Kanu wanted to ask Mahen a question. He looked up and saw Mahen staring at him. He folded his book and asked, 'Has the world changed for you, Mahen?'

'The world?' Mahen smiled shyly. 'I do not know. Do I know about the world? We live in a small place. I had no idea the world was like this.'

'I mean your own world Mahen, the world that you live in. Has that changed for you?'

Mahen thought over it. 'It is now different from what we used to have earlier, in our younger days. My father called me to the field as soon as I could carry a plough. Daily living was much more difficult then. Going some place would mean a bothersome journey for hours on foot. Food was available only in measured portions. But everything else was simpler. We knew less and cared less.'

'But were you happier then?'

'A poor Rajbanshi is happy so long he gets two handfuls of rice twice a day and a cloth to cover his shame. That was about all we needed.'

Kanu asked, 'Didn't you ever think of a change Mahen? Don't you think it should be otherwise for you?'

'Yes, when the hardship becomes excessive even for us to bear; when for days we have nothing to do. No work is available; food is scanty and meals irregular. In bad years the people shrink, sit down with arms and legs tucked in. A day is cut down to only daylight hours. We prepare only one full meal for a whole day; retire with the dusk so that no fuel is burnt. We then live from one day to the next. Now we see everything around us changing — new roads, electricity, machines doing the tilling and reaping, even milking buffaloes — but for us poor Rajbanshis two ends are never met.' Mahen turned around and lifted his shirt to expose his back. A long ugly scar like a furrow bisected his midriff. 'We tried, even took to fights for a change but didn't really understand how our conditions could be changed!' He eased himself back into the berth but repeated his own confusion again. 'How?'

The book Kanu was reading told him about that confusion. Mahen's confusion, his clan's confusion. The Rajbanshis, for five hundred years, except for a few big landholders, have been mostly poor peasants, without education, without prosperity. Their own confusions about their identity had defeated them when they wanted to assert themselves by demanding a separate state, the Uttarakhand, the *northernland*, for their tribe. Their own King himself introduced the confusion by declaring his family as caste Hindus. He wore the sacred thread, built temples, and denied their origin from the Koch tribe. His family turned out to be one of beautiful men and women. And when they could wear enough jewels and build a big enough palace, they became a part of the Raj, played polo and cricket, dined in Delhi, danced in London. His subjects had followed him declaring themselves as part of the mainstream Hindu population, ignoring their flat noses, small eyes, scanty and slanted eyebrows, and their Koch customs and social practices. Now how could they become a separate tribe again to claim a separate land?

There were other confusions. What would be the boundaries of such a state — would it be determined by the languages spoken or by some dug up legacies about an ancient Koch kingdom, the Kamtapur? Peasants like Mahen who fought on the ground had to contend with a new confusion. Against their triangular red flag with a white sun in the middle was raised a bigger red flag. Those who carried that bigger red flag believed that the lot of the Rajbanshis would change only when the lot of all the other peasants in the whole world would change. People like Mahen should wait for that to happen. Nearer home, thrifty and prudent economic issues divided the clan further. Those who had land, opposed equity to the landless, raised objections to vesting of land by government to build barrages, to set up industries, or to expand tea gardens. Besides, over the years, other communities had immigrated to settle in their land—the Lepchas, the Bhutias, the Madesias, the Mechs, the low caste Hindu refugees from East Bengal who had reclaimed the *char* lands on the Teesta. With whom should the Rajbanshis share their forests and the rivers? Unable to resolve those confusions, the clan largely continued to linger back in time with their totems and village deities, their ancient tools, and austere lifestyle.

'Poor people everywhere suffer the same miseries but a Rajbanshi poor is the most wretched, displaced and unheeded in his own land.' Mahen summed up his clan's woes.

Kanu stirred in his sleep as he felt uncomfortable in the narrow space of a berth. In the dimly lit compartment, where only two or three night lamps were burning, all forms were comprehensible only in vague shapes. From his side birth, Kanu could see fragments of human bodies. A woman slept opposite Keka's berth. A blanket partly covered her face; he could see only the nose, some portion of the lips and an ear with a large earring. Locks of curvy hair lazily rested on the exquisitely sloping jaw line. The train rocked sideways as it passed an uneven stretch of track. He drew the curtain on the window over his head and looked out. The train crossed an unimportant station. A few blurred globes of lighted lamps passed by. Kanu sat and watched.

After some time, slowly, very slowly, the veil of darkness began to lift. Now he could make out a tree at some distance, or the outline of a thatched roof, then some indistinct shrubs. The train crossed a bridge. The darkness over the ravine was different from the darkness elsewhere. It was foggier, spreading out like a blanket. The train gathered speed and its regular soporific movements made him slumberous again. Images he saw in the semi- darkness outside dissolved into images conjured up behind his heavy eyelids. He saw Ludwina, as a little girl, dancing in front of an ivory white monument with a high dome and tall tapering minarets. He was standing on the bank of a mighty river, one dip in the flowing waters of which could absolve one of many past misdeeds. He saw Dukhiram coaxing him to swim. A priest chanted mantras and helped him to make offerings to the sky. He dreamt of yellow eyes; saw himself as crawling back to the womb he was born from, as if the sacred of sacred places was calling to him for a last repose at the end of his journey. He sensed passing through a dark tunnel that gradually lightened up and he began to feel bright light seeping through his closed eyelids.

He heard someone calling him in the voice of his son. He extended his hand and then he woke up.

'*Saab, chai.*' The coach attendant stood in front of him with the morning tea. He smiled at Kanu. 'Good morning sir, we shall reach within an hour.'

***

The dak bungalow, where Kanu was to stay initially in Monabari, was about ten minutes walk from the station, which had unusually long platforms for such a small place. The bungalow was on a high ground skirted by a road that looked like a black ribbon amidst the surrounding green and tawny land. One could see the faint outlines of the hills etched against the northern horizon but the land nearby was mostly flat, barely undulating with only minor elevations and drops here and there. Clusters of houses could be seen farther south on the other side after two large playgrounds and what looked like a school. Somewhere there a house was being made ready for him with the money he had paid as advance.

'It's old, but habitable. Absolutely,' pointing to the bungalow said Deep Saha, the local doctor who had received Kanu at the station, as he opened a wicket gate and stepped on the foreground covered with thick unmown grass.

'How old?' Kanu asked as he looked at the thick columns of wood supporting a sloping roof over a wide deck like verandah. At places the paint had peeled off and the woodwork looked splintered and raw. The dak bungalow, erected over a chest high wooden parapet, still looked impressive. If the railway station, so inexplicably big for such a small place, had baffled Kanu, the dak bungalow pleasantly surprised him.

'So, in here it will all begin!' Kanu said to himself.

As if to make that thought come true, he took out his camera and stepped back a few steps to view through its lens the amazing relic, built like a hunting lodge by a Maharaja who rode beside Edward the Seventh during his coronation. An old khansama still stayed here and served the occasional guests since nobody here bothered to know if he had been retired. As he pointed his camera to view the bungalow from different angles, his viewfinder captured the aged khansama standing at the far side of the deck, leaning on the nearby doorframe, as if transported from a bygone era, and Kanu had his first snap. He had his first meal in Monabari at a dining table that could seat twelve guests. On the opposite wall, there was a built-in fireplace and the stuffed head of a deer looked down on it from the wall above.

Dr Deep Saha came again in the afternoon with Dhar Babu, the sub-assistant engineer in the public works department, officially responsible for the bungalow. They discussed Kanu's stay in Monabari. The house of Rajen Ganguly, a settler from East Bengal and now a prosperous landowner and planter, had been chosen for him to stay as a paying guest for the time being.

'The rooms will be done in another day or two,' Deep Saha said, 'but you may wait for another few days. Ajoy-da will come next Friday and let everybody know about the arrangements made before you move in. That way everything will be smooth. Ajoy-da is very happy that you'll stay in Monabari. Absolutely.'

Ajoy-da, Kanu learnt, was the local Member of Parliament and had been returned form this locality for a record eight times. 'Did Ved have to take the matter that far?' Kanu was perplexed.

'Don't worry,' Deep said. 'It's just a ploy to keep everyone happy.'

Dhar Babu got up from his chair and began to do some bending exercises. He grimaced, fisting the back of his waist. 'This waist, it seems to get solidified if I sit for even a few minutes.' He bent sideways and talked from that position, 'You need not sit here in the meantime. Wander about and use that camera of yours. Go to Sevoke; see the Baghpool. What beauty! The photographs will come great.'

A day later Kanu was to witness that dizzying beauty of a river gushing through a deep chasm between two ledges of a hill. The western sun sent slanting rays through the slim tendrils of a cement and concrete latticework that bridged the gap in the land. The green steep obverses on either side looked vivacious where the sunlight had stayed, but below, down in the abyss, the umbrage looked thicker and shapeless under the shade. Through the middle, the fast waters of a river whooshed through, rustling and creating white foam against the large rocks and boulders scattered in the stream. From there a steady rumble filled the quiet air as the only proof of shifting time.

Kanu was stupefied. He had envisioned this spectacle in the operating room at the University Hospital in Amsterdam. He felt terrified at first and then tried to reason with himself. This was perhaps a much-photographed overpass where human artistry had expressed itself in perfect unison with nature. He must have seen somewhere sometime a photograph of this bridge built to honour the coronation of a queen of England and then had hallucinated about it under the influence of a pre-operative sedative. Looking at the river Kanu now felt an exhilaration warming up his heart gradually. He had come to the right place.

'What do you say?' Deep Saha asked, surprised at Kanu's visibly moved deportment.

'No words, absolutely.' Kanu turned back and hugged the doctor.

Thirteen

Kanu understood later the reason why Ved and Deep had selected Rajen Babu's house for his stay when he saw the new annexe in Rajen Ganguly's household. Rajen Babu had built this new annexe to his house but had left it unfinished, as he did not plan to use it before another six months. Workmen now worked overtime to make it ready for Kanu. The fact that Kanu was a Brahmin and Ajoy Pradhan, for some reason, had favoured him, might have had quickened Rajen Babu's acceptance. Ajoy Pradhan did not pay a visit as promised but had sent words.

Three days later when Kanu went to the Gangulys', that unfinished brick and cement irregularity was the first thing he saw. He was trying to recover from a sudden jerk as the cycle rickshaw abruptly left the main road and entered an uneven brick-laid approach to the house, the entrance to which was guarded by a tar painted tin door fitted in a wooden frame. Rajen Babu and his two sons, Chapal and Badal, greeted him at the entrance and took him inside. The inside of the house contrasted with its rough cortical presentation. The main residence was an L-shaped one storied house with a sloping corrugated tin roof hoisted on wooden beams standing on a two feet high porch at the far side of a large clean cemented courtyard. Two women stood on the porch of the house with a ten-year-old boy wedging himself between them. Only his head protruded from the wraps of the women's saris. The elder one came down from the verandah wobbling and tumbling, supporting her short pudgy body on the cement columns and cried in a peculiar croaky voice, 'Come, come. This house, can it be good enough for you…? Oh! this knee will kill me...old age means only trouble.' Suddenly she changed her tone and shrieked. 'Wait ...wait, do not come inside now.' She said the last two words to Kanu indicating with her hand for him to move back.

Kanu stopped, baffled, and was not at all prepared for what happened next.

The younger woman hurried to where he stood with a pitcher in one hand and a small brass plate in the other. She poured some water from the pitcher near his foot carefully so as not to wet him. The older woman had reached by this time. She took some flowers and leaves from the plate and touched Kanu on the forehead. Her hands danced, touching his eyes and ears. She took a portion of a homemade sweet from the plate and put that in his mouth.

'Please be our guest. What can be a better deed than to be able to serve a proper Brahmin?' She said gently.

'She is Kalyani, my elder son Chapal's wife and this is Badal,' Rajen Babu started introductions. Jugu, the minion of the house, introduced himself and carried Kanu's luggage inside.

Badal took him to his room. He was the younger son and had no job. He asked Kanu, 'Do you have a transistor? It would be better to buy a TV set. You can view quite a few foreign channels here, relayed through Bangladesh.'

The medium-sized room, recently white washed, had fancy light brackets. Wires drawn from the main building lighted the lamps in them. Someone had thoughtfully placed a bedside table and a cupboard against the wall. The attached bathroom had modern fittings but no water supply. Large tin drums stored water instead. A look through the window on the east cheered him. A fair amount of open land stretched on that side between the house and a pond surrounded by tall trees at some distance. The house was actually on a gentle slope.

Kanu began to unpack under the watchful eyes of Sona. 'Do you eat cows?' the ten-year old boy suddenly asked.

Kanu was stupefied for a moment. Then he was amused. He said, 'Well, one shouldn't, isn't that right? Do you know what happens if one eats a cow?'

'I don't know. Thakuma was asking Dadu. She said Brahmin or no Brahmin, where you stay everybody eats cows.'

'And what did your grandpa say?'

'He said he didn't know and that Thakuma must not ask you this question. We don't even eat chickens. A true Brahmin shouldn't eat all those things, birds, cows, snakes.'

'Are you a Brahmin?'

'Not yet. I'll be next year when I get my *poite*. Do you have one?'

Kanu was bowled over. He had not prepared himself for such an inquisition and a demand to produce his sacred thread as a proof. 'I've this for you.' He picked up a small folding binocular from his bag and held it in his hand.

The boy's eyes opened wide. He held his breath for a second, then his hand swooped down upon it and he ran away from the room.

An uninterrupted wall blocked the north side of the room but the west had a window that opened on to the courtyard, and through that Kanu could look at the L-shaped house. On the verandah, Rajen Babu sat on a cot reading a paper. Sona tried to balance himself from a hammock hanging from an overhead joist. At the far end, Rajen Babu's wife sat cutting a large pumpkin into small pieces. Through a door in the brick perimeter of the courtyard Kanu could see a heavy bosomed muscular woman rising up the steps from a pond carrying a pitcher. She came in and poured water from the pitcher on a basil tree springing up from a small pedestal and on some small flowering plants lined against the wall. Kalyani came out from the kitchen and stood there watching her. Suddenly, Rajen Babu's wife started rebuking the maid pointing to a large plastic tumbler full of turbid slop near the kitchen and a wooden ladder leaning against the wall with clothes hanging from its staves.

A little after five in the afternoon Rajen Babu called Kanu out for a walk. One of his friends accompanied him. Kanu joined them but when he saw the light in the sky he went back to fetch his camera.

'Namaskar, I'm Umanath Chakrabarty. I was the headmaster in a school in the nearby town. Now retired and waiting,' Umanath raised his hand to point to the sky, to indicate the place he was waiting to go. 'I hear you're a Brahmin too.'

Kanu shook his hands and said, 'Namaskar, Your village is beautiful.'

Umanath's hands were soft, quite unlike the large callused hands of Rajen babu. Together the duo presented a study in contrast. Umanath shorter and bald with a round kind face; Rajen Babu a head taller and brawny, with a large nose, bushy eyebrows, and a thatch of thick gray hair.

Umanath had a snuffbox readied in his hand; he tapped on that and pointing to the bag of camera strapped on Kanu's shoulder said, 'Last year a few young men and women came with TV cameras; they wanted to make some films about the Rajbanshis. My God! How they were disappointed to find that Rajbanshis have no *ghotul* system.' Umanath sneered as he placed a small pinch of snuff in his nostrils.

Rajen Babu chipped in, 'Monabari is no more a village. It's now almost a town.'

'Is it?' Umanath snorted. 'In the fifty years I've been here I've seen some changes. But call it a town only by its vices. Nothing else has developed, no factories, and no jobs for the young. The health center is the same for the last twenty years. Everything is languid. Only the boys have become unruly and the girls smarter.'

Rajen Babu laughed, 'That's the typical headmaster in you. You reduce everything to your students.'

Kanu changed the subject. 'Which way is Mahen's house?' Mahen surprisingly had not met him since he had come to Monabari.

Umanath looked at Kanu and asked, 'How do you know Mahen?'

Kanu told them about Mahen and how Mahen and he had become friends. When he said that he had come to Monabari following Mahen and he intended to use his short stay in taking photographs, he saw Rajen Babu and Umanath grin and exchange meaningful glances. They smiled as if they knew better than to believe Kanu's story. Clearly, what Kanu had declared as his reasons had not convinced them.

They were now outside the village, into the fields, now mostly reaped, empty for a better part after harvesting of the summer crop. 'Summer, autumn, and winter,' Umanath explained to Kanu the age-old cycles of cultivation, 'that is changing. Farming now goes round the year and not necessarily follows the rice-jute-rice schedules. Why, maize and even tobacco are now major crops in some areas, then oil seeds and potato.' He pointed to a few plots lush with young saplings looking expectantly to the sky for more libations. 'All Rajen's,' he added. Rajen Babu went down to a furrow and stooped to feel the crop. He had a faraway look as he whispered, 'Umanath, remember those days? Fifty years ago we fled as hunted animals.'

Kanu watched as the two old men peregrinated back and forth

through time. Between them, they told Kanu the story of their lives.

'We came here as refugees, after partition, and then we worked and worked,' Rajen Babu said. 'We worked throughout the day, even through the night if the night had a strong moon. We've tilled the land, dug ponds and canals, made roads. We teased this land to no end and then only it yielded gold for us.' He rose on his toes, spread his arms on both sides, and extended his head. To Kanu he looked like a proud tree.

Mahen, who lived a few miles outside Monabari proper, came next afternoon. He had been busy the last few days trying to put his household in order, neglected for the one and half months he had spent in Calcutta.

With Mahen around, Kanu thought, he could venture for a walk by himself. He was eager to test the lights at different times of the day, take a few pictures, and see the results. They walked to the station. Mahen wanted to reach his home before dark so he would take a bus rather than walk back. The bus would take a longer route that skirted around Monabari and the drop would be a mile away from his house but it still would be quicker. As they stood at the bus stop, some people who were watching them for some time approached Kanu.

'My regards. You… from Calcutta… a friend of our good doctor, right?' said a middle-aged bald man, dressed in a fine dhoti and full sleeves shirt. He reeked of perfume and the condiments he was chewing.

'Good afternoon. I am Krishna Mohan Chatterjee.' Kanu extended his hand.

'A Brahmin! My regards then.' Another man in the group folded his hands.

'I'm Bhola Pal,' said the first man after he had thrown a blob of red spit on the ground. 'And we're glad that a person like you has come to stay in this small place of ours.'

The other men nodded enthusiastically, 'True. You've chosen the right place. Monabari might look passed out now but a few kicks in the butt will send it running again,' one of them said.

'I'm grateful for your hospitality,' Kanu felt Mahen tugging at his elbow but he persisted out of politeness, 'I'm happy to be here and what I've seen so far ...it is a nice place.'

'It's very good of you to say so,' Bhola Pal said. 'We hope something good will happen to Monabari, now that a person like you has come all the way from America to stay here.'

They had got their geography wrong but Kanu did not correct them. It was quite beside the point. Bhola Pal accompanied him back to Rajen Babu's house.

Reception to Bhola Pal was cold at the Ganguly house though both Rajen Babu and Chapal were polite to him. Bhola kept on pestering Kalyani with requests for a cup of tea or a pan as he openly ogled her.

'Your stay here will be nice; enjoy that but when you buy land, you buy only through me.' He whispered to Kanu before he departed.

Rajen Babu immediately seized Kanu. 'That man is not welcome at our house. You had better avoid him,' he said.

'He invited himself.' Kanu tried to explain his position. 'But who is he?'

'He? A snake, that is what he is.' Rajen Babu hissed, '...found lot of powers recently, a wily local politician; pries in every household. He thinks he owns the world here.'

Fourteen

Three days later Mahen invited Kanu to observe a puja to the goddess Bishahari at his house. Bishahari, if appeased properly, can extract all poisons from a sick body. Her power drives out all evils from family households.

Mahen led Kanu to his home through a path that wound between two smelly ponds covered with thick slime. Two huts stood there at right angles to each other under the shadow of a large tamarind tree. One hut was larger than the other and had thick earthen walls; its straw top looked discoloured and shrivelled. The smaller one was built more feebly with walls made of only bamboo plaits. Mahen began to recite a couplet — areca on the north; open on the south; duck on the east; and bamboo on the west — that is how a Rajbanshi should construct his house. By that, he ensures that the tall areca trees would protect him from the chilly north winds. Ducks on the east means to have a pond on that side of the house, so that the water can reflect the early sunlight, which is good for health. Open south allows the pleasant southern wind to blow in, and bamboo trees on the west protect the house from the glaring afternoon sun and keep the house cool.

Keka was standing in the yard, her bun tied tightly at the back of her head. Her face lit up as she approached Kanu with an amazing fluidity. She seemed to bounce through the air as she began to chatter.

She said many things but Kanu hardly heard her. He stood staring at her. She looked not a bit like the bashful docile woman he had seen before. Her smile oozed warmth and happiness and her movements had all the springiness of a young girl. The forenoon sun washed her with bright rays; the air around her powered her movements and she looked as if she was sailing over the ground that receded beneath her feet. When she came near, she stretched her body straight up and tilted her head to one side, regal as a queen. Without realising what he was doing Kanu held up his camera and clicked.

'Come Dada,' Keka cried, looking embarrassed but happy. 'You, at our house at last! The roof here has become old but it has no mind to leak yet. Now, if this has thrilled you, you can stay at the poor sister's house for two-three days. But Kalyani Boudi is perhaps taking greater care of you!'

Mahen frowned at his wife. 'Stop this needless talk,' he said. 'Why aren't the provisions needed for the puja kept ready? Where are all the other people?'

'Everything was made ready hours ago and now this man comes to find faults,' Keka said. 'Look,' she pointed to a portion of the yard in front of a basil tree.

A portion of the courtyard in front of a basil tree, on an earthen pedestal reinforced by a few uneven bricks, had been smoothened with a thick paint of clay.

'Talk less, talk less,' Mahen said. 'Send for Balika. Let her bring some drink for Dada.' Turning to Kanu, he added, 'Come Dada, sit here and rest while we take our bath.' He went inside the room and came back with a tambour that he placed under the shadow of a tree.

Women looking fresh after a bath put large plantain leaves containing flowers and sliced fruits in front of the basil tree. An old man came and sat on his haunches on the ground beside Kanu. He smoked from a hookah. 'Poor girl!' The old man said pointing to Keka walking to the basil tree. She was wearing a new sari made from unwashed yarn, yellowish-white with a red border. Her long hair, wet and loose, draped her back. A large vermilion mark adorned her forehead.

'My poor girl!' The old man said. 'She calls me Baba as my own daughter. And look, how this unkind wrathful Bishahari has put her to all sorts of trouble! That hoggish woman wants blood.' He spat on the ground.

Kanu remembered Ved telling him about Keka, 'A year at the most.'

Mahen followed his wife. He too wore a new dhoti, and had a yellow cloth around his neck over a bare body. Husband and wife sat on either side of the priest who threw flowers on the plantain leaves, which contained rice, bananas, sugar and beaten rice as offerings. Some milk waited in a tumbler; a smaller pot had honey in it.

Large trees cast uneven shadows around them. The air became thick with aromatic smoke from sticks of incense stuck in a lump of clay and from pastilles burning in large earthen pots. The smoke swirled around the priest who chanted mantras with a peculiar primitive drone. Everyone sat silently with folded hands. The atmosphere was charged with anticipation, with an expectation of transcending all that was around and known, the house, the earth, and even the sky above. The mood was heavy with a hope to reach beyond the ordinary and the humdrum and to connect up to something spectacular that was divine and merciful. Kanu felt that eeriness somehow entering his soul and making a connection to a dormant sense inculcated in him eons ago and borne by him through many ages. The feeling was uncanny but not unfamiliar, as if he had sat like this before, many times, through other past births.

The priest produced a pigeon, sacrificed it and then smeared the ground with its blood. A man took away its head and set that on fire at some distance but where everyone could see it. After the ritual, the priest sprinkled water from a dented copper urn marked with verdigris. All who were present bent their heads to take that water on their heads and shoulders. When he came to Kanu, Kanu readily bowed to take the sprinkling on his head. The priest's chanting became louder as he began to circle the larger hut presumably trying to cast spells around it. Though Kanu could make little sense of the mantras, his gesticulations and showering of water and flowers to invoke the invisible powers did not appear to him as something that he should doubt. 'If this works, let it work for Keka,' Kanu thought and with everyone else in the crowd he too prayed for the blessings of goddess Bishahari and departure of all evils from the cursed home and for the recovery of the woman of the house from her illness.

Mahen lived outside Monabari proper, a few miles to the east of the main village. If Kanu walked south from the Ganguly house, keeping the health centre and the doctor's quarters on the right and the panchayat office, the new houses of the teachers of the school on the left, crossed the ground where a circus team had erected a tent a year ago, crossed a small rivulet spanned by a bamboo pole, turned left to cross the railway line, and walked for another two miles, he could reach Mahen's place. Alternatively, a local bus service, which plied four times a day on the district board's road, drawing a semicircle on the northern side of Monabari and the nearby villages, could get him down to a stop from where Mahen's place was just a mile away. However, one could walk in these areas so long there was light in the sky. After that, darkness reigned, darkness as solid as the stone walls of a fort. If there was a hut here from where children went to school, a lone lantern would burn for one or two hours in the evening but in most houses around here, wicks soaked in oil, producing more smoke than light, offered some light if there was a dinner to eat.

'Never walk alone in the dark,' Balika cautioned Kanu when, on later occasions, she felt close enough to him to unravel the mysteries of their secret world. The tall and fair Chan or the headless Magar wait in ambush. The goblins would get inside him and make him crazy. Kanu must not respond to any unidentified caller at night, unless the caller had repeated himself at least thrice and he must have fire or weapons made of iron in his hand while coming out of the room on dark nights. Balika gathered other children around Kanu and he told them other stories. How, once upon a time, all animals lived only in water, and how one day some of them ventured to come out and began to crawl on the land to explore what was beyond their world. Those who came out gradually evolved into cleverer animals and ultimately became man. Those who remained in the water remained fish. Those fish have no stories to tell one another.

'Absolutely,' Deep Saha said when he heard that. 'Presently I am that fish, condemned to squirm in the smelly pond of Monabari.'

The field that Mahen tilled was nearer to the Ganguly house than his huts. One day, Kanu sat under a small grove of trees, perhaps left to stand as a marker to distinguish between rival possessions, and watched Mahen at work. Mahen set off from the far side and came nearer, all the time pushing down the handle of the plough dragged by two bullocks. His whole body became taut with tension, his arms joined in front to steady the plough that bounced on the earth. As he came nearer, Kanu could see the pointed head of the plough emerging from the surface of the ground and sifting soil. Mahen reached this end of the field and then turned back. A mild drizzle started. Kanu now looked at his back, catching the raindrops. Mahen followed an invisible line, creating a new furrow, just by the side of the earlier one. This he did repeatedly, coming and going back and forth, propelled by the combined drag of two foaming bullocks, until the furrows became pliant and began to yield easily. His movements became easy, his hand rested loosely on the plough handle, his titillating the bullocks became less pronounced.

There were a few distant noises earlier in the air, perhaps from the generators powering a few pumps; now they were gone. The sky was slate coloured; it sent down fine white tendrils to the earth. Under a pale sky, in a soft but illuminating light, the earth around looked like a checkerboard with patches of different colours, sizes and shapes. Some of the fields were green already; some still waited in preparation, they looked gray. Sheltered by the trees and his umbrella, Kanu stood alone and watched. Around him, there were only the open fields and a few toiling men upon them to look at, almost no sound to hear, and only a faint familiar fragrance of wet soil to smell. Still the picture looked complete and the experience was satisfying. Kanu forgot that what he was looking at was quite unspectacular, flat, one dimensional, and that for many many miles around this place, there was no lift to ride.

On the day the replanting was to begin, Mahen and other peasants propitiated the powers lording over the crops. They cleared a small place near the northeast corner of the plot of land selected for the ritual. They performed a symbolic plantation of a sapling there, and then cooked a feast for the gods with rice, milk, banana, sugar and camphor. They prayed. 'Oh, gracious god, be kind enough to help us in our plantation. Give us ample rain and good weather. May we prosper with abundance of crops this year. Oh god, make this year a better one and keep us in health and prosperity.' After that, they fanned out one by one in the fields around.

***

The mornings in Monabari were beautiful, the afternoons dour, and there was no evening in the countryside, only long dark nights. Every morning and afternoon, with an umbrella, Kanu walked along the railway line following it for some distance, visited the fields where Mahen and his friends worked, and then returned by the same route. On days when someone could accompany him, he went inside the villages to meet people and take photographs. By now, he had found out that it could be perilous to wander in the villages unescorted with a camera in hand as unknown women should not be photographed at any time. Neither could he wear his jeans and photographer's vest and hat. It made a spectacle of him and he had to devise less conspicuous attires.

The monsoon broke late and poorly. It rained little at first and cultivators were unhappy though nobody feared a drought. When the rains came ultimately, they added a different smell to the air— the stink of wet soil mixed with the musty sweetened smell of decomposing leaves and overripe jackfruits. Usually the land here does not hold water for a long time, and the earth does not become muddy easily. Still, with the rain, the ponds become fuller, and weeds and shrubbery overgrow and rot on the narrow village paths now made narrower by heavy showers scrubbing off the earth from their sides. The paths to Mahen's village became treacherous.

Meanwhile, one by one, the curious lot of Monabari and even of the nearby settlements had visited Kanu: a policeman, the block development officer, panchayat leaders and their detractors, even a forest officer. Some were happy just knowing him. Others expressed shock at the meagre comforts he had to accept at Rajen Babu's house. They offered him extras — a comfortable couch or an extra fan; some even offered an extra serving of milk and butter, fruits and poultry. Some people wanted to sell him land, for a farmhouse he might want to build. All, however, wanted to know Kanu's story, its beginning and how it would end, to try to understand this unique incident in their world, the why and how of it, its logic, the cause and effect chain. That was important, to know what caused what in a story, the sequence of events, as the old storyteller reminds every time he finishes one. He has to end the story because a cow has devoured the tree of imagination. The cow had done that because the cowboy had not taken it for grazing. The cowboy had not because the maid did not give him his lunch. The maid did not because her baby was crying. The baby cried because an ant had bitten him. The ant had the best logic–it did so because it just felt like it. Kanu offered that to Monabari as an explanation. He had come to Monabari just because he chose to come. Monabari took Kanu's story in its hands, turned it this side and that, sniffed at it but did not swallow the whole. However, largely, it became friendly, tried to assimilate Kanu within its senses, in its daily living, and unknown to him for a while, even within its ambitions. It wanted to make Kanu a part of its own history.

A visibly elated Badal brought Manik Babu, a district level political leader, late one night. 'Manik-da will help us,' he gushed.

Manik Babu talked about his family and how his great grandfather, an officer in the princely native state which once ruled these lands, would make four men stand entire nights to hold the four corners of a mosquito curtain if he had to sleep in the open on tours. Manik Babu had inherited a large estate but he said he cared less about that because he wanted to work for the poor. He had a flag to carry and naturally had a duty to find people to follow it. He was very polite. 'Let's not hurry about it. First let Chatterjee sahib recover. Moreover, he has to know this place also. If what Chatterjee sahib has in his mind is as big as I hear it to be, then it'll be lot of work. Everything must be planned meticulously.'

Kanu looked at both men sitting complacently before him and

tried to guess what work the men were talking about. Of the two, Badal looked more animated.

'No, of course we must not hurry,' he said. 'But right now, I've no work to do and I could do the running around. Somebody has to do that and if I get that license for an agency, I'll be busy afterwards. I might not be available then.'

Manik Babu smiled. 'How can you say that Badal? Without you, Chatterjee sahib will be without an arm.' He turned towards Kanu and said, 'Chatterjee sahib is perhaps not yet ready to talk about the details. We'll do that sometime later but I must keep my district leadership informed. I'll look like a fool if suddenly one day you announce your project and they hear it from other sources.' Manik Babu departed, his smile intact but his eyes flaring. Badal shot an admonishing look at Kanu and then hastened to follow him.

That was it then, Kanu thought. Someone had spread a rumour about a project he would undertake even before he had come here. But who and why? Was this why Ajoy Pradhan had instructed everybody to make his stay in Monabari trouble free, and was this why Rajen Babu and Umanath looked in disbelief when he said that he had followed Mahen to Monabari?

A few days later Kanu saw Manik Babu again in the farmers' market, which did business twice a week, spewing venom at Jamil, a fisherman friend of Mahen. Jamil had failed to deliver fish for a feast arranged for the district leaders at Manik Babu's house. The yokel had since then played truant and evaded Manik Babu's summons but today the leader had caught him.

If Monabari had Mahens with their world of goblins and handheld ploughs, the *jotedars* and their vassals, a few Manik Roys and Bhola Pals who schemed and twisted everything to make it political, it also had Gopal Shahoo. Like one two hundred years old fictional gypsy, Gopal had been bringing all the latest wonders to Monabari for the past fifty years. The wheat grinding machine, the generator, the pumps, the power tiller. With one clever machine after another, he had kept Monabari impressed and flocking to his doors. He guarded the commercial frontiers of Monabari as his personal fiefdom. One day he sent an invitation to Kanu.

Gopal was in his office of lending and mortgaging business-cum fertiliser agency-cum saw mill-cum shop for tilling tools. He sat on a sprawling white mattress spread on a knee-high platform with a wooden box in front of him. The box served the dual purpose of a cashbox and a writing desk. The platform occupied only about one fourth of a very large hall. On the far side, lay heaps of all kinds of things — sacks of fertilisers, tins of paint, pumps, drums, some new, some broken and out of use, dust covered and forgotten.

After Kanu had drank the *sarbat* offered in a tall tumbler made of stoneware, Gopal leaned towards him and whispered, 'Don't keep your money lying idle with you. Money has wings. If you keep it with me, I'll give you good interest. Moreover, later, when you start your work, if you ever need cash, I'll give you a loan. If a good thing is coming to Monabari, Gopal Shahoo will carry his share of the burden.'

'Is he a very rich man?' Kanu asked Badal when they were out on the road.

'Very rich. Perhaps the richest in the entire district or even beyond it. On this side of the Ganga, except Ekanath *Jotedar*, and Hafiz sahib who is the owner of the North Bengal Construction Company and has fruit orchards in Sikkim, no one has so much money. Even the Lahiris, the old tea merchants from Jalpaiguri did not have so much money in their heyday.'

'That does credit to him, based in a small place like Monabari and being that rich!' Kanu observed.

'He is into many other things, from illegal cutting of trees in the forest to smuggling,' Badal said. 'Besides, he has ways to make money. Ask Mahen how he cheated them a few years ago.'

Kanu heard that story later, in bits and pieces from Mahen and others. For generations jute had helped the cultivators in these areas to earn cash with easier schedules of cultivation. That year, the cultivators found no ready buyer for their jute in a market increasingly reduced by machine made packing materials. While the government delayed in declaring its procurement policy and price, the market was further lost to jute smuggled from across the border. Local jute growers panicked, their leaders came, and a movement started to force the government to take steps to protect the cultivators against smuggled jute.

Both parties agreed that each genuine cultivator would get a certificate and the Jute Corporation would buy only from the certificate holders and in fair price. The cultivators in Monabari shed their worries briefly only to find that those certificates were hard to obtain. The piles of golden fibers of raw jute stacked high in their courtyards, which should have been solace to them, became their eyesores. They became desperate to sell their cash crop. Gopal Shahoo then started to buy in secret, without the certificates but at the price for hay.

Umanath pointed to a larger plot that was eternal, and involved many. For ages, big landholders, usurers, and agents of power here had connived to keep the farmers in perpetual debt, pulling off one smart con after another.

Fifteen

'So far!' Umanath sneered and took out his handkerchief to wipe his nose with a peculiar sound, the tone of which, Kanu had observed, varied with his mood.

'At least Monabari doesn't seem to disagree with me.' Kanu had said just then to the assembly of evening walkers gathered on the empty platform of the railway station, which was the only public place in Monabari to have some benches to sit with a shade overhead to prevent the evening dew from settling on their elderly heads. Kanu was responding to Umanath's assertion that Monabari like many other places was just waiting to become corrupt by the vices seeping backwards from the towns.

Umanath pulled up his legs on the bench and covered them well with his dhoti to deny the mosquitoes feasting on his blood. 'Who ever thought that Monabari can be a place for a layoff? I've heard that many sahibs and memsahibs now come to live in remote Indian villages in order to develop the third eye, awakening the Kundalini and all that. But Monabari is rustic, not mystic.' Umanath wanted to share his assumptions with the other evening walkers.

That was true, Kanu thought. Monabari was, as he had found, neither here nor there. Step a few miles away from it and one was in a grand wilderness running away towards the hills with white tops but nearer, the surroundings were grimy and haphazard. The people residing here used different dialects and did not care for the totems of other communities. It took very little for the local people to retreat from that grand wilderness to the ordinary and often naive suppositions and bickerings of daily life at and around their small huts — who stole whose goats or whose cow munched whose little vine. No commerce had come their way to change their plight.

Located away from the highways through which the chariots of development progressed, Monabari had gradually fallen back in time with its populace clinging to their hand-held ploughs and old ways of doing things. Other than seasonal work in the fields, nothing else here existed that could put food in the mouths of the masses. Yet everyone, even those from the remotest and the meanest of huts, had to follow a political flag. The boatmen here wore Bermudas and the girls wore English skirts, used dresses donated to the flood victims on the other side of the border and then smuggled in and sold cheap. On the balance, Monabari had fresh air, time moved slowly, and daily life had a sense of remoteness to offer a good enough hiatus for Kanu to hibernate and recuperate. Each day, all twenty-four hours of it here belonged to him. He could walk a few miles if he wanted, or sit at a place to read a book, had time enough to exercise his mind, to develop control of his mind over the body and he had prospered. The radiation induced sores in his mouth had healed and though he had a dry mouth because he did not make any saliva, he now ate with more ease.

'But a simple visitor or a tourist you can't be, not for a long time,' Umanath said to Kanu. 'In school, I used to teach the boys an English proverb that says: fish and visitors smell after three days. You've to know the people and the people have to know you.'

Dhar Babu picked up the tourist part of his statement. 'I told you Mr Chatterjee, move around a bit and once Dooars gets inside you, you may never want to leave this place again. Besides, in the jungles and mountains, you don't have to be careful with your cameras!'

Umanath and others began to discuss the historical places around Monabari that could be of some interest to Kanu as a photographer. Besides a big temple at Jalpesh, relics of the past here were few, a broken fort here, the ruins of a palace there, strenuous efforts of small kings.

'There isn't enough history preserved in this area, political or religious, anthropological maybe.' Umanath concluded.

The stationmaster, though an avid drama enthusiast, was usually a quiet listener. He now spoke, 'It depends on what one wants to see. I watch people boarding and getting off trains everyday, but each day I witness one or two uncommon astonishing incidents. Fascinating scenes from everyday life. This is not a peak that you stand on and watch nature, frozen for ages, with its timeless charms. Here, you've to get down in the stream and feel the current. The small *thans* of the deities in various villages have enough stories to tell. Mr Chatterjee here is a sahib, probably doesn't believe in god's doings but people have their beliefs. It wouldn't be a bad idea for him to look at those *thans* and throw a flower or two to the deities there, even if with a backhand flick as the Chand Saudagar did in the ballad *Manasamangal*.'

Kanu said, 'But then, you've to tell me the story. I don't remember it.'

Umanath chipped in. 'It's more than folklore. Singing ballads used to be the lifetime passion for many people. Boys began to train early to be a part of wandering performing groups, to be a lead singer, or a choirboy, even a simple drummer. Then they would pass a life of little money and much privation to make these ballads alive. Mr Chatterjee, these tales are complete only when the people who sing them and the people who hear them perceive the characters of the ballads as real men and earthly gods they know like their own families.'

The stationmaster said, 'Umanath Babu is right; someday we'll take you to a performance and then you'll know. For now, I can tell the gist of the story about Chand Saudagar, which is in fact two different tales, woven together … from a time when the gods used to interact directly with their followers or detractors. Chand Saudagar, whose merchant vessels braved the seven seas, had a running feud with the goddess Manasa or Padma as she was locally known. The goddess ruled over all the snakes and wanted to be idolised in each household, but Chand Saudagar, the most influential man of the region and an ardent devotee of Lord Shiva, declined to accept her as a goddess and called her a one-eyed wench. He refused to relent even when she had his six sons killed and all his ships destroyed. She then killed his seventh and last son by ordering a snake to bite him on his wedding night. The boy died but Behula, the young bride, refused to part with the body of her dead husband. With the lifeless body, she set sail on a raft determined to find the gods or means to bring her dead husband back to life. Braving many hazards, she found the gods ultimately, charmed them with her singing and dancing and made them broker a deal in the feud between the snake goddess and Chand Saudagar. Manasa gave back all the seven sons of the Saudagar, his riches, and the ships she had destroyed on the seas. In exchange, the Saudagar offered a flower to the goddess with his back to her.'

'So,' Umanath said, 'Mr Chatterjee should take a tour of these thans and see if he can strike up a bargain with any one of those gods.'

'Well, if one has to petition god, any deity is as good as the other,'

Kanu said and others nodded with much geniality.

***

'The thirty-five-year-old businessman had a heart attack,' Kanu read from one of the many small pamphlets the husband-wife duo he had consulted in New York had given him. 'Doctors told this man that never in his life again would he be able to do outdoor work.' One day the man asked his wife to bring the Bible to him. When his surprised wife brought him the Bible, he opened it at random and found the text, 'Jesus Christ the same, yesterday, today, and forever (Hebrews 13.8).' The man thought if Jesus Christ had really done it before for others, why would he not do it for him also. He prayed all day asking Jesus to heal him. When he had said his prayers all day, he seemed to hear Jesus say, 'Believest thou that I can do this?' The man answered, 'Yes Lord, I believe that you can.' The pamphlet described how a sense of quiet and tranquility enveloped his mind, and how within three days he was out again to do his work, and he lived to be seventy-five, never falling sick again for even a day.

The books and pamphlets Kanu brought had many such examples: a crippling disease miraculously cured when all hope had been abandoned; an inoperable tumour stopping to grow and then a chance meeting with a doctor who had faith in God and had the courage to cut it out; an intestinal obstruction relieving itself just when the doctors had decided to undertake a very risky and major operation. Kanu had gone over them before. It now occurred to him that those fables were no different from the one he had heard that afternoon.

The radiotherapist in New York had discussed these issues. 'God or no god, there is a higher force, a part of which resides in you, unawakened, untapped. Tap that and persist. Total healing might take a while but you must retain your calmness and persist. Be prepared to accept any outcome but remain calm.'

Kanu had long passed the time for his first checkup but he wanted to delay that for a few more days to take some more photographs and then take them personally to the studio in Calcutta he had started working with. He took a hand mirror, opened his mouth and carefully examined the insides of his mouth. He protruded his tongue, made it narrow and pointed, and moved it from side to side. The old ulcerated area had thickened a bit, and it was sore. The white row of teeth stood as a large stone wall of a castle bordering a pink red valley that sloped up again to merge with the thicker furred tissue of the tongue, and there, Kanu noticed, an area had become thick again, losing its normal lustre. He tried a closer look. It had certainly changed appearance, it was sore, and it was tender. Was there an ulcer on top of it? Kanu moved to have better light. He put a finger there. It definitely hurt. He removed the finger; the area now looked redder. He examined the tip of the finger. On the tip, mixed with a small amount of saliva, there was a fine, but an unmistakable streak of red, as a portent for more ominous developments there. Just the way the tumour had started to develop in the beginning.

He dropped the mirror. Must remain calm. Must not panic. As if powered by a gale, he moved with considerable agility to close the door and the windows, brought out the tapes, and ducked under a pillow on the bed with the Walkman plugged in his ears. Music and a calm voice filled his ears, '...Breathe in, breathe out, let the thoughts pass, make your body soft...see a light, a beautiful white yellow light, visualise it entering your body, spreading through every tissue, every fiber, every minute cell of your body and then let the light focus, concentrate in a beam, and pass through your mouth and throat...'

Next afternoon, he made a trip with Badal to see a deity known for its peculiarity. The many-handed black stone idol, with snakes around her head and neck, sat on a lotus. Oddly, in the place where there should be the roundness of a full belly, there existed a cavernous hollow inscribed upon with the distinct image of a large scorpion. The rest of the image had normal attributes with five hands on each side, although some were broken. The hands held a severed head, a skeleton, a gong, and a musical instrument. Ornaments made of snakes adorned her ears, neck and the head. A doll that looked like a woman sat at her feet, flanked by a jackal on one side and a peacock on the other. Kanu looked at Badal and waited for him to explain the strange deity.

Badal whispered, 'Great tantrics come here to offer puja to this *pet-kati* Kali. On the night of the Kali puja people will come from far and wide — have been coming here since when nobody knows.'

'*Pet-kati* Kali,' Kanu thought about the name of the deity. The name literally means an incarnation of goddess Kali with a slashed abdomen. That succinctly described the deity but did not explain the conception. Moreover, why the scorpion? Kanu asked Badal.

'I don't know. The goddess Kali has so many aspects. Ma might know; she recites hymns dedicated to the ten different female forms of goddess Durga and this may be one of those.'

Kanu sat on a stone slab and looked around. The stone idol might be ancient as was apparent from the chipped off black stone at places and the image's broken nose and arms but it had no formal temple. Just a common tin and timber structure housed her. The middle-aged son of the old priest had very little information to give. Yes, they had been doing this job for three or four generations but did not know who made this idol. All they knew was that it was found buried deep in the nearby ground and the villagers felt obliged to establish a *than* for a deity that looked so imposing. The old priest was indisposed and did not come out of his room. His son, though, did not think that there was anything extraordinary in the conceptualisation of the deity. It, he said, depicted a simple fact. If one has hunger in his belly, every other thing becomes inconsequential but he flatly declined to stand for a photograph with the deity.

Within a few days, it began to happen all over again. First, the sore in his tongue reappeared. Then the area hardened and its top developed an ulcer. There was pain, and every time Kanu put something in his mouth, the ulcer bled. Deep informed Ved, who consulted his seniors.

One afternoon, Deep came to deliver the consensus of opinions from the hospital in Calcutta. 'You must go back, absolutely,' he said. 'Get the operation done.' He drew a circle. Then he divided it into three equal parts. 'This one is for your mind. This one is for divine power. This one is for modern medicine. Even if you grant them equal status, still, without the medicine the other two add up to only sixty six per cent and medicine for you now is surgery,' he explained.

That evening Kanu did not go out for his evening walk. An operation would mean a further period of rest and though this family had been very caring, overstaying his invitation might not be sensible. He chided himself for the fact that though he was supposed to move on after a period of rest in Monabari, he had not made any plan to do so.

Kalyani came several times on the pretext of doing one thing or the other. She called on Jugu, 'Come here. Smoke the room now. Kanubhai is not going out today.'

Kanu came out of the room and sat on the verandah as Jugu came with an earthen censer with burning pastilles. He took it to each corner of the room, under the bed and the couch, behind the small cabinet and in front of the windows. The heavy smoke filled the room with a smell that would drive away the insects and the mosquitoes. Kalyani watched over him, indicating the corners he had missed. As she turned to step out into the courtyard, she paused, 'I shall go for a wash now,' she indicated the pond behind the house. Every evening women had their wash there, enjoying a little time with themselves. They cleaned their feet with stones, washed clothes and gathered water in their pitchers.

Kanu looked at her. Her eyes were restless and her lips pouted.

'Is it true that you are going back for an operation?'

'Yes. A minor one.'

'How can they operate on someone like you…so weak and not yet able to have proper food?' She started to leave but turned back again. 'My mother-in-law was mentioning about the fakir saheb who has presently taken residence in the Pir Saheb here. The old man, she hears, knows charmed medicines. People are thronging to meet him in hundreds. From Assam and Bangladesh. Looks like the great annual fair at the dargah has started already!'

Kanu had heard about the fair from Sona, who had seen camels there, live, for the first time in his life. People who lived by rivers bought the desert animals chiefly for Qurbani during the Eid. Presently, he tried to drown the worries of Sona's flustered mother by bursting out in a deep chested laughter, 'Don't worry, I'll be fine. This operation, it had to come sooner or later. Send me an invitation for your son's *poite*, and you will see how I come back like an express train.'

'But these operations! Aren't they risky at times?'

Kanu shrugged his shoulders. 'Who cares, I know I'm not going to make old bones!'

'God forbid! You shouldn't utter these words when the evening is mellowing. It is the time to come back home and thank the gods. Who will be there with you? You could ask Badal to go with you; he has no great business here, just twiddling his thumbs for nothing.'

Before she finally left, Kalyani swivelled on her feet once more. She stood half-turned, facing the courtyard but her voice was clear, not quivering at all, 'This house says, and says in one voice, that this room will wait, ready and keen, if someone cares to come back. Sona will wait. Hasn't someone promised him to stay put till his *poite*!'He was still sitting in the verandah when Kalyani returned after her wash. He saw her lighting the lamp in front of the basil tree. She had a fresh sari on, her chignon well set and a large round vermilion dot on her forehead. As she retreated within the household, Kanu heard her warbling, 'I'm coloured with the colour of the dusk, O Rana, and I'm coloured with the colour of my lord.'

Sixteen

The sounds came through muffled at first. Then they became harsher, guttural sucking sounds intervened by angry rasps. Kanu woke up from his drug-induced sleep. The lights were on in his double-bedded cabin. The night staff was trying to suck out phlegm from the throat of the other occupant of his cabin with a tube attached to a whirling contraption that purred much and sucked little. Another staff came and pushed some drugs through the IV line. A few moments later, the patient became quiet.

Kanu took a fuller look at the man lying next to his bed, swathed and doped. That patient, Samar Banerjee, had returned to this room from the operation theatre only a few hours ago. It must have been a long operation, continuing until the late hours of the evening. The first night could always be turbulent, Kanu had heard. He had shared this cabin with that man for the last two days, since his second admission to this hospital. Today he had been to the table, a day later Kanu would be.

'Never have been to a hospital before in all my life,' the man had said to Kanu when they first talked. Kanu paid no particular attention to his story. He knew it would not be very different from what most other men would tell, probably no different from Kanu's own tale — how they had struggled and never taken to vices, and how just when years of labour were to bring them some comforts, this had to happen. 'But going to a court to settle property disputes between brothers is worse. No one knows what'll happen in the end.' Banerjee had said and that had made Kanu listen to him with more attention.

'Delicate affairs, when it happens in a family,' Banerjee had concluded with a wry face waving the file holding sheets of paper he had been reading all through the day.

His words struck Kanu. Was that what Rajat and his other cousins were afraid of, that he would take them to court? Kanu himself had never considered such an eventuality and he cringed at the thought.

That was yesterday morning, and tonight Banerjee was engaged in a battle to keep alive. 'Carry on, Banerjee, there is always another day,' Kanu whispered and then turned towards the wall on his side of the room and tried to concentrate on a damp spot there. The southern wind that came in from the open window was breezy and made the room cool. Kanu drew a light cloth over his head to block the light burning over the other bed. He closed his eyes and let his thoughts meander to other images. Happier images. The tulip gardens in Aalsmeer, the sunflowers of Avignon. Soon, however, those images faded behind long rows of headstones weathering out in the older desolate part of a cemetery on the bank of the Amstel River. Kanu had left Ludwina there to sleep by her parents' graves. He would not be there to give her company. He could not, not being a Christian himself.

He opened his eyes to a sunny morning. There was a flurry of activities around the other bed. A fright slashed through him. 'What has happened?' Then he heard one of the nurses instructing Banerjee to move his legs. He looked through the corner of his eyes and saw that two trainee nurses were busy making the other bed tidy. Crumpled and soiled sheets from the overnight toil lay discarded on the floor. Banerjee moved his legs under instructions from the senior nurse to prove that he was alive and well. Kanu breathed easier, the operation had been a success. Satisfied with that evidence, the nurses returned to their stations. Banerjee returned to his slumber, probably from another dose of sedation, unaware that an insect, looking like a big black ant, was crawling up his leg. The insect inched up, feeling its way onwards with its proboscis. Kanu studied its progress with interest. Its legs made slow movements and its head at times veered indecisively to find its way but it moved with a definite purpose. It crawled up and up, passed the hip and suddenly it changed track, went towards the flank and then started to climb down. It was now clear to Kanu that it was heading to the arm that was taking the IV fluid.

Kanu got down from his bed, tiptoed to scoop the tiny raider in his hand, and brought it to his eye to see if he knew that one. He took it to the window and looked for something to swat it with but then he just extended his arm outside the window and released it. As he turned back from the window, he saw Banerjee stirring in his sleep. Banerjee drew up one leg but could not keep it balanced. It bent at the knee and then dropped sideways, on its own weight, and rested awkwardly on the rail guard of the cot. Kanu held the leg at the ankle and gently pulled it straight and drew the cover over it.

The wards outside got busy. Kanu listened to the usual pitter-patter of the doctors and the sounds of nurses trotting between the beds followed by the screeches made by the dressing trolleys. It was time to get up.

When he came back from the bathroom, he found Mina, the young nurse with the Julie Andrews face he had befriended during his earlier stay, crouching over a newspaper spread on his bed. She smiled when she saw Kanu walking up to her and blushed. She looked happy with a thick vermilion streak going straight back from her forehead along the parting of her hair in the middle of her head. Mina had got married!

'Congratulations!' Kanu said, 'Where is my share of sweets?'

Mina was in high spirits and she babbled a lot. She went out of the room to call the staff who would dress Kanu for the operation. Kanu heard her yelling, 'Bed 32A, operation tomorrow, ASD due.' The professional tone of her yelling lessened his own ebullience — as it underscored a plain truth that to some people he was only a number. It then occurred to him that Mina should have been actually sorry rather than happy to see him back so soon.

In the afternoon Rajat came. 'I'll be here by ten tomorrow morning. They'll take you to the theatre around eleven, the nurse told me,' he said.

***

More than the pain, a mingling of various disquieting feelings and an intense thirst irked Kanu. He wanted to sit up but felt dragged down by a heavy weight. Someone was pulling him through a dark tunnel and he was unable to see where he was or where he was going. He began to struggle to free himself, and then he heard someone calling and talking to him. He sensed a shadow falling over him and felt a painful tug at his mouth. With that, he opened his eyes but could barely make out the blurred outlines of a face, with a hood over its head, speaking to him.

Kanu felt an urgent need to pass urine but could not speak out. His mouth and throat felt gagged, jammed by a thick tube. He tried to remove the gag in his mouth but he could not move his hands tied to the cot.

The apparition leaned closer. Sounds of it screaming and yelling some commands at him entered his ears, grating the insides.

Kanu felt vulnerable and unequal to meet the authority of the voice.

That made him angrier. His lips and mouth were dry, aching for water. He wanted to speak again and made gestures to the figure by his side. It then came to him slowly. He was waking up in a hospital ward and it was late at night.

Another figure leaned over him from the other side. It spoke with a softer voice, calling out a name repeatedly and said something about an operation being over. Slowly the words became clear, 'Mr Chatterjee, Mr Chatterjee, your operation has gone well and you're doing fine.'

That figure seemed to be familiar but it was not Dr Nolan. Kanu tried to focus hard but the figure moved away. The other figure with the hood on its head leaned again. 'Quiet, quiet, don't be so restless,' the hooded figure rasped. 'Oh, my god, this man is going to ruin all his drips.' She was holding up a syringe in front of her eyes now. She bent down on his bed and lowered the syringe. Gradually her face became indistinct again.

He became fully awake towards the afternoon of next day when the doctors removed the thick tube from his windpipe. It took him one more day to sit up. Two days later, when he sat on a chair without his nightshirt, he looked at his own hands as the nurse sponged and rubbed them. They looked like they belonged to someone else, skinny and wasted. Thick and ugly veins leaped out from underneath the dry skin, some of them just blackish blue streaks, dead channels without any flow, vestiges of past therapies. They looked like an old man's hands.

Kanu stood at the porch outside the ward, taking the sun on his back. The warmth felt good on his sore back. In another day or two, his stitches would be removed. He looked at the green and gray land lying beyond the hospital boundary. A meek solitary two-storied house stood there so inexorably immersed in sunlight that it created no shadows. From its terrace, a sari dived down, bathing in the abundant sunlight. It seared in the heat, but also reported the presence of someone inside.

The greenish-yellow cloth, luminous in the bright sunlight, played with the breeze, folding and unfolding upon itself.

Kalyani had such a sari; Kanu could imagine her wearing it. She must be eager to know about his operation. A letter would be inappropriate but he felt a desire to end her anxiety. News, though, must have reached them from Ved via Deep Saha. Another thought crossed his mind. Gently passing a hand over his face and neck, he mused if his scars would hurt her feelings.

A couple with sandalwood paste smeared on their foreheads climbed up the stairs. The woman, her long hair wet and loose, carried a plate that had some flowers and sweets on it. Her eyes brightened as she recognised Kanu.

'You have recovered well!' she cried as they moved closer.

The couple stopped when they reached Kanu.

The woman continued, 'Who knows what awaits us? Khokon will be operated tomorrow.'

Kanu knew this couple well, from his earlier admission. They were the parents of the young boy who had sarcoma of the arm and who detested losing it for he wanted to be an engineer and had been undergoing some tough chemotherapy so far. Kanu wanted to say a few words of encouragement but refrained. It troubled him now to say even a full sentence. The stitches did hurt. He pointed his finger up and mumbled, 'Pray to Him.'

'That's what we've been doing all these days. Just have been out to the temple,' the woman said.

'Uma, offer some *prasad* to Dada,' her husband said and after his wife had taken a flower from the tray and touched it on Kanu's forehead, he added, 'This temple is very famous. The goddess there is truly alert and merciful and is known to grant people's wishes. One of my cousins told me about this place. His son was cured after praying there.'

'That boy is going to college this year,' Uma interjected.

'Exactly.' Her husband said with a catch in his voice, 'He has grown into such a lovable young man but this place sets very tough conditions. Chanting the *Mahamrityunjaya* mantra for one hundred thousand times is no joke. We could do only ten thousand each day and the whole affair made us fifteen days late.'

More people, patients from the ward and some relatives, gathered around them. Uma distributed the blessed flowers and the sweets and they encouraged her.

'You've done a great job,' one of them said.

'Your efforts will be rewarded. Have faith; I know of such miracles myself,' another one added. 'The important thing is to approach the right place.'

Uma listened with attention, her eyes shone with a faraway look. With blotches of sandalwood paste on her forehead, vermilion smeared thickly at the parting of her long hair let loose on her back, and clad in a new but coarse red-bordered sari she appeared to be in a trance.

Almost everyone present knew of places where miracles took place. They talked about incredible cures and divine interventions they had witnessed or had heard about. Stories effervesced as the group exchanged notes and advised each other. Soon the conversation veered to recent newspaper reports about a shrine where a top industrialist had offered prayers for his MIT trained son and where the central minister for education had performed elaborate religious rites. Both had made offerings considerable enough to make news and that shrine since had gained importance because of their patronage. Perhaps it was always like that — the grandness of any place, be it a shrine, be it a cenotaph, always owed its importance to the money that went into it.

Rajat came beaming, with a touch of benevolence in his smile. He opened the bag he was carrying to show tins of health drinks and cartons of fruit juices packed in it. He had also bought a few high neck polo shirts that Kanu planned to wear in order to hide his scars.

Back in his cabin, Kanu took out the pad of slips he used to communicate with the staff and the doctors for he had not yet got back his normal speech after the operation. That would take another two weeks, Ved had said. He first wrote Rajen Ganguly's address in Monabari on the pad and then scribbled below that, 'Write a letter on my behalf telling about the operation. Ask them not to worry and to inform Mahen and the others.'

Rajat read the note. 'Will do,' he said simply and then as he pocketed the note he asked in a very matter-of-fact tone, 'When shall I write them to expect you back?' As if it was already decided that Kanu would go back to Monabari. As if that was the most natural thing to do.

Kanu shrugged his shoulders at first but then showed two fingers. '...weeks, about,' he said turning to the bed.

Seventeen

The lavatory in the railway compartment had become dirty after the overnight journey and the mirror above the basin looked pock marked as mercury had fallen off at places. Kanu stood and peered intently into the glass to see what it was that itched in the scar on his neck. A thick brown line lazily skirted the upper portion of the right side of his neck horizontally, starting from under his chin to the back of the ear, joined by another line that dropped vertically down to the collarbone. The neck seemed hollowed beneath the swollen right side of his face and the jaw line looked fuller. The right corner of his mouth had drooped a little. Another few minutes and he would be back at Monabari. He got back to his berth and selected a high neck shirt to wear. At the station, besides Mahen, Rajen Ganguly and Deep, a sizeable crowd waited led by Bhola Pal.

At the Ganguly house, Rajen Babu's wife wailed, 'What have you been reduced to Kanu Babu? Didn't that big hospital have anything to give you as food?'

Badal held his hand up. 'Ah Maa! Why don't you stop? He's fine. Anybody can look a little thin after an operation. Be careful now about what you give him to eat. Not anymore of your god damned *chaccharies.*'

Half-an-hour later when Kanu emerged from the bathroom he found Deep, Badal, Mahen, and Kalyani assembled on the verandah in front of his room. Kalyani had seized Deep. 'Advise me about his food before you leave. What should I get him for snacks and for dinner? Everyday he can't have soups and soft-boiled foods for all his meals!'

Deep had his attention turned to Sona, whom he tried to tickle. He cooed, 'Yo...yo… you'll manage all right for your Kanubhai.'

Kalyani whined, looking angry at Deep's snub, 'Let his son come and bring home a bride, and then you'll see how nicely they'll look after him.'

Kanu smiled at Kalyani. 'Don't be upset at his words. I know I've you here.'

She looked sharply at Kanu and turned around dragging Sona with her. 'Let me bring your food. And i've to look after the whole world after that,' she said hastily leaving the place.

Kanu quickly reentered his room. A minute later, he emerged with the packet of medicine that Ved had sent for Keka, Mahen's wife, who had not been doing well. He gave the packet to Mahen and said, 'These are for her pain, brought from England by a doctor friend of Ved. Be careful where you keep them and give her only one or two tablets per day for the first three or four days. If she can take them well and does not feel drowsy then you can give her more.'

'Let me see those tablets.' Deep extended his hand and exclaimed as he examined them, 'Good Lord, these are morphine tablets. Mahen, you better be careful with them. An overdose will simply kill her.'

To his surprise Kanu found that settling back in Monabari caused him much less embarrassment than he was afraid of. First, unlike its usual self, Monabari let him be, without the eager visits and efforts to draw him into its life. The chief reason for which was that perhaps other thoughts and businesses occupied Monabari for the time being.

Jute was planted late this time because of the late monsoon and it was now time for the jute growers to have their crop harvested and be busy with the work of retting and drying the golden fibres and take their produce to the market. Though Aus crop or autumn harvested varieties of paddy are not popular in this region, people connected with farming were busy tending to their Aman or winter crop. More importantly, the annual festive season was little more than a month away and that had sent the gentry to other pursuits. Some set up new shops, some travelled to cities to gather wherewithal to decorate their puja pandals on scales grander than before. Still some more started to polish their acting talents for the annual drama.

Both, the stationmaster and Dhar Babu were lost to the last cause, locked in a duel for the post of the director. Kanu, left alone for better part of the day to his solitary walks, each day ventured a little further exploring new spots. Although the villagers talked about forests with their perils and mysteries, there was no real one nearby deep enough for a prowler to stalk him or a wayward tusker to come charging. He, however, kept his evening excursions shorter, usually returning by dusk as darkness posed some real dangers to a lone walker in these areas. Snakes in the grass or thugs from the other side of the border only a few miles away, both were equally perilous.

This evening, he lost his way back. When he got back his bearings and set forth on his return journey, he was already late. The sun had set for some time and a full moon was up in the sky. A little away, he could see the gleaming steel lines of the railway track running through a wide strip of clearing. The track would lead him straight back to the station, at the heart of all the lighted areas in Monabari. He left the trail through the fields and began to follow the railway track back to the station, stepping carefully on the wooden ribs connecting the two steel lines. The moonbeams became brighter and the sleepy land seemed to come alive with an unspoken desire. The little bushes and shrubs on either side gradually looked like shadowy heaps that absorbed moonlight and presented their insides as damp patches on a dark green sheet. Further away indistinct bushes bordered vast stretches of lands on which a gossamer fog settled gradually and condensed to cover the unevenness of the fields like a white cotton quilt. The steel lines, now shining under a brighter moon, seemed to be converging at some distant point but with each step that point moved further ahead. He followed the lines blindly because he knew they had gone beyond where he was going.

The moon shone on a hypnotised earth, which sulked as a woman asked to wipe off her smile. One, two, three, he began to count the wooden sleepers to ward off disturbing thoughts. Suddenly on the right, he saw the big transmission tower and up ahead the lights at the market and the station. He stopped, realising his mistake. He had overshot considerably the point where he must leave the railway track and turn right to cross the highway and follow the district board road to return to the Ganguly house. He turned back, annoyed that he would have to walk so much more. There was a shorter route, he remembered. Instead of going back straight along the railway line and turn left, he could walk the field diagonally and bring himself to the rear of the Ganguly house.

The shorter route was in reality a trail, wide enough only for a lone traveller, beaten by successive steps through the dense infestations of shrubs and the heavy undergrowth of a jungle. Trees with heads full of foliage serried at places and made the path dark where it had passed under them. Kanu followed the path through alternate darkness and the milky shine of the moonlight. The fog had become more condensed and white, girdling the earth and closing in gradually. The faraway fields were now less visible. The path entered thicker woods, nearing the backyard of the Ganguly house. In the semi-darkness, his vision was tricked by the hazy light and fleeting shadows. The bushes assumed ethereal dimensions, their margins blurred; each one flowed effortlessly into the next without demarcation. In places, thickets or tree trunks took the aspect of human forms — a bent head here, two arms hugging a torso there. The path took him near the pond that marked the boundary of the Ganguly house. On the left, trees continued with a grove on the backyard. In front, supple overgrown branches of young trees hovered on the path, running along the bank of the pond, obstructing vision and progress. He parted them with his hands, breaking a few twigs and startling some frogs, which jumped into the pond.

He emerged into a clearing and halted, transfixed. The image of a woman, who came up the stairs of the ghat of the pond and stood under a tree, held him. For a moment, she looked like a fairy in the moonlight. Then the image transformed into a real being, asserting itself in the form of a woman, alone, in a rare moment of her being herself. Was it Kalyani?

At times Kanu had wondered, if she was all to everyone all the time, then what she was to herself and when? He looked on stunned by the gentle slope below her shoulders, her shapely arms, the curve of her loin, a partially covered body hinting barely of a heavy bosom and round thighs. All made more mystifying by the moonbeams, more perceptible and affecting. She also saw him. The unexpected encounter numbed them into staring at each other for a very fleeting moment as measured by the time. For them, the moment however held, prolonged into a timeless existence, becoming indescribably longer than any other they had shared together. A twig got broken under his foot and that broke the trance.

The woman gasped, brought her hands up to cover herself, and then retreated into the shadows of the larger trees. She let out a muffled cry as she sat down. She had hurt herself; probably a thorn had pricked her foot. Spurred by a reflex, without thinking what he was doing, Kanu stepped forward but stopped as the woman frantically cried with a stifled voice, 'No, no. Go away, please,' while her arms crossed over her body and her hands joined to form a cocoon to hide her face. Kanu retreated and ran back in the direction he had come from.

He ran for some distance, sat down on the ground panting for breath, and got up again to keep moving, making a lone shadowy figure ambling aimlessly across a moonlit land. Twice he attempted to sneak back into the cloistered corner of his room but turned away again. On his third attempt, a visibly irritated Jugu confronted him. 'Where were you?' he demanded. 'Ma and Boudimoni kept pestering me to go out and look for you!'

Kanu felt relieved. Kalyani then had not misunderstood him. He touched Jugu on his arms. 'Oh! Jugu! Why do you care for me so much?'

Jugu got angrier. 'You gentlemen from the cities!' he sneered.

***

Monsoon had departed for sometime. The sky had dropped its dark looks and fleeces of light white clouds now drifted carelessly in an autumnal blue sky. The countryside had divested itself from the dank waters and the muddy grounds and crops of tall kans grass with their plume like white flowers, the long slender *kashphools* claimed all the wetlands. They transformed the gray and green fields into white seas that undulated as the wind blew.

On the four special designated days when the goddess Durga supposedly comes down from her abode in the Himalayas to pay an annual visit to her paternal house on this earth, people hopped around the puja *pandals* and food vendors put up roadside stalls selling chow mien and egg rolls. Even after the immersion of the idols there was gaiety all around as families called on one another to exchange greetings and embrace each other, forgetting all past disputes. Kanu was glad to receive some of them and offered them sweets he had specially delivered from Siliguri. Before long, within a month and a half, the weather became cooler, the sunrays gentler, and the gardens around the houses began to sport colourful flowers. The kitchens luxuriated on varieties of winter vegetables and smelt of newly cropped rice and fresh juice of date palm trees.

Kanu gradually got back to his old rhythm but three things happening simultaneously got in his way. Keka Burman deteriorated steadily; Deep received orders for transfer and impatiently waited for his reliever; and political tensions in the alliance of parties ruling the country from Delhi created a ripple effect to end some of the hastily cobbled up unhappy cohabitations in the peripheries. New political alignments saw some of the village councils changing hands. A few needed fresh elections to fill up vacant seats as council members changed political affiliations and resigned their posts. For some reason, Monabari needed to elect a good number of representatives to its panchayat samiti, a third of which was reserved for women candidates. The last one brought unexpected troubles for Kanu.

Small shanties on the main road near the market transformed into busy little hubs. The offices of the major political parties fighting the election brimmed with workers. The educated in the local community left their sinecures to manage those offices, and peasants and labourers from nearby villages thronged in to swell the ranks of the processions that snaked through the main thoroughfare of Monabari twice a day — once in the morning, once in the afternoon. Many afternoons, Kanu saw long lines of people, men, women and children, following each other like ants in a line, traversing the distant fields to go somewhere. The banners were different for different groups but the slogans were mostly the same. One day, a small group of men stopped Kanu near the market.

'Regards,' a man said as his companions gathered around him.

'You can count on us,' another one said.

The first man raised his hand and signalled to the others to be quiet. He said, 'If Kalyani Boudi stands in the election, we hear that you want her to, we're on your side. Leave everything to us and we shall see that she sails through. No son of a pig shall be able to whine a bit.'

'Do you know me?' Kanu asked.

'Of course we do. We know about your project too. We shall help you there also. But if you've your own nominee in the council, that'll help.'

They saw that Kanu was looking towards Badal who had seen them talking and was approaching them. One of them moved closer to Kanu and whispered, 'The two brothers are going to fight now! We shall talk to you later; you can always find us here.' As the group departed one of them abruptly turned around and hissed, 'Don't act naive. We know everything. If you had thought you'd stay here and fornicate with our women and we'd sit by, then that won't happen.' The man made an obscene gesture before parting.

Kanu recoiled in shock and scampered in the opposite direction before Badal could catch up with him. For quite some time he aimlessly wandered about, away from all crowds. He did not try to return until the sun had set and darkness provided him a cover.

By this time it was apparent to him that someone had spread this rumour about his desire to build a big community project like the few coming up in adjoining districts with foreign aid or NRI money. Those projects, real and happening, and widely canvassed, had given the rumour its legs and the local people had added their imagination to give it a soul and a body. Now they were giving it an ugly face. How could they? Could they not see that he was sick and old? Well, almost old, Kanu corrected himself.

He returned a few hours later. However, the Ganguly household did not take much notice of his late return. Sona had developed a fever during the evening and that made every other thing unimportant. Kalyani became invisible for the next few days and then, when nearly a week later, Sona still remained sick and began to refuse food the Ganguly household lost its balance. Rajen Babu's wife became hysterical.

That morning Kanu stopped a grim faced Deep on his way out after a visit to Sona.

'What's wrong with the child?' Kanu asked.

'Something more serious than ordinary fever,' Deep said.

'Typhoid then, it is,' Kanu said.

'No, it's not typhoid,' Deep shook his head. For a minute or so, he kept his gaze fixed on Kanu and dwelt on something that apparently troubled him. Then he raised his right hand to his own neck and placed two fingers like the arms of a divider at two points on his upper neck. 'Sona has got two large nodes there. They are bigger than I last saw them and they are hurting him, absolutely.'

'Nodes!' Kanu felt an unknown anxiety raising an alarm somewhere deep inside him. 'Why nodes?' he cried and immediately realised it was a silly thing to say. 'Do you think the fever is due to those nodes?'

'I think so,' Deep said. He looked grave. 'I don't like their feel. Nodes are fairly common findings with children, but these ones, sc big and tender!'

Kanu found Deep irksome. Nodes are ominous things; he knew that from his own experience but what did they mean in a ten-year-old child, a perfectly healthy bubbly little something, who always ran and now just had happened to have a fever! All children have fevers and stomach upsets occasionally. Didn't Nanu's paediatrician always tell that to Ludwina! But this man was a doctor and he should know his business.

'What's your diagnosis?' he asked with a certain sternness in his voice.

'Could be just plain infection, one of a bacterial kind. I hope it doesn't turn out be something more sinister, like Hodgkin's. I should ask Ved-da.'

'Hodgkin's!' Kanu did not know what that meant. Deep's nervousness and his mention of a need to take Ved's help, unsettled him. He was afraid to ask anything more.

'Don't worry.' Deep kept his voice low. 'It's curable, no doubt, but the child will have to go through a lot.'

Kanu walked with Deep up to the rickshaw waiting to take him back to the hospital. 'This afternoon I will come and see you in your quarters,' Kanu said when the rickshaw started to roll.

He reached Deep's quarters when it was already dark. Deep was not home; neither was Mahen who was expected to come. Keka had deteriorated considerably. Kanu waited in a room with bare lime washed walls and large windows with iron grills. He sat on a lone chair placed in front of a study table, books and magazines heaped on it. A bookrack fixed on the wall above the table held some books and magazines.

One small book attracted his attention. It was an old book with a green cloth bound hardcover and a maroon spine, on which the title of the book was embossed in gold: *Notable Names in Medicine and Surgery*. Kanu took down the book and opened it at the front page. In the beginning, the authors explained the need for a new edition with 'many departures' from the past editions. The reason for this was twofold, they wrote — fashions in medicine and surgery change and advances in knowledge often bring with them other names. The paper of the book had yellowed and the pages were at places moth eaten but it had the smell of those books that are not disposed of until their last pages fall off by themselves.

Kanu thumbed through the pages that described the men perpetuated in the history of medicine by naming after them the parts of human anatomy they had described, the diseases they had identified, or the instruments they had designed. A known name attracted Kanu's interest. Glauber's salt. He read on. Johann Glauber was born at Carlstadt in Bavaria in 1604. He never frequented the universities, nor even 'had a mind to do so'. It was his opinion that had he had a university education, he never would have arrived at the knowledge of nature he possessed. A stomach disease that was rampant at that time struck Glauber himself and then something happened that changed the course of his life. The authors had quoted Glauber, '*On the advice of friends I dragged myself to a certain spring situated about a league from Norstadt. I had brought with me a loaf of bread, but with no hope of being able to eat it. Arriving at the spring I took the loaf from my pocket and made a hole in it so I could use this as a cup. As I drank the water my appetite returned, and I ended by eating the improvised cup in its turn.*' He made several visits to the spring, and soon was miraculously cured of his illness. He discovered, along with many other novel compounds like the fertilizer ammonium sulfate, a universal solvent but declined to let out its secret on the plea that it 'would encourage luxury and Godlessness.'

Kanu began to open the book randomly at different pages and read the headings: 'Bright's Disease', Richard Bright 1789-1858; 'Roentgen Rays', Wilhelm Conrad Roentgen 1845-1923; 'Syme's Amputation', James Syme 1799-1870; 'Hodgkin's Disease', Thomas Hodgkin 1798-1866.

Kanu sat up straight; was this not the name that Deep had mentioned about Sona's illness? He began to read, '*Thomas Hodgkin, the discoverer of Hodgkin's disease, was not appreciated in his day and generation…he was the first in England to use the stethoscope, which his contemporaries called a new fangled contrivance.*' Kanu read how the physician, an unsuccessful practitioner, given a 'blank cheque' by a satisfied patient, entered only ten pounds. The patient felt insulted and never again asked Hodgkin for his services. However, all physicians soon learnt that Hodgkin had identified a disease process, in which the patient suffers from a mysterious fever and then the lymph nodes get swelled up, and that this disease was generally a 'sentence of death'.

Kanu dropped the book. Sentence of death! Sona! Kalyani would be devastated. He looked at his watch. He had already waited nearly an hour for Deep. He uncurled his legs from under his buttocks – in Monabari he had learnt to sit like that, during the nights, to escape the mosquitoes honing on to his feet. Before he could get up, the power went off. He slumped back in the chair. Now he would have to wait until Deep's servant came to rescue him.

In the dark, the mosquitoes descended on him with glee. In the dark, he could not read the book to see when it was printed but it must be years ago. Surely, what it said was not valid any more but had Deep made the Gangulys aware of the danger that threatened Sona? Deep Saha was a good doctor but his style was very prosaic, his attitude minimalist, even puerile at times. Kanu had not seen Rajen Ganguly's wife organising any special function to propitiate her gods either! Even though he was sitting in total darkness, Kanu still closed his eyes and offered a prayer. Cure this boy and prove to me that you exist, he implored.

Deep's help came in with a lantern. Deep could not come, he informed. Kanu would have to go and see him in the hospital itself.

Outside, it was as shadowy and mysterious as only a countryside can be with a waning moon in the sky. Between the doctors' quarters and the hospital building, stretched a dark ground lined by large silent trees with shaggy heads. On the other side of the dark ground the windows and the doors of the hospital rooms showed as dimly lit up rectangles from the timid lights of kerosene lanterns. Kanu stepped cautiously to cross the ground but slowed as a voice reached him from behind one of the trees. He knew the voice. It was Rajen Ganguly. He looked in the direction from where the voice had come. Two indistinct figures huddled in the dark behind a tree and talked to each other. Kanu was about to pass them when he heard his name being mentioned. He stopped.

'You must press your Kanubhai,' he heard Rajen Babu saying. 'He is not committing anything. If he has not decided what to do, he could at least offer something to Badal!'

'I don't know. You better ask Ved *daktar*.' The other man spoke. Kanu knew that voice too. It was Mahen.

'If both of them press Ajay Babu, then there would be no difficulty for Badal to get an agency. This Deep doctor is very clever. I have heard that he had extracted a promise for Jairam Haldar and his cuckold brother to have a big contract if Mr Chatterjee builds this project here. I asked Kalyani to persuade him but she refused. She is not a hussy to flatter this man.'

Kanu retreated in a flurry of hate and anger. He waited for Rajen Ganguly to leave and then watched Mahen climbing up to the verandah of the health center. A lantern burned on one side of the landing and as Mahen passed that light, a huge shadow formed on the opposite wall and then it quivered to shrink into a sharply outlined silhouette. Kanu stood on the ground near the steps without making a noise. The light from the lantern blinded him to some extent and he could not make out Mahen's features but saw the angularly projected dark image on the wall, which was now still without any further movement.

When Kanu retraced his steps to the Gangulys' after talking to Deep, he was more worried than when he came to Deep's quarters. There was no good news for Sona and for Keka the time was quickly running out.

The Gangulys had no formal hour or place for their meals and Kanu had always been served in his room. Kalyani, or at times her mother-in-law would come and stand outside the door of his room to enquire about his progress with the meals. This evening Kalyani came to supervise his dinner after a whole week.

'Sona ate some food today,' she said standing on the doorsill and leaning on the frame. Her poise looked relaxed. 'His fever did not spike since yesterday. Seven days of fever and no food for such a small boy, sustaining only on barley and milk!' She said with some anguish and then added with a smile, 'The boy's grandma has gone nuts. For three days, she did not perform any puja, none of her hour-long prayers and offerings to her idols. "If my grandson can't eat, let those wretched gods not eat also," she is saying.'

Kanu was surprised. He had expected the Gangulys to behave otherwise but then they were not aware of the danger they might be facing. Kalyani had not talked about Sona's swollen nodes and it was not Kanu's business to make her aware of that. Even then, he asked, 'Are you not going to make a trip to the Jalpesh temple to make some offerings?'

'*Na baba*,' Kalyani jerked her head back. 'There's no time to do that. Let my son recover. Then there will be time to thank the gods.' She left.

Kanu took his medicines and went to the bathroom to gargle his mouth and throat. When he exited from the bathroom, he saw that the lights were out in the rooms of the main house. On the verandah, Rajen babu, Chapal, and Badal sat in a row taking their meals. Kalyani and Rajen Babu's wife waited on them. Rajen Babu looked particularly animated. Kanu closed the window facing the courtyard, put out his own light and switched on the new bedside lamp he had got in place recently. He picked up the book he was reading in the morning, which was about a man who wanted to build a house of his own. That man was from a different world but Rajen Babu fitted much of the description. Reading about that man his earlier annoyance at Rajen Babu's behaviour softened to some extent. That man tried to build a home for himself and his family, and his story summed up more or less most stories about men.

Eighteen

Keka died two days later. Alerted by Deep on the previous night, Kanu reached Mahen's house before the day had broken fully but by that time, it had become evident that the end was not far. After a particularly restless and painful night, towards the dawn her tussle with the inevitable had begun to dissipate.

Standing just outside the door of the dimly lit room Kanu looked at her. She no longer moaned in pain. Her hands, busy for sometime in smoothening imaginary peaks in the frazzled bed sheet around her recumbent body, gradually became limp. Her eyes sank and their tired lids drooped. She would see no more light even if the morning was glorious. She would not notice this morning how the rooster would crow in the courtyard, how the goat would impatiently bleat, or how the ducks would flap their wings anticipating her visit to free them from their cage. When her world would await her outside, she would silently cross to another world, not to care about these things anymore.

Mahen woke up from a slumberous position at the foot of the cot. He came out to meet Kanu stretching his arm that had cramped under the pressure of his head and body resting on it. Looking at him Kanu's inside twisted. The poor man had probably fallen asleep towards the wee hours of the morning, unknowingly, after a nightlong anxious vigil. They looked at each other; no words passed between them. Mahen came to the door and stood leaning against the frame. Kanu stood outside and looked in. Together they watched the listless body before them.

Her breathing had become shallower but the chest was still moving. Mahen went back inside, put out the kerosene lantern burning through the night, and opened the window. The light from outside leapt on her body. The curtain of darkness had lifted and the world was set to unfold its daily drama.

Mahen came out of the room and picked up a washcloth hanging from a rope. He stopped briefly before crossing Kanu and mumbled, as if talking to the wind, 'For the last few days she was in great pain but last night it became almost unbearable, even for us to watch.' He did not look at Kanu and only made a gesture to indicate that he was going to wash his face in the pond.

Kanu watched Mahen's back as he slowly ambled down from the porch and walked past a small cage. Inside the cage, the ducks quacked and flapped their wings. Mahen stopped and then stepped back to release the latch of the cage door, to let them out. The geese filed in a column and wobbled hastily to enter the water. Kanu got down from the porch and sat on the frame of a broken cot, its bed of *madur* strings ruined into shreds.

'Areca on the north; open on the south; duck on the east, and bamboo on the west,' Kanu remembered Mahen reciting the couplet to him on the first day he had visited his house, to describe how a Rajbanshi house should be planned.

Balika appeared at the door of the room that served as the kitchen, her face flushed and eyes watering from the effort of lighting a stove that used wood as fuel. 'Shall I bring her some hot milk?' she asked.

Kanu nodded silently though he knew it would do no good to her mother, anymore. A minute later, he saw Balika tiptoeing to Keka's room carefully holding a tumbler with her sari.

'Don't give her that very hot, it'll be difficult for her,' Mahen said mildly to his daughter as he came back and sat on the terrace just outside the room leaning on a wooden pole supporting the thatched roof above. Kanu followed him and sat leaning on the pole on the other side of the door.

Mahen turned his face towards Kanu and spoke with a half smile, as if he knew what Kanu was thinking. 'Twenty years,' he said and turned his face away again. Kanu felt Mahen had used those two words to conclude the story of their lives that he had been telling Kanu in bits and pieces through all these days. Death was not unfamiliar to them. They lived lives in which dates, months, and years, the units of time, were counted and remembered by only such happenings as the birth of their children and the death of the elders. It was her pain and the sufferings, which she wanted to endure so valiantly, that prompted Mahen to take her to Calcutta, at the risk of losing whatever earthly possessions he had. But this, such a hasty end, and with so much suffering, he had not bargained for.

Without the morphine tablets that Ved had sent, it would have been much more painful. Kanu knew Mahen felt betrayed. 'Couldn't the doctors have done a little more?' he had asked many times.

A sudden gush of wind raised dust from the courtyard and from the porch where they were sitting. The earthen surface of the porch looked untidy. It had not been swabbed and had missed for some time the usual daily coating of mud and cow dung mixture that kept the floors smooth and clean. Kanu looked around; everything spoke of a missing hand. He looked at his watch. A man had gone to fetch a local quack doctor. The old man who called Keka his daughter hobbled up and sat near them.

Inside the room, Balika tried to part her mother's lips and pour some milk through them. Keka tried to swallow the milk, fighting with all her will to accommodate the renderings of her beloved daughter. Her efforts to swallow compromised her already strenuous breathing. Most of the milk did not go down but trickled outside down the angle of her mouth. Her eyes became wide in desperation and she began to choke. Scared, Balika turned towards Mahen who shook his head slowly. The girl understood; quietly she put the tumbler and the spoon down. In order to suppress the onrushing tears she bent her head cradling it with one arm to rest it on the knees of her mother and began to massage her legs with the other hand.

Outside the goat stood silently; the ducks filed back on their own; even the squirrels did not run. The entire household, down to the insects crawling on the ground, waited anxiously holding its breath, for the departure of its central soul. The breeze fell. The sun rose higher. The day became warmer and the still air made it more stifling.

Suddenly someone breezed past them. It was the quack doctor. Kanu and Mahen watched as the doctor tried to find Keka's pulse, first at the wrist, then on the elbow, and then even higher up as if looking for some lost thing. His face changed colour as he continued to examine, opening the eyelids and looking at her eyes. Mahen did not stir. He seemed to be looking at the doctor's actions with a dispassionate interest. Kanu could see that he already knew what the doctor was trying to know. That Keka had died.

A thought suddenly flashed through Kanu's mind and his head throbbed. Mahen perhaps had done what he had done once. Mahen too had chosen to end the sufferings of Keka. The morphine tablets had made it easier for him to do so.

Nineteen

For the Gangulys it was good news. Sona's reports were all normal — his fever subsided and the nodes became smaller. The Ganguly household was back to its daily routine.

The days now were shorter and nights longer and colder. Kanu learnt to devise situations to avoid the gentlefolk of Monabari. He discovered a few quiet spots, out of the way, which the busybodies of Monabari did not frequent usually. A grove of coconut and date palm trees on a knoll looking on the railway lines a few miles up became his favourite haunt. The knoll materialised when the engineers of Indian Railways dug around to lay a straight track and, in order to spare the cultivation all around, heaped all the displaced soil in one place. Over the years, trees had grown there and had made it a beautiful resting place. Moreover, on these winter days with clear skies, from that spot he could clearly see the distant icy peaks soaring up in the sky. Kanu marvelled at the snow-covered mass that reposed across the northern horizon with a majestic insolence. Nagadhiraj Himalaya. What a beautiful name! The lord of all mountains, the abode of snow. The eternal resting place at the end of mortal journeys. For his photographs though, he wandered deeper in the small hamlets outside Monabari proper. He used an umbrella rather than a hat, and carried it with him in a large side bag along with his camera, a folding cushion wrapped in plastic, a bottle of water, some fruits, and books.

His nearest refuge from the Ganguly house was the ruins of a temple with a once paved courtyard and a broken flight of stairs on the banks of an unfrequented water body. Nandatalao was large enough to be called a lake. Anglers came there occasionally and sometimes during the winter, tea merchants from the nearby town came there to shoot teals and birds.

Mahen had not come since Keka had died. Umanath was away visiting his grandchildren. Sona was his only solace for the time being, the elders of his family being busy. The little boy came running to him as soon as Kanu returned to his room that day. 'Letter for you,' Sona cried. He was visibly excited.

Kalyani followed her son. 'A letter for you? From whom?'

'My brother. He has written about you,' Kanu said, glancing through the letter.

Kalyani knitted her brows and her lips twitched. Her face coloured but unlike before, she did not leave immediately. Glancing up from the letter Kanu saw her looking at him with innocent curiosity but her eyes were bright.

'He knows how diligently you look after my needs and he is thankful,' Kanu said gently.

After a minute or so she left, and Kanu settled down to answer the letter. He wrote slowly from lack of practice and as his thoughts were all over the place. Addressing his letter as 'Dear Rajat', he wrote,

'Your letter was just in time. What you wrote braced me up, against a little despondency. Regarding that, later.

'You have wondered how my relationship with this family is taking shape. I myself have thought a lot about it. I have discussed the problem with Umanath Babu. Here, we are talking about relationships beyond consanguinity. How much can they evolve and in what direction? Umanath tells me of a Sanskrit *shloka*, which says, "A life responds to another life." That is natural. And they form bonds. Nevertheless, beyond a certain point that relationship needs to be formalised, with the seal of approval of the society.

'Among the native communities, I find this practice of formalising relations between non-relatives to be very popular. If two adults, as head of their families, form such a relationship, they call it making *mistar* (friends). Younger girls become *mita*. Then they take vows. With a bow and an arrow in their hands they say to one another, "If you look at my husband with lustful eyes, I will gouge them out; if you fornicate with my husband, I have the right to kill you." One must admit that it is indeed a very practical charter without any ambivalence.

'But seriously, as it is, my relation with this family can grow only up to a point. I can look at my relationship as a simple business relation, paying up for what I get—but that, I feel, will be a great injustice to this family. So if you ask me, "Where to from here?" Or if I ask myself, should I leave this place? And if the answer is yes, then how and when would be that point of departure? More important for me—what should I like to be the point of my departure from this world?'

'The staid atmosphere that I first found here had been made murky by the sudden intrusion of things political. My relation with this family has come under scrutiny. That is eternal India, as you keep reminding me, where nothing is private or sacred.

'Rumours have been floated that I have come here with a large sum of money, ostensibly to build a community centre. It is good publicity, you would say. But that is not the point. The irritating part of this is the clandestine aspect they have given to the whole affair, as if I am on a dirty secret mission, trying to execute some underhand deal. People have started scheming behind my back, in order to grab the imaginary spoils from that project. After a look at the whole scenario, I cannot blame them altogether. The neighbouring subdivision of the adjoining district has a World Bank or WHO project coming to it for sometime. This project has not yet taken flight because the work is not distributed equitably amongst the major political players. The district administrative agency has itself conspired to send the project to another subdivision, probably for extra political mileage. Such things happen here regularly and the general populace is quite accustomed to experience big money coming to these rural places in the name of various aids and public health projects. The suspicion is that all this money is not well spent; the commissioners themselves siphon off major portions.

'Keka, Mahen's wife, is dead. Her death has put Mahen virtually out of circulation, which is a loss to me. I passed time most comfortably with him. Besides, when he is with me I can photograph their people more freely. Deep, the local doctor and my guide has received orders for transfer. He is itching to move out but has to wait until someone relieves him from his duties here. When he is gone, I shall be in further quandary. I now travel to more and more distant places for my excursions and exercises.

'All these, put together, have made me despondent. Doubts now creep into my mind if it was prudent to do what I have done. You have said that it helps to be a believer in such situations. I never had strong views about religion. The debate, about God existing, never besieged me before and my own belief has never been so strong that it would make me go to find Him. Kalyani is a strong believer and she plagues me to go to various sadhus. For my illness of course. She virtually maintains a diary of all ascetic men in this region. However, you are right: when one is alone, and nothing else matters, mysterious thoughts come to mind.

'Do you think pilgrimage is more about knowing life than renouncing it? Come then, as you said, and let us travel—travel as roaming hermits do, without a care, making all notions of time and space irrelevant —and your lifetime ambition to flee from it all can find fulfillment. But, you are too involved, unable to take that one first bold step. You are like Rajen Babu. Or, like the man whose story I am presently reading. It is about a man who wanted to be careless, to drift, and to witness amazing things in life but allowed himself to be worn-out in building a house of his own. "Is a trap," the man would constantly say about his life. Yet, he found bliss in papering the covers of his children's books, in giving them grammar lessons, and in energetically bickering about the food. That "is you, man!"

'Sona, Kalyani's son, just dropped by. He was annoyed to see me otherwise engaged but when I showed him that I have written his name, he left happily to break the news to his mother. He is anxiously waiting for his *upanayan* to take place when he will be twice born and will be able to wear the sacred thread and then he will be one up on me since I do not have one. That ceremony has been postponed. He missed a rare auspicious date because of his illness and then the pundits ruled that he must wait for the sun to begin its northern journey, which is favourable for such events. Do you remember if we did that runaway act during ours in which the new Brahmin, his head tonsured, an alms bowl and a staff in his hands, pretends to run away to a far off place in search of knowledge and deliverance while his relatives pretend to lure him back to the mundane world? We must have done it because in New York I dreamt about it. It was your chance Rajat. You missed out on it early.'

Kanu read the letter carefully and put it in an envelope. He would send it by courier along with the rolls of film he needed to send to

Calcutta. One reputed studio in Park Street, which had handled some of his photographs, had agreed to take special care to develop and print his photographs. He caressed the rolls with fondness. Soon digital cameras would send them to the pages of history.

Twenty

Monday, the first day of the week, is usually the busiest day for most hospitals. After a brief lull during the weekend, activities pick up to recapture lost grounds. This Monday though, back in the hospital in Calcutta, did not at all progress well for Ved and his colleagues. A patient died from operative bleeding. The entire unit went into a huddle to discuss what went wrong. This was a bad case and needed drastic surgery and without the risks taken, the patient had no hope. He would perhaps have been a castaway in a terminal care ward, to pass a few agonising days in pain or in stupefaction from heavy doses of sedatives.

'Drowse with the fumes of poppies...' Ved remembered. It remains to do only that when every other measure has been taken. When all ugly sprouts from the body have been excised, all known claws burnt, all runaway cells poisoned enough but when the hideous crab still crawls resolutely, gnawing, nibbling the very fabric it resides in, and death is sure to follow, then it becomes the time to palliate, to daze and deaden the patients enough to make them insensate, bereft of all wits.

Jamaj telephoned right at that time. Manoj had turned critical and Ved needed to rush to his house. For Manoj it was going terribly for the last two weeks. He could not even leave the bed. His family had decided to nurse him at home.

'No urine since this morning, and the pressure is low, no sense either,' the nurse informed Ved when he arrived at his friend's bedside. Ved took Manoj's hand in his and what happened next stunned him, gave him a memory that he would not be able to forget ever. Manoj curled in his fingers and scratched Ved's palm, a faint smile quivering on his lips, as if saying, 'What did I tell you, you fool?'

A few hours later when Ved got up from his friend's side, he saw Jamaj looking at him with the unavoidable question in his eyes. Ved simply nodded and moved away. Jamaj hurried to the bed and pulled his brother's head on his lap. He had a silver urn in his hand. He looked at Ved again.

'Yes,' Ved said.

Jamaj took a spoonful of the holy water carefully stored and kept ready in that urn and poured that through the half parted lips of his brother. At the doorway leading to an adjoining semi-darkened room, a pundit, his face partially lit up by the yellow light from a brass oil lamp, sat reciting *shlokas* in a restrained voice from a book held by a trivet. Now his voice rose. Two other pundits busy performing some rites in the depth of that room, hurried to join him. Their voices joined in a forceful chorus in order to guide the departing soul in its wondrous flight.

Ved stepped outside. The house physician could prepare the necessary papers.

A terrible exhaustion and sleep overpowered Ved when he returned to his quarters. When he woke up a few hours later, the serenity of night had settled outside. A fax and a letter left quietly on his table awaited his attention.

The fax was from Mr Chatterjee's son Nanu. He was coming to Singapore on official work and was taking a few days off to come to visit his father. He had requested Ved to book a connection to Monabari, by air or by train, whichever would take him there immediately. His date of arrival, Ved calculated, was only three days away. Nanu phoned often, but if he had something important to say, he would fax. He would put his points in writing, in black and white, documented for future reference. Ved wished he could keep in touch with Nanu through electronic mails. Though it was now nearly three years since the chief minister of this state had uttered the first few words carried through the wireless world of communications in India, and people had started to call handwritten letters as 'snail mail', this hospital had only recently decided to rope in that service for the daily use of its staff. Soon, Ved hoped, he would be able to have an electronic address for people wanting to contact him.

The letter was from Gola-da's daughter. A week before, Gola-da had passed away quietly in his home. Ved had not seen the news carried in the newspapers. Samar Roy, the beloved poet who wrote so many famous lines, did not get even one line on his death. Perhaps the news was there, in fine print, on an inside page. Gola-da had remembered Ved before his death, his daughter had written, and he had donated his body for the enrichment of medical knowledge.

Ved wondered how Golada would look lying on the cold marble-topped table of an anatomy hall. He remembered his own days of anatomy lessons. Surprisingly, what came back to him more strongly was the stink. The stench of rotting flesh made more pungent with the aromatic odour of chemicals, mixed with the heavy oppressive smell of eucalyptus oil. Would the students know whom they would dissect? Did he himself, during his dissection classes, ever realise that what he was dissecting was not only the muscles and bones of a cadaver but, perhaps, in addition, the wish of a living being? What is it that prompts a man to wish this ignominy — is it truly the fulfillment of a noble desire for a total sacrifice for the good of others or a desire to walk a different path even after the mortal journey has ended? Could it even be a stronger pathological craving to be vanquished totally, a culmination of an inherent tendency toward self-destruction?

There were a few more handwritten sheets along with the letter. They were the last few poems that Gola-da had written.

Before he went to bed, Ved read Nanu's fax again. If he could book a ticket for Nanu in the Darjeeling Mail, Ved decided, he would accompany Nanu. That train had a coach that went to Monabari tagged behind a connecting local train.

Three evenings later, by the time the railway caterers started to serve dinner, Ved and Nanu had settled well in a compartment of the mail train. They talked sitting face to face keeping their dinner plates between them. Ved did not expect Nanu to speak in Bengali but was surprised to find he could understand a few words. He even could use a few Hindi or Urdu idioms, picked up from his colleagues from the subcontinent. Everybody used those idioms there, including the Tamils.

Nanu talked between the casual pickings he made from the vegetable stew and a tough chicken portion. He worked as a technical expert in a firm that specialised in designing big civil constructions like bridges and barrages. He handled the load factors, specifically. 'While designing them,' he said, 'we test them against possible wear and tear for the next two hundred years. And against some calamities like excessive rain or even an earthquake.'

'That makes you a stress specialist!' Ved said.

'Yes,' Nanu said, 'my work does teach me to handle stress. Its principles are similar to yoga. Both call for a distribution of the load so that stress is not maximised at any particular point. You're a Hindu, aren't you?' He abruptly asked Ved.

Ved nodded, Yes, naturally. What else could he be?

Nanu discarded the knife, which was doing a poor job, and began to eat with his hand. He ate in silence for some time and then said, 'In school I was often asked what my religion was. Ours was a predominantly Protestant school. A boy from a Buddhist family, from Ceylon, and I were the odd ones. Most of my friends knew what they were, what prayers they had to say. I was never sure. My parents somehow avoided telling me and no one in my school had any idea what a Hindu was.'

'Is it very important to you,' Ved was curious but he made his tone playful, 'to know if someone will stand guard outside your door on dark stormy nights?'

'My mother was a good Christian and I knew she was happy with her beliefs. I am comfortable with the idea that I have a creator, even a patron saint. Tell me, what do you make of my father? Do you think he's crazy?'

'Your father is a great believer in fate. That's what he is battling with, not this disease.'

'He's a great guy otherwise, isn't he?' Nanu said. He had finished his meal and stood up to put the plates away.

Ved nodded. Secretly, he had hoped that Nanu's father would agree to finance a community project in Monabari as he had hinted to Ajay-da. If Mr Chatterjee really stayed back in India, Monabari could be as good a place as any other for him. Serampore, he could guess, was a lost option to Nanu's father. He hoped Mr Chatterjee, by this time, had developed an affinity for Monabari. According to what he had heard from Deep, Kanu Chatterjee seemed to be in good spirits in that place. Besides the Gangulys being good hosts, he had acquired other allies and was happily shooting around. Ved got up and pulled the drapes around their berths. The other two berths were empty, marked as booked from Malda, a midnight stop. Changing into his nightdress Ved made two beds with the pillows and blankets supplied by the railways.

Nanu brought out a book. Ved helped him to put the reading light on but Nanu did not open the book. Obviously, he had something on his mind.

'Do you have something to say?' Ved asked as he lay down on his berth and pulled up the blanket.

'Yes.' Nanu said, 'How good are his chances?'

'Reasonable.' Ved said simply to Nanu but he himself had to reflect, 'The operation Mr Chatterjee had undergone was not radical enough and that was a cause of worry. He insisted having it that way to preserve his look and speech but that also meant that the margins of excision were closer to the tumour. On the other hand, the operation had gone well. The margins were all reported as clear.' He had already discussed these details with Nanu but the boy now wanted a definite answer, in absolute numbers, in percentages, in numbers of years or months. 'I wish he had had this operation earlier,' Ved added after a pause, 'but he did not want to look like a cubic picture.'

"Like what?' Nanu's eyes became wide. Then he smiled and nodded, 'Yes, he would say that, even to cancer.'

Ved pulled the blanket further up to ward off the next question, which he knew would inevitably be about what caused cancer and if there would ever be a remedy.

Nanu asked a more personal one, 'Do I carry it in my genes; I mean the trait for developing cancer?'

***

The compartment was still, gone to sleep. Nanu slept without a care. He had a program at hand. Flying down to see his ailing father, then flying back again — an amicable and satisfactory completion of his duty. Unable to sleep, Ved began to read what Gola-da had written in the last few days prior to his death. The poems spoke of a disturbed and cluttered mind and described grisly images. When he went to sleep, he dreamt of those images. A girl with a white flowing dress came in with white pigeons fluttering around her but the red of her blood stained the white of her dress. Men and women in a silent procession followed her; men with misshapen faces and truncated limbs, women with bulging abdomens and charred chests, consumed and wasted. Together they walked past like parading in a masque.

Twenty One

A number of people, one after another, held up Kanu returning from his walk that morning and when he reached the station, the morning train was already in. Few people were on the platform and an old worn out diesel engine was shunting on another track with hisses and whooshes blowing out little puffs of blue white smoke. A lone family sat on the platform, amongst scattered bundles of tattered clothes. A young woman, in a coarse red sari, thick with dirt and frayed from overuse, sat on her heels clutching the elbow of a half-naked small boy wearing only a torn coat and trying to run loose. The boy had his gaze riveted to the engine as it shunted back to position itself in front of the coaches. His little body arched backwards in excitement and he began to pee.

Kanu hurried through the gate of the railway station and walked down the slope to go to the dak bungalow. A makeshift video hall had come up in the vacant land opposite to the bungalow. Two curious boys gazed in awe at posters displayed on the fragile structure with walls made of bamboo mats and a tarpaulin top.

As Kanu opened the wicket gate to the lawn in front of the bungalow, he saw Nanu with his back to him talking to Ved.

Ved saw Kanu first and cried to Nanu, 'Look who is behind you?'

Nanu whirled around and then froze.

Kanu saw his lips parting but they failed to emit any sounds. Kanu could see Nanu taking in his physique that, he knew, had become lean. The skin of his neck was discoloured, and his complexion had got swarthier under a tropical sun. He dropped his umbrella and rushed forward to embrace Nanu.

'I've taken a vacation myself,' Ved said, 'And am I glad to see you! You look to be in good shape and don't look bored.'

Kanu freed Nanu from his embrace and stood by his side. He saw his son taking in the scene around them. He followed his gaze. The station road was deserted again and it would be another hour before people would come to board the returning train. The morning mist was long gone and the vision was clear as far as one could see. The air was peaceful, cool, and carried only the faint sounds of birds twittering and trees rustling.

'It's nice around here, isn't it?' Kanu asked his son.

Nanu did not answer immediately. He looked at his father's eyes, as if searching there for an answer to some question he had in his mind. Then he pointed to the video hall across the road and said, 'But this … not your Shangri-La! I thought I would have to search through some unfrequented caves to find you.'

'Wise men compromise,' Kanu said smiling. 'This place serves me well, gives me something of both worlds. The air is good; the food is healthy; I even get some medical help that I need occasionally.'

They climbed the steps to the wide wooden deck running along the cabins on all four sides and guarded by a railing made of wood. Kanu sat down in an old-fashioned armchair. He got excited when he heard Nanu's plan. 'Two full weeks!' he exclaimed.

'Yes, why not?' Nanu laughed.

After breakfast, the three of them proceeded to the Ganguly house. Before they took the branch road that went to the north side, Kanu took Nanu to show a bit of Monabari. They sauntered through Monabari's main thoroughfare on both sides of which stood the few modest buildings of Monabari: the library, the school, a few small quarters for the staff working at the block development office and the health center. The trees on either side of the road provided shade.

'That one is a jackfruit tree, and this big one is a neem tree. Local people use its twigs for brushing their teeth,' Kanu said stopping briefly under a tree.

'A medicinal plant, I know.' Nanu said.

They came near the health center and were about to turn back when the yowling of a man under a jackfruit tree caught their attention. The man saluted Ved and said something incomprehensible.

'He appears to be drunk,' Kanu said.

'He always is,' Ved said. 'He is Balmiki, the hospital sweeper.'

'But how does he work if he is always like this?' Nanu asked.

'Oh, he hardly works, but he has a large family and anyone of his sons or daughters, whoever is free or sober when a service is required at the health center, fills in for him. The nurses do not mind so long as a soiled bed gets cleaned and a bed pan gets washed.'

'Why is he not fired then?' Nanu asked.

'Because no one else can do his job.'

Nanu stopped walking and stood to look at Balmiki. He turned to Ved and asked, 'The untouchables, right?'

***

Kalyani screamed, 'Oh my god, what a beautiful son you have

Dada. He is so handsome. Any family will be fortunate to have him as a bridegroom.' She did not press when Nanu and Ved declined an invitation to lunch.

When Kanu returned to the bungalow in the afternoon Ved was asleep. Kanu and Nanu pulled two chairs and sat on the wooden deck facing the western sun just as Kanu did on the first day he came to Monabari. 'Imagine,' he said to Nanu pointing to the foreground and smiling, 'the rajas and their English friends are alighting from elephants there, returning after a day-long hunting party, and the khansamas are barbecuing ducks in the light of burning torches. Oh! I can almost smell the smoked meat.'

'Nice thoughts,' Nanu said, 'but pointless. No use of trying to romanticise this place. If this makes you happy… well, I do not know, but you should have at least completed your treatment there.'

'They did not give any guarantee either.'

'But the odds would have been infinitely better.'

'I was not sure. If you remember Murdoch, he had the strongest family support and the money to buy the best treatment. Still he broke. He could not take it anymore and ended his own life. Nothing could save your mother.' Kanu added.

'Yes, I remember Mr Murdoch. He had no faith and chose the Dutch way.' Nanu remained silent for some time. He turned to face Kanu and said in Dutch, 'But mama certainly deserved better.'

'Maybe that was her destiny, and this is mine. Perhaps the stars decide ultimately.'

'The stars!' Nanu pulled his chair closer. He continued to speak in Dutch. 'I'm willing to believe that there is a God, but to think that stars can decide how we fare, makes me weary. The universe is huge, not just a Mars here and a Jupiter there. Forget that nonsense and think rationally.'

'I've done that all my life.' Kanu spoke slowly, swallowing thc small amount of saliva pooling in his mouth. He found it easier to talk in English than in Dutch. 'I've passed days and nights peeved with the thoughts of how to make things happen the way I wanted them to happen...losing sleep and peace of mind over such little things as an extra holiday or a discount in the instalment due. In trying to anticipate other people's movements and checkmate them, manipulating them to my advantage. But ultimately when the chips begin to fall, one realises that for most of us, it's a *phoot*... if you know that word.'

'We've gone into these in New York and I am certainly not going to go over them again; all those decision analysis and probability modeling, all those ever existing truth-seeking questions of life. Nevertheless, consider what you can tolerate for a long time. This dust, this humidity, so much filth... this is certainly going to get you sooner than later. At least a genuine retreat in a cool, clean, peaceful place would've been different. You aren't with your family either. What happened to your plan of living with your blood brothers?'

Kanu was afraid that Nanu would ask this question. He did not know what exactly to tell him. 'I met one of your uncles. He came to see me a few times in the hospital. He even stayed the night they operated on me, on his own, without my asking him to do so and did not allow me to pay for his expenses. I have not visited Serampore though. To tell you frankly I was disappointed with what I learnt about the conditions there but they all dote on you. Maybe we will go there together one day.'

Nanu shook his head. 'What good will that do me? Visiting a place and a memory that you yourself are afraid to experience? And this! Living in such gross conditions! I won't argue if you say you enjoy what you've here but it can be tough after some time. Eventually you might have to go back. You'll do well to keep other options open. Consider also the possibility of coming to USA and living somewhere near me.'

Kanu stared at his son for a long time. Then he said slowly, 'Live here; go back to Amsterdam; or migrate to USA? Well, I know I have to make that final decision one day. But I need more time.'

'You won't have much time left if you continue to live in this filth. If you really want to live here, look for a nicer spot where you can build a farmhouse or a cottage or whatever. Install air conditioners and be comfortable. You are no hermit.'

'Send Scotty and I'll do that.' Kanu joked and felt immediately sorry for it hurled them into a past when he and Nanu shared many intimate evenings together living in the fantasy world of the faraway galaxies and stars. He leaned forward, placed his hand on Nanu's shoulder, and said, 'You can at least believe me when I say that since I came here, I have never wanted to have a smoke or a drink, never—not for a day.'

Deep came in and roused Ved from his sleep. They settled on the verandah. Ved held a book in his hand. He showed it to Nanu. 'I saw this book on the table, must be yours. What is this fuzzy logic?' Ved asked pointing to the book's title.

Nanu laughed. 'That is what dad and I were discussing. A and non-A. When precisely does an apple you are eating become a non-apple?' He took the book from Ved's hand and gently caressed it as if it was a valuable object.

Ved, Deep and Kanu listened quietly as Nanu briefly explained to them the theories in the book.

Deep was the first to respond. 'Wow, that sure is a tough one. Why some people make life complicated is beyond me.'

Ved appeared thoughtful. He put a hand on his face and said, 'Then, when each day I see myself in the mirror, what do I see — do I see more of me each successive day or less of me?'

Nanu nodded. 'You got the drift.'

'You're reading too much science fiction,' Kanu said.

'And you're reading too much about the occult,' Nanu said and then changed the subject. He expected to hear from someone after two days and only after that would he be able to decide about his tour program in India. In the meantime, he would like to see a bit of the forests and the mountains.

'Good idea, absolutely.' Deep said but he appeared morose. 'I wish I could come with you too. Surely, it'll do Mr Chatterjee some good. He should be out of this place for a while.'

Ved concurred. 'We can certainly do a hill station and one jungle resort in two days.'

Kanu saw Deep getting ready to leave. He said, 'We're invited to Umanath's house for afternoon tea. You're included.'

'I've to go back to the hospital first but I'll join you later and then probably Ved-da will have to go with me to see a patient.' Deep hurried out.

Twenty Two

Umanath was ecstatic. He scrambled down the steps from the terrace of his house to welcome Nanu. Kanu watched from a distance, concerned that the old man might get tangled in his dhoti. Another man, whom neither Kanu nor Ved had seen before pulled out chairs for them to sit.

'This is Priyo,' Umanath said. 'He teaches economics in a college.' Priyo was a local lad, a Rajbanshi, who had studied in Delhi and had now come back to a nearby town appointed by the College Service Commission. He had married Umanath's niece, scandalising her puritan tradition-loving Brahmin family, and had come to visit for the first time in order to ease relations with his reluctant in-laws. Priyo readily agreed to arrange a short tour for them, to a hill or a jungle.

The house was smaller than Rajen Babu's was, built at the far end of a clean square courtyard, fenced on all sides. A table, which Kanu suspected was used by the children to study, was laid on the porch under the usual slanting roof of tin and timber. Chairs of different sizes and shapes were scattered around the table. Umanath sat on a stool and hurled instructions as Kanu and his companions were served tea.

A little girl watched them.

'She is Subhadra,' Umanath told Nanu. 'Do you know who Subhadra was?'

Kanu listened as he expounded, trying to impress Nanu with stories from the Mahabharata, the great Indian epic. Nanu knew about Arjun's predicaments regarding duty but he was lost about the other characters and about the complex story of an epic that is many times larger than the *Iliad* and the *Odyssey* put together. Kanu smiled. Umanath was getting into dangerous turf there. There are stories within stories in that epic, at times denying all logic of time and probability.

Umanath talked while the others ate and listened. Kanu saw Ved casting occasional furtive glances at a man, apparently a minion in Umanath's house, who sat on the floor looking at Ved as if they had a dialogue going on. The man had slanting brows, a flat nose, and a toothy idiotic smile that broadened each time Ved glanced at him. After a couple of half glances, Kanu saw Ved confronting the man with a full stare, as if challenging him to explain his conduct.

'My name is Haren Roy; we live in Bhubandanga,' the man said. 'Do you remember?'

Kanu saw Ved wincing and slowly putting down the cup in his hand on the saucer. For a few moments he gazed at that man who now waited expectantly for him to speak out. Then Ved nodded, as if affirming something.

The man bowed and folded his hands. 'I never thought I would be so fortunate to see you again. Mahen is smart. He could go all the way to you and do what he did. Maa Bishahari is equally unkind to us both. I heard that Mahen's woman had the same disease as mine!'

'Champa Roy, wasn't it?' Ved asked.

The man was counting on his fingers. He looked up and said, 'You remember then! So many years have passed but our lot has remained the same. When Mahen went to your big hospital we all said he was trying his best but who would care to offer the right treatment to a poor Rajbanshi!'

Umanath noticed his minion talking to Ved. Without interrupting his narrative, he motioned to Haren to go inside. Kanu felt that Ved was about to ask that man something but before he could do that Haren disappeared inside the house.

Umanath coaxed Subhadra to speak a few words in English to Nanu and she finally opened up. When she saw Nanu giving her attention she quickly retrieved an illustrated children's version of the epic tale and began to introduce the different characters to him.

Kanu turned his attention to Ved who appeared thoughtful.

'Did you hear what he said?' Ved whispered to Kanu. 'My name is Haren Roy. We live in Bhubandanga – those were the exact words he said to me one morning when I worked here. That was many years ago but he is right in one sense, not much has changed for a lot of people.'

'Did his wife have the same disease as Mahen's wife?' Kanu asked.

'Yes.' Ved nodded. 'I still remember him following me to my quarters one day. It was a busy day in the hospital, one of those days when people had no work in the fields and found time to come to the hospital. Then they had all sorts of ailments to be treated, all their old coughs and indigestions. And they would drag their fatigued women and worm filled itchy children in tow. You seldom knew what exactly they came for. One had to coax them. What is your age? Where does it pain you? here? there?' Ved rubbed his eyes with both hands.

Kanu had walked past that hospital frequently enough to know that the hospital had two wings, two large halls to serve as a male and a female ward, joined by a single row of four rooms with a wide verandah in front. An outpatient clinic was held every morning in one of those four rooms, male, female, and children all together. On some days, the queue would be so long that it would stretch through the verandah, down the steps, into the open ground in front of the hospital and snake around the building to its back.

Ved resumed his story. This man had followed him that day, matching his pace but keeping a respectful distance and throwing in a sentence after every few steps, 'My wife is very ill from a bleeding that will not stop.'

Next day that man had come with his wife. A look at her did not suggest any heavy bleeding to Ved though she was weak and very frail. Her fair complexion looked whiter from loss of blood. 'My youngest can walk about,' she said when asked about her age.

When Ved had done a pelvic on her, he immediately knew that she was suffering from an advanced stage of cancer of the uterus and in all possibility was beyond any attempt for a cure. He had then decided to keep her admitted for some time and then find a way to shift her somewhere else.

'Please give me some medicine, I'm terribly distressed.' Champa Roy had implored. Outside this man was waiting and Ved had told him what he thought about his wife and that she might need a transfer to the medical college in the city. The nearest medical college was fifty miles north. A passenger train went there every day and tickets would not cost much but such things were outside this man's known world. All that Ved could extract from him was endless gestures of bows and folding of hands.

Champa Roy was admitted to the female ward, which was a large room that had ten beds placed in two rows along the longer walls of the room. When these beds were full, the intervening space on the floor between the rows of beds would keep another five or six patients. They would lie down on whatever bedding they had come with or could be provided by the health center. That would then become an extra bed, marked with a number on a strip of adhesive tape fixed on the forehead of the patient so that the nurses could read it standing afar. It was important to have a bed number because otherwise the daily quota of ration, both food and tablets, could not be sanctioned. In busy times, three or four patients shared the space that could hardly contain one.

'It's no better even today—peep into the ward one day and you'll be shocked,' Ved said as he narrated to Kanu the story of Haren Roy and his wife.

By next morning, it was apparent that along with cancer, virulent bacteria had invaded Champa Roy's weak body and then Ved had a long talk with Haren.

'My name is Haren Roy, we live in Bhubandanga.' Haren Roy had said then, by way of introducing himself in exactly the same way as he said those words a little while ago. On that day, many years ago, he had sat uneasy, shrinking and shifting his body on a stool in front of Ved. He was late, having had to walk all the way from his house. He opened up gradually but he spoke more about his travails than his wife's illness. Jute did give a little money that season and Haren had toiled much for the paddy crop but most of the crops he had produced that year he had sold while still in the fields to repay the usurers. He had then planned to sell his small plot of land to Nabin Jotedar, a big landlord, who had been eyeing that piece of land adjacent to his own for a long time. He would till only the northern plot of land and in spare time would act as a sharecropper for Nabin. He knew Nabin would agree to that if he became his vassal. Haren that day had sat before Ved as a troubled man about to lose the two dearest earthly possessions of his life, his wife and his land.

A couple of days later in the afternoon Ved had been sleeping in his quarters. A knock at the door roused him. It was a call book from the hospital. Ved had read with sleepy eyes what the nurse had written for him. The message was cryptic but final in its delivery. 'Champa Roy, bed no extra 5, stopped respiration at 5.15 pm.'

'That was very unfair,' Kanu now heard Priyo saying to Nanu. He emerged from Ved's story and turned his attention to what Nanu and Umanath were discussing.

Nanu objected to Priyo's assertion, 'If it's a war, it is a war,' he said.

Kanu realised that Umanath was still on Mahabharata, talking about the epic war, which lasted eighteen days and in which all the kings of Bharat fought for one side or the other. Umanath had just now narrated the account of the young warrior Abhimanyu. He was telling how seven great generals of the Kauravas ganged up to trap the teenager prince of the Pandavas by tricking him into isolation away from the protection of his father.

Nanu found no fault there, for he held that there was little ethics involved in wars, then or now. 'But I think it was a blunder from a military point of view. They could have held the Pandavas for a ransom if they had their prince as a hostage. A killed idol only inspires vengeance.'

Umanath quipped, 'Probably there was no practice of taking prisoners then. Wounded soldiers were mostly left to die in the field, others returned to their camps after sunset.'

How those men died, Kanu thought. Many of them surely died slow, painful deaths from poisoned wounds or broken bones and from thirst and hunger. Haren reappeared from inside the house in cleaner clothes. His work done, he was ready to leave for the day.

Kanu looked at him. Could this man be of any interest to him as a photographer or an artist illustrating an epic story? His face? His hands? His bearing? His conventionality or the antiquated soul persisting in him? This middle-aged man with slanting eyes and a flat nose, who one day left his home on a journey to find a cure for his ailing wife, a lone man cutting through the empty fields to gain time — could he be the character of a tale?

Kanu visualised this man walking steadily one sunny morning ignoring the hot sun above his head. Plodding through the reaped open fields of paddy he comes to cross a small rivulet, an offshoot of the Teesta, which is now only a thin stream between the dried up sandy and rock filled riverbeds on either side. He finds that the river has become a little fuller suggesting melting of snow in the mountains. All rivers will be in spate once it starts to rain. He stoops to touch the cool water and sprinkles some on his hot face and shoulders. He offers a prayer each to the Teestaburi and to the Jurabandha Thakur and then begins to walk again.

Umanath hurled an instruction at Haren, who vaulted down to the courtyard from the verandah and lumbered to a corner at the end of it. He fetched a water pitcher from there and from it sprinkled with great care a few sprays of water on the basil tree housed at one side of the courtyard and on some flowering plants lined against the fence. Returning the pitcher back to its particular place with much gentleness, he came back to the verandah with his sandals in his hand. He placed the sandals in front of his feet, and then bowed, bringing his head down almost to his knees. He folded his hands together and brought them to his bowing head. Umanath paid no attention but both Kanu and Ved felt embarrassed. Haren's courtesy was too pronounced to ignore. They stood up to acknowledge the salutation.

There was something theatrical in Haren's gesture. Kanu did not understand what exactly he had wanted to convey. Perhaps he had said something to Ved. Perhaps he said that with treatment or without, Champa Roy and Keka Burman had met the same fate.

Kanu turned to Umanath and Nanu.

'Our life is steeped in myths, held by abstraction,' Umanath said. 'Look around, and you'll find every one, every thing, every custom has some myth to lean on.' He pointed to the place where Haren stood a few minutes ago and said, 'Even that man, Haren, carries a myth.'

'And what is that?' Kanu asked.

'Once in mythical times, some warrior kings killed a great Indian sage Jamadagni. His son Parashurama, though a Brahmin, was the fiercest fighter of his time. He swore to wipe out all warrior castes from the face of the earth, a proclamation he affirmed by carrying out his campaign repeatedly for twenty-one times. The warriors or Kshatriyas who could avoid his wrath by fleeing to this region settled here. 'And,' Umanath added pointing again to the place where Haren stood, 'according to that story, he is a descendant of those warriors—a Kshatriya.'

'Myths are myths,' Ved said glancing at Priyo, who looked at some distant object and feigned to be oblivious of the present discussion. 'Could the Rajbanshis be really serious about this story?'

Umanath shook his head. Myths had many levels, he said, and thousands of years pass by before a myth is finally born.

Ved began to laugh. Umanath looked offended. He pushed a bit of snuff in his nostrils and produced a piece of cloth stained with yellow powder from his pocket. He used it to wipe his nose with a disapproving sound.

Ved raised his hand and said, 'You're speaking in terms of centuries, while I was thinking about a decade being a long time. That made me laugh. Haren Roy could well have been from any other time in their history.'

Umanath demurred but picked up the thread of conversation he had dropped a moment ago. History was important, he said. No one, let alone a community, could advance without it. When there is not enough history, not enough remembrance of the previous and the past, people make them up. The Rajbanshis were no exception.

The sound of a motorcycle arrested them. The bike stopped in front of Umanath's gate and Deep got down from the pillion of the bike. The rider in front was a young man who looked glum. Deep hopped up the steps to the verandah where Ved and others were sitting. 'Sorry I got late ...two bad cases of malaria at the same time ...neither going to make it through though ..,' he said munching on a piece of fry he had picked up from a plate.

Nanu looked anxious. 'Malaria! Do people here die from malaria too? I thought that happened in the jungles of Africa only.' He invited Deep to sit by his side. 'Have you told these things to my father? He is a careless man.'

Ved changed the subject. 'Is that the younger son of Haldar Babu?' he asked Deep pointing to the young man now getting off the motorcycle and approaching them.

'Yes, that is Balaram. He has come to take us to their house. You've promised to pay a visit to old Haldar. Are you ready?'

Balaram came nearer and stood looking curiously at Nanu. Umanath dismissed him with a wave of his hand. 'Send Fokir; he can take them in his rickshaw. I do not think Ved would like to be the third rider on your pillion.'

Twenty Three

'What is wrong with the old man?' Ved asked when they were on their way to Haldar's house in a rickshaw.

Deep rolled his eyes and said, 'Aversion to food, and that, you know, is a serious condition for the old humbug.'

Once, during his stay here, Ved had treated the senior Haldar and the family believed that he would have died otherwise. Deep now looked after the old man, paying him regular visits and prescribing medicines. 'For money,' Deep said to Ved. 'The Haldars have enough to part with.'

Ved felt discomfited by Deep's frankness. Many doctors serving in rural health centers earn some money on the side but most would not trumpet that. He chided Deep, 'You shouldn't make money from the people here. Aren't you in government service?'

'Who cares a hoot, Ved-da? Everybody wants extra privileges and they pay. My duty does not include visiting patients in their homes but can I refuse the bigwigs here?' Deep asked. 'I'm an outsider here.

Besides, I need the money. I've a sister to marry off. Forget those small matters and tell me where you got this shirt. It is real chic and you look smart, like the doctor you are.'

'Really?' Ved laughed. 'You guessed right. Mr Chatterjee's son brought this.'

Deep caressed the fabric of the shirt and drooled, 'They make nice things there. I wish I had some real nice suits, three-piece, and could buy a mobile phone. I feel mortified when I go to Calcutta these days. All those new swanky shops, everything so glitzy and posh. Last time I went to see a relative admitted to the Birla Hospital. My god, I could hardly walk the floor, the marble was so polished.'

'With a suit here you will look like the doctors in our films. I always wondered how they could keep their shoes shining after treading through the dust and mud of village roads!'

Deep agreed, 'You are right. Yet, a doctor needs to dress like a sahib. Is it because we practise western medicine? We write prescriptions in English; even the doctors practising in godforsaken villages do that.'

'Yes, I too wonder why.' Ved said. 'Do you know of any famous *kaviraj* or a hakim here? Or a mystic? I know Mr Chatterjee is looking for one. He nurses hidden hopes to find a miraculous cure one day.'

'This Mr Chatterjee of yours is a nice man, but he is crazy.' Deep looked thoughtful. 'I cannot remember any good one in this region. Charlatans there are many, probably one in every small shrine. I have heard of a Muslim fakir, who does see a good number of cases; some of whom come to him from quite far.'

'Is that so? You can then take Mr Chatterjee to him one day.'

'I can,' Deep said but he sounded doubtful. 'But from what I gathered, this fakir mainly treats those with unnatural afflictions of mind. The hysterics. Basically, he is a ghost buster. You can call him a psychiatrist as well, dealing with the subconscious and the hidden layers of mind, not with any physical illness. Perhaps that is why he is successful. But tell me Ved-da, are you and Mr Chatterjee really planning to set up a hospital here?'

Ved did not answer. He was looking around as the rickshaw puller heaved to paddle forward against a strong wind. 'I see many new shops and pucca houses; these areas have changed a lot,' he said.

'But not the health center. It has not changed a bit. Still people come and get admitted only to get some food and a place for a shelter on rainy or cold nights, even if that means sharing a mattress with three other ill persons. But you didn't answer my question!'

'It depends on how Mr Chatterjee fares,' Ved said. 'I'm not very happy about the operation he had. He didn't agree to a full radical operation. He was more worried about his looks and speech. He wouldn't take chemotherapy either. Another few months, and then we will know.' Ved formulated his words carefully. He himself did not know if Mr Chatterjee would be interested to finance a project but if he remained well for some time he would have to find a place to settle and then he might consider the possibility—anything was possible. Ved continued to look at the shops— a neat row of about a dozen spacious half-masonry structures with cemented walls and asbestos roofs after a boardwalk made by mortared layers of brick.

'All owned by the Marwaris from Siliguri or Jalpaiguri,' Deep said pointing to the shops. 'The folks of Monabari are as they were.'

'But,' Ved said, ' take Mahen; could you have imagined a few years before that someone like him would go all the way to Calcutta to get his wife treated?'

'That is true. When I first proposed to him that he should go to Calcutta, I never thought he would actually do it. These people do go out from here; they go out all the time for business or jobs, to earn money. To Siliguri, to Cooch Behar. But all the way to Calcutta! Just to get treatment, that too for a woman! I must say it was extraordinary for a poor peasant like him.'

The habitations became scanty once they crossed the railway crossing. Between long stretches of fields on either side of the road going to Purbapara, clumps of mud walled houses with thatched roofs appeared with uneven regularity. The rickshaw puller was familiar with the location of the house and piloted his vehicle without any direction. They passed some young boys and girls playing a game of Dhassa in a field in the failing light of afternoon. A young boy was coming towards them trundling a big iron ring with an iron hook along the dusty road. Spotting them on the rickshaw, he stopped and immediately turned around to run in the direction he came from.

The rickshaw puller laughed, 'That was Babu, the grandson of Haldar Mosai; they will get the news of your arrival.'

The new boundary wall of the Haldar house looked imposing, complete with regular cement plastering and paint. Haldar lay on a cot on the broad verandah resting on two large pillows behind his back. A chair was kept waiting by the side of the bed. Ved jumped on the verandah without going to the small stair a few more steps away. 'How are you today Haldar Babu?' he asked.

'For us old men all days are same; it's now only waiting for the call.' Haldar raised his right hand in greeting and motioned Ved to take the chair.

The old man, Ved noticed, had become thin, his supine body only a hint of the large physique he once had. His voice had become husky and his speech slurred. He could move the left side of his body with great difficulty, the result of a paralytic stroke six years ago. Only his eyes looked piercing and even more rapacious than before. Two young women, apparently his daughters- in- law stood by his bedside covering their heads with their saris. His wife sat near the foot-end of the bed.

One of the daughters-in-law from time to time fanned the old man with a hand fan made of bamboo plaits and flounced with a strip of coloured cloth even though the afternoon was cold.

'He is doing fine; aren't you Haldar Babu?' Deep shouted a bit louder than was necessary, and then pointing to a bunch of keys peeping from beneath the pillows he added, 'He is still in business, absolutely.'

The women giggled and Haldar frowned. Ved too grinned but felt uncomfortable. 'If you see a mirror peeping out from under the pillow of a lady after a prolonged illness, then that is a sure sign of improvement.' One of their professors used to quote this old medical saying. The keys under the pillow of the old Haldar might not turn out to be as prophetic for him.

Haldar signalled to his daughters-in-law to remove one pillow from his back. He lay flat and took Ved's hand to place it over his belly. He said, 'Feel this place; here I've the greatest pain. Something is hurting inside there. At times it becomes unbearable.'

Haldar flinched as Ved probed his abdomen. The upper central portion of the abdomen was full, suggesting a swelled up organ in that region. Haldar had lost much fat and a lump was somewhat palpable there. At the base of his left neck, just above the collarbone, Ved found a node, rising up from deeper tissues, enlarged, ominously hard and unmovable. The Virchow's Node! The seat of the devil! Its presence made all other examinations redundant.

'Have you examined him recently?' he asked Deep quietly so that others could not hear.

'I did, but that was about a month back.'

'Come, feel again.' Ved stood aside to let Deep examine the patient. For him there was nothing more to know. Haldar Babu had cancer of one of the internal organs, most probably of stomach, and the disease had already spread to his liver and other parts of the body. He began to formulate in his mind what he ought to tell the family of an eighty-year-old man, paralysed on one side, and suffering from a fatal disease. It would be tough to keep this frail grumpy old man comfortable at his home. A blood vomit, an attack of pneumonia, or accumulation of water in the chest or abdomen—any of those happening and he would have to be rushed to a hospital or left to die in agony at home, with his helpless family watching, unable to do anything except to close the eyes when the time would come. On the other hand, it would be equally inhuman to send this old dying man to some distant center, separating him from his family in anticipation of those complications. Smaller centers, nearer at home, but willing to take care of him would have been more helpful. Ved looked at the expectant eyes of Haldar Babu with a renewed interest. This idea about smaller centres in the peripheries would be a good one to broach with Mr Chatterjee.

'What did you find? Is there a serious concern?' Jairam, the elder son, asked.

'Give me some good medicine. I can't tolerate this pain anymore. Also, see to it that I can eat properly. Look how thin I've become!' Haldar begged.

'We'll certainly do that,' Ved said as he sat back in the chair.

'Please arrange everything before you go back to the city. Have your tea,' Haldar said, mustering some cheer in his voice.

He looked on for some time as Ved and Deep sipped tea and then asked, 'Tell me *daktarbabu*, is it true that your friend from America is going to settle here?'

'Who told you that?' Ved laughed to minimise the significance of the question.

'What is his full name?' Haldar queried.

'Krishna Mohan Chatterjee.'

'It is good that he is at least a Brahmin! What is he doing here?'

'Nothing, except trying to get well after a big operation.'

'I have never cared to know him or about his business here but I keep hearing stories. We live with a family and we need to be careful. There was a lot of talk ...not now, but previously ... about this man's having a bad disease that they have in those countries for having loose morals. We of course trust you. Whatever you say is good for us. But people talk.'

Ved was aghast. The possibility of this kind of speculation had not occurred to him.

'Doesn't he have any family?' Haldar persisted.

'I told you that Mr Chatterjee has a son and right now he is in Monabari visiting his father. Why do you forget everything?' Balaram looked irritated.

'You be quiet.' Haldar disregarded his son. 'Let *daktarbabu* tell me about his friend and why must we welcome him in Monabari.'

Ved told him briefly what he knew about Kanu's family.

'True, very true.' Haldar nodded. 'You must be right. But we heard that he has some distant relationship with Rajen's in-laws.'

'That's not true at all.'

'Then what interest does our Rajen possibly have in being such a good host? I've heard that his daughter- in -law takes very special care of him. How old is your Mr Chatterjee? Could he have a daughter like Kalyani as his own?'

'Oh father, we shouldn't be talking about other people's affairs. It is their business and why should you bother?' One of the girls demurred.

'Of course it's none of my business but I've been with this land for so many years. I am witness to so many incidents, good or bad. I've seen enough and I don't want to be bothered anymore. Still, people continue to ask me. Tomorrow morning elders from Paschimpara will come to me and I have to give them my advice about this. I can tell you one thing;

do not think that Rajen is doing this thing without a motive. I hear that the numskull younger son of Rajen is not doing anything creditable. Is your Mr Chatterjee really comfortable at Rajen's?'

Ved told Haldar what Kanu Chatterjee had told him about Rajen Ganguly, that Kanu saw him as a tall proud tree.

Haldar closed his eyes and lay quiet for some time. Then he whispered to Ved, 'Yes. He is like a tall tree and like some trees he will die from the top, suddenly. Here, I am dying from all parts of my body, slowly, like a poisoned weed.'

'Tell me what I can eat?' Haldar asked again as Ved and Deep started to leave.

'Can you make a diet chart for him?' Jairam,the elder son, asked as he put on a shirt and looked for his slippers.

'Deep will do that for you.' Ved did not want to waste any more time in that place.

Jairam did not press him further. He accompanied them to the door to call the rickshaw puller waiting outside. He said to Ved, 'Please do not take offence at what the old man has said. He has lost all senses. You're like my own brother and I shouldn't hesitate to make this request to you. If something comes up let me know. I'm trying my hand in civil construction recently. I've already built two culverts for the village council and Balaram can run errands for you. He has no job now.' Jairam stopped only when they reached the rickshaw. 'Fokir, take back *daktarbabu*,' he motioned to the rickshaw puller. Ved held up his hand. 'Do not bother please. Fokir you don't have to go. This evening is so pleasant; we'll walk back.'

'Jairam-da, I'll collect my fees later,' Deep shouted at the hastily retreating figure of Jairam and said in a lower voice, 'No curtseys, not even an offer for fees to you!' He shook his head in disapproval. 'Oh... absolutely!' Deep kept saying that shaking his head and laughing.

Ved was having other thoughts. 'I was thinking about Haldar Babu. He has so much desire for life still,' he said. 'He is crippled and old; yet he is busy planning and plotting. I used to think that after a certain age people accept death as a natural event and become less concerned about worldly matters.'

'People do not want to die, whatever they might say.' Deep observed.

'Maybe,' Ved remarked and then turning towards Deep recited slowly , '...and there he must remain, on a hand's breadth of ground, all his life, it would be better to live so, than die within an hour.'

Deep chuckled, 'Wow, that sounds classy!'

'It is. Copyright Dostoevsky.'

'Is it from the Russian film they showed us in the '92 youth festival?'

'That one, that book.'

'Getting on with life is tough enough. Why bring questions into it? I'll make money a little, make merry a little and that will be it. When it'll be time to say good bye, I'll say good bye, not hang on like Haldar.'

'What would you do?'

'Take something that acts quickly and causes no pain, a large dose of insulin perhaps.' Deep jumped to catch a leaf from an overhanging plant creeping on the banyan tree under which they passed.

Ved watched Deep tearing off the tendril and rolling the leaf between his two hands with an easy careless manner.

'And what would you do as a doctor to a patient who has no hope to get well and has only pain to suffer?'

'I will help him to bring an end to his sufferings.'

'How? For how many? Surely you would not like to be known as "Doctor Death"!' Ved watched as Deep threw the leaf in his hand with a forceful bowling action but the leaf did not carry and dropped near his feet. 'How about that?' he repeated.

'Mr Chatterjee tells me that in his country, doctors are allowed to put an end to such miseries, if the patients or the relatives so want. He has hinted to me he himself would want such an end, quick and painless.'

Ved shook his head, 'That is a long shot here; we cannot even guarantee him a supply of morphine tablets, for terminal pain.'

'You sent some for Mahen's wife , that did her some good but Mahen might have overdosed her and ...' Deep hesitated to complete the sentence.

'And?' Ved asked, somewhat perplexed at Deep's reticence.

'I won't blame him if he had done that intentionally, to end her sufferings.'

'Are you sure?' Ved looked quizzically at Deep. 'If he had done that willingly, then it goes to prove that at least some people would rather see their dear ones die quickly than suffer. They do not do so because of the shackles put by the society. Mahen perhaps felt less impeded on that account.' Ved said and stopped to see what had caught Deep's attention.

'Look Ved-da.' Deep pointed his finger to a pond by the side of the road. It was dark out there and the water must be very cold. Two boys did laps in that pond, racing one another. Two girls, possibly of the group they had seen playing in the field before, giggled, standing on the bank. Both Ved and Deep looked at them for some time. 'Tell me, Ved-da, can you scoff at that!' Deep asked.

'No. Why should I?' Ved said.

Twenty Four

The events next day took an abrupt turn. A Rajbanshi nurse was gang-raped and murdered in Cooch Behar district hospital. The Kamptapuris promptly declared a 12-hour general strike next day throughout the whole district. Priyo came panting, when Kanu and others had just had their lunch, to give them the news. His face showed the strain of cycling hard for a long distance. Trouble might erupt, he said, and they should leave as soon as possible to move into the adjoining district, outside the area of the strike. He suggested that they pass the night in Shanti Babu's shelter, which would be midway to their destination. Nanu was excited when told that Shanti Babu was a revered ascetic and ran an ashram for meditation and yoga, along with a social service center. 'On the way you can see a hay market also. The ragtag of rural Bengal is best seen there,' Priyo said. He himself would accompany them to Shanti Babu's ashram from where Kanu and the others could travel on their own.

The initial part of the drive was through an open land; few settlements came by. Crop growing fields extended on both sides of the road. At times only uninhabited stretches of ground, patchily green, holding aloft steel lattice towers carrying unbroken lines of cables, and occasional ponds with coconut and date palm trees made up the scenery. A while later, the grassy land on the right gave way to a sandy and pebbled terrain, and beyond that, towards the far right at some distance they could see the outline of the bank of a river, but not the river as the bank was made high with concrete slabs. Priyo extended his hand to the right and said, 'That side... there was a ghat ...used to have a ferry service once.'

Nanu looked dismayed. He asked, 'What happened to that? It would've been nice to be ferried across the river.'

Priyo looked back and said, 'Gone. With the '68 flood.' Priyo raised one hand, moved it in the air like a helicopter rotor indicating all things around, and said no more. As if, the '68 floods needed no further description. As if everyone should remember the sufferings of a generation wrecked, their villages washed away, their land sealed against future cultivation for years. Kanu had heard older people talk about incidents with the 1968 flood as a pointer in time. They described incidents as happening either before or after that flood when an impatient river Teesta flowed high over the Jalpaiguri town. Local residents knew why. Dolia, Teesta's daughter, languishes as a poodle on the other side of the town, deprived of any flow of fondness from its riverine parents. In her craziness to meet her daughter, Teesta at times swells up and sweeps over the town.

There was a bridge, broad and mighty to cross the river. They stopped their car on Ved's request at the bridge. Nanu went down to take a closer look at the solid embankment of the river and at the spurs made of boulders, cemented and encased in thick iron meshes. The spurs extended into the river like the ugly talons of a prehistoric monster. Kanu stood in the middle of the bridge. An unsteady wind that rose from the river greeted him as he leaned on the railing and looked ahead. The day was cloudy, and looking at the horizon, they could only make out the nebulous presence of the hills, like the rampart of a distant fort. If the day was clear, they could easily see from there the golden peak of the Kangchenjunga; they could see how the icy peak rose up and up towards the sky and how the sunrays painted it with molten gold. Somewhere up, Teesta had rushed down from the constrictions of the alpine region to the plains and had spread with abundance.

During winter, and if it has not been raining for sometime, the river shrinks. It becomes a narrow sinuous stream of water zigzagging through a vast gray and white terrain of sand and boulders. In a few places, craters and shoals trap the tides and create small isolated lakes . Then again, when the sun crosses the equator and comes south to make this part of the world warm, the snow in the mountains begins to melt. Suddenly one day the people living on either this side or that side of the river wake up to see turbulent water whooshing past their homes.

After a few miles, they entered a side road winding between ploughed fields. They passed a few bullock carts with rubber tyres squeaking along slowly.

'Going to the market,' Priyo said indicating the carts. 'Markets are where people meet. Everyone comes — local landlords, politicos, and touts. Even the tillers come straight from the field. This one does business once a week; luckily today is that day.

A sharp wind blew from the north and brought them the first greetings from the market. The sound of a microphone blaring out the trendy beats of a popular film song greeted them, rising above a faint din, an indefinable sound that had no cadence but extended its presence from a distance. The road veered to a narrower road and the market rushed to them, drawing them into its turbulence of many feet and many voices.

This market though comprised only a few shanties made of tin and bamboo. Behind them, some temporary structures of bamboo and thatched boards stood in rows creating lanes between the shops. Petty vendors sat on the ground with vegetables and dainties displayed on torn jute sacks or even on banana leaves. An aged woman sat with just two pumpkins she had probably grown on the thatched roof of her hut. Inside the market dust settled easily on the products on sale. Outside, discarded leaves swirled in the unsteady wind. Everything moved at a slow slovenly pace. Even the few goats and cows roaming in search of vegetables dawdled. Some men coming straight from the fields with muddy feet and sweaty bodies looked around, shopped very little, but laughed incessantly. Kanu could see that Nanu was keenly observing the poor ill-clad men and women, their meagre merchandise, their tottering rickety tin and bamboo huts. He looked annoyed and Kanu knew why. More than the poverty, the diffidence in the existence of these men affected him. For some reason Kanu felt a twinge of shame. He felt he owed Nanu an explanation.

'Soon, much will change here; a big barrage has been built on Teesta and when the entire project will be completed, the conditions of these people will change.' Kanu said as they began to walk back to their vehicle.

'Teesta is no longer the Teesta of one's dreams,' Priyo said and shook his head. 'It's now a controlled flow of water. The forest will disappear. The deer and the rhinoceros and the elephants will have no place to stay.'

Kanu told Nanu which new industries were planned.

Priyo stopped him with a brazen wave of his hand from the front seat, 'No one is building them a small hospital, or a decent school and they are asked to wait for grand things!'

Ved was listening silently so far. Now he spoke up. 'The government has no funds. It's sad that there are so many NGOs working in other parts of West Bengal, but very few in these areas. If anyone takes up a community project here, it'll be a good deed to do.'

'See that man,' Priyo said pointing to a man standing at some distance with the full attire of a sweater over full sleeves shirt, his dhoti hitched up to his knees, and his laced shoes presently bedraggled with mud. 'Do you know that man?' Priyo asked Kanu.

'No, but should I?' Kanu asked.

'Yes. You would know him for sure once you complete the book I gave you.' Priyo smiled. 'He is Ramnath Paikar but he is just like that fictional *jotedar* made so famous by that book on Teesta. These *jotedar*s had begun to own land here since people had first started to settle in these places and nobody had any measure of how much land and cattle one could claim since no one was there to check. That character is present here before you in real life.'

The man saw them looking at him and came closer. He spoke to Priyo who interpreted his dialect for the others. It was amusing to listen to what Ramnath had to say about his lands and court cases against the government, about his woes — his land forcibly vested by the government, about his difficulties to acquire more land.

'Look, he has no quarrel with himself. He knows what he wants to do,' Kanu said aside to Ved.

***

About his ashram, Shanti Babu began to tell an old story that every child learns at sometime or other. Kanu heard him expounding on how a hermit was presented with a cat by one of his disciples to scare away the rats that were chewing up his only loincloth. To give the cat milk the hermit had to bring a cow, to tend the cow a cowboy, to give food to the cowboy a woman, for the woman a man, and so on till his cave was not an isolated cave in the mountain any more. It became a part of the everyday world. 'All for a loincloth!' Shanti Babu spread his arms and shook his head. The ashram now tilled its own paddy fields, grew vegetables, ran a few workshops to make baskets of cane, and artifacts of wood. The tea gardens bought them all.

Shanti Babu's place was larger than Kanu had expected it to be — a two-storied house extending on one side with a long unfinished one-storied wing with a wide cemented verandah. It was on a high bank but dangerously near the river. The ground was well manicured with trimmed shrubs and flowering plants and bordered by a verdant shrubbery. Shanti Babu invited Nanu to sit on his deer skin covered seat. Just to let him know how it felt.

'At least it saves worries about snakes and insects; they don't get on these animal skins.' Shanti Babu smiled and added, 'Quite an important consideration for the yogis meditating in open spaces.'

Priyo drew Nanu's attention to a minion and said, 'This Jhagru had to give up his land for the barrage. He has lived in this area for many years; suddenly you come and tell him, he does not belong here. Where would he go, with his habits, his stories, his songs? How would he teach his son to know the elephant paths from the tiger paths and teach him the innumerable mysteries of a jungle?'

Jhagru listened without a word.

Kanu looked at Jhagru standing mute like a tree with his long limbs, and wondered what was passing through his long narrow head behind those slanting eyes and arched brows. Jhagru and Mahen, Priyo and Ajoy Pradhan, stand on different rungs of the ladder of a society, and perhaps even in different times. Later, when Shanti Babu gave them a tour, Ved called his attention to a man squatting outside the workshop polishing a cane basket held easily between his two large knees, his large head tilted back as if he did not need to see what he was doing and was apparently listening to some distant sounds. The man was old but his muscular body had not stooped with age and there was something unnatural in his face that looked crude and brutal. Kanu saw Ved looking at the man with a shocked expression, his mouth half-open. The man had no eyes! Both the sockets in his face were empty, without the eyeballs.

'Gouged out by a mob, as retribution,' Shanti Babu explained when they had passed that man. Baburam was the leader of a fearsome gang of dacoits in his early life. Caught during one act of crime, his punishment was swift but final, one that would last through his life.

'I shall die happy if I can complete that wing,' he said laughing, pointing to the unfinished part of the building.

'Is that your goal?' Nanu asked, disappointed.

Kanu took Shanti Babu's picture with that building in the background.

It began to rain. Kanu stood on the verandah and watched the sky pouring down water with an unchanged monotonous intensity. The trees soaked up serenely and the soft earth sopped the raindrops in silence. Below a dark sky, over the fields, and over the wide bed of Teesta, in the diffuse low light, and through the haziness of the downpour, the outside world looked unreal. He could hear Nanu engaging Shanti Babu inside about the nuances of Hinduism. Kanu knew Nanu had a complex about religion. He wanted to be a believer for his mother's sake but his training prevented him from being ritualistic. With a religion to follow, it would have been easier then for Nanu to drop the intellectual pursuit and just be a believer.

They stayed the night in two large rooms, sparsely furnished but clean. In the dead of the night, Kanu was roused by a deep sonorous chant outside his window, a sombre chorus that kept rhythm with the hurried steps of people carrying a heavy object and repeating the same words, '*Bolo Hari, Haribol. Bolo Hari, Haribol.*' Kanu listened. The import was unmistakable.

Unable to sleep, he went outside. Far down, at one place along the river, in the all-pervading fog and darkness, a fire burnt. Mourners had gone down the pebbled alluvium to cremate their dead there, near the water. A pyre needs water to douse it when the consecration is done. What came into being from the air, from the earth, and from the water, was being returned to the air, to the earth, to the water.

A person came and stood behind him. Kanu turned slowly, hoping that in the darkness the person would not be able to notice the tears running down his cheeks.

'You're thinking of something?' Shanti Babu asked.

Kanu nodded and told him about his parents.

Shanti Babu remained silent for some time and then said, 'Everyone who is born as a Hindu should pray for his ancestors. Tomorrow at sunrise I'll take you to the water and help you perform a rite.'

A rising sun was just about to make the earth warm but the river water was still cold with a mist hovering above it when Shanti Babu made Kanu take a dip. Shanti Babu performed his own rites first. One by one, he called the names of his ancestors and then poured holy water brought in a copper receptacle from the river Ganga with a smaller copper ladle held between his two palms, begging his ancestors to accept that water to quench their thirst. He turned to stand facing all the four directions one by one, and chanted mantras with an unhurried but fluent rhythm. After that, he prepared a sacred thread for Kanu and slung it from his right shoulder. Kanu stood in knee-deep water facing the south and called the wandering souls of his father and then of his mother and poured water into the river. Shanti Babu asked him to chant, 'Let this water truly and fully please all those who were our friends, all those who were not our friends, all those who were our friends in other lives, and all those who desire our offerings.'

Nanu had also woken up early in the morning. He went out with

Ved to do a bit of cycling, towards the north, to get a feel of the forest. Besides, he had to find a public call office to make a long distance call. His cell phone received no signal here. He came back looking happy. A Canadian girl he had met in Singapore would come to Delhi in three days. If Nanu could board the flight on Saturday from Bagdogra, he could join her for a trip to Agra and Bharatpur. Moreover, from a vantage point, under a sky that had become clear after the rain last evening, he had obtained a grand view of the Kangchenjunga, the 'five treasures of snow'. Under a radiant morning sun, the golden peak had generously exhibited to him all its splendour.

Twenty Five

Nanu's decision to go to Delhi brought a sense of immediacy and direction to their wandering. Kanu narrated his experiences about the small trips he had made as Ved and Nanu pored over maps and guidebooks to select spots they could visit in the next two days. A few miles up and to the north from Shanti Babu's ashram the openness had disappeared into the evergreen jungles of Sal, Khayer, Madari, and Sisso trees. They had only to follow the highway going up north into the forest and then, where the road has forked into two, could turn either to the left or to the right. They could even go straight up, look at tea gardens, go up the hills through the kingdom of pines, firs, and rhododendrons and peek at the mysterious land of Tibet across the mountains. Kanu wanted to make a day trip to the frontier town of a neighbouring small country, a country that rested peacefully cuddled by the soaring peaks and impassable gorges of the Himalayas. An ancient monastic monarchy still ruled it.

The last part of the drive to that town was through a road that tore through the Hasimara forest with the grandness of a king's drive. The trees on either side created an unbroken canopy. The light was low and often for a length of time, they could hear no other sound than the hum of the engine of their car. Nobody talked.

Kanu was thinking about what Shanti Babu had hinted to him before they left. He needed money to build the new wing but he was in urgent need of a multipurpose pick-up van and he would be grateful if Kanu could see to that. He felt a mild twinge in the operated side of his tongue. The first time it was there just for a fleeting moment. Next time it stayed longer. Kanu leaned backwards on the back seat of the car and looked out, trying to peer beyond the impenetrable walls of the thick foliage and the high undergrowths on the roadside.

'That's brilliant.' Nanu cried out suddenly from the front seat, looking up from a travel guide he was glancing through. 'Look here, it says, if you cannot go forward, you go back.' Nanu read out the story to them. More than a hundred years ago, when the mountain railway to Darjeeling was laid, the engineer was stuck at some point beyond which he could not advance the lines. One night while he worried, his wife remarked, 'If you cannot go forward, go back.' He did exactly that, creating an ingenious zigzag pattern of railway lines that bypassed many seemingly insurmountable obstructions.

'If you cannot go forward, you go back.' Kanu repeated that to himself — go back in order to come forward again through a different way. If that were possible to do in life, which things would he have done differently? Would he have gone back to some point in life and then set off on a different track to correct some of his misbegotten actions? Even then, he would not be able to know which course would be more rewarding. He would never know; no one would ever know because no one can live any particular moment in two different ways. As a photographer he knew, no one could snap up a moment twice. From now on, Kanu decided, he would only go forward and never look back at roads not taken.

The road ended in a filthy dirty square but on the opposite side stood a huge majestic Tibetan gate, and beyond that, once they passed under the arch, magically it was a different land.

The border town mostly meant a market square built around a rectangular park. The morning air was nippy. Kanu fished out a scarf from his bag and tied it around his neck. He and Ved sat at a teashop while Nanu and the driver went to find a local car to take them a few miles up the mountain where they could visit a gompa. In the adjacent shop that sold small statues and photographs, souvenirs, key rings attached to medallions, and handicrafts, a teenage boy lighted sticks of incense in front of some statues sitting on a small shelf. His eyes measured Kanu for a prospective customer.

Some old men, clad in *gho*—heavy robes with long overflowing sleeves, sat absolutely still on the steps carved out of rocks with the sun on their faces. Not a muscle on their faces moved and with eyes shut, they too looked like statues. Behind them at the slopes of the mountain ranges, triangular flags of different colours fluttered on poles erected here and there.

The gompa was a few miles up but had a motorable road reaching up to its doorstep. As the road climbed higher, the land around began to look like a wrinkled green carpet, soaring up here a bit and then sloping down to a valley only to rise again. On the ledges, a few small houses, all remarkably similar in pattern and colour, stood. The trees became taller gradually and so did the flagpoles. The flags were also bigger and now they were square. It made sense, Kanu thought. Just as the trees have to become taller to get light and air, the flagpoles have to be made higher and the flags bigger so that the rise of the land around them does not hide them. Nanu looked excited. At last, he would meet people who could tell him the oriental lore. He kept talking about Tibet, the primordial mysterious land, where, he had heard, thousands of years of consideration had frozen solid into a granite hard wisdom.

The gompa stood on the edge of a flat square of the size of half a football field with only the sky as its backdrop. The vast expanse of open space around it exalted it into something more than a man made structure. Amidst stretches of green lawns full of colourful flowering plants, on a piece of tawny land the medium sized gompa stood like a citadel, almost like the last frontier post of the known world.

Nanu was the first to get down from the car. He ran to the temple and spun the prayer wheels lined in front. Ved and Kanu followed him to the atrium. Two monks sat in front of a statue reading from the scriptures in the illumination of some butter lamps. Paintings of Lord Buddha adorned the walls. Near the entrance, where there was more light, a small group of people, some of them obviously tourists, sat around two monks in sleeveless red robes.

Kanu and Ved advanced towards the statue.

'This light is terrific,' Nanu said, stepping back to take photographs. He was carrying Kanu's camera.

They trooped back towards the entrance; one of the monks holding forth there was actually European. The other one, apparently the senior one, was yellow skinned, with an exceptionally large physique and a radiant smile on his clean-shaven round face under a tonsured head.

The monk looked at the three of them with clear eyes. His smile was friendly and his stare so intimate that they felt obliged to sit down with the group.

The monk was talking about monasteries, the famous ones in Paro, and in Thimphu and about the wise lamas there who had mastered the gifts of nature and could use them to heal any wound. 'The monks were not supposed to stay in one place; they were supposed to wander to beg for their sustenance, and preach. Monasteries came much later, probably a full century after Lord Buddha. This gompa had only been built three decades ago because the royal mother wanted a suitable monument to adorn her tropical garden.'

Kanu was amused to see Nanu's disappointment. He would have liked to imagine that the gompa was at least a thousand years old. He had inherited his mother's likes and dislikes. Ludwina lived in the past. Medieval castles and ancient churches, old edifices that had 'spires that could dream', were her favourite haunts.

The sunlight that came through the open door dimmed and the hall got darker. Perhaps a cloud was passing across the path of the sunrays. The flickering lamps near the statue looked more beckoning. Their flames appeared timeless and seemed to carry memories that were extraterrestrial in origin, memories that went much beyond those first terrestrial dusts and hot rocks on the shore of an ocean of liquid nitrogen where it all began. There seemed to be an elemental force flowing through the sanctum. Kanu began to do a set of *pranayams*, trying to absorb the vibes from those lamps and the statue.

A sound of laughter broke his spell. He looked at the group sitting around the monks. They looked happy. A younger monk came and whispered something to the senior monk. The monk smiled and nodded his head emphatically. The younger monk trotted back somewhere inside but soon returned with a few strips of capsules and a glass of water. The senior monk took them. 'I had an operation, in Delhi,' he said indicating a cut on his abdomen, 'am still recovering from that.' He laughed.

Kanu came out of the gompa, alone. The sun had come out again and the ground in front was awash with light. The air was fresh but cold. The verandah was clean and a he chose a spot to sit. An old man in dirty robes hobbled up to him. He said something but Kanu could not understand his language. He looked around and saw the driver of their hired taxi squatting at some distance. He was a Nepalese; he should be able to understand this man. Kanu called the driver.

The driver exchanged a few rapid words with the old man and then explained to Kanu. This man used to copy scriptures and read them at people's houses. Now he had become old and had lost his eyesight. He had a pair of spectacles made for him but still could not see well.

The man began to say something animatedly to Kanu. Apparently, he was trying to convince him about something.

The driver intervened. 'He says that the eye doctor who gave him the spectacles had cheated him. Now his eyes have become solid and he will need an operation to make fresh holes in them so that light can pass through. He is now saving money for that to travel down to an Indian hospital.'

Kanu smiled at the old man and showed him a thumbs up sign.

The man came closer and made a gesture of writing with his finger on his left palm. The smell of his heavy coat disturbed Kanu. He tried to move away. The man pulled at Kanu's jacket and said something to the driver.

The driver spoke on his behalf. 'If you can keep some money with him, he will use that to light lamps here daily for your well being.'

Kanu gave him fifty rupees and moved away to Ved and Nanu standing at the doorstep watching him.

'Smell of all senses bothers us most,' Ved grinned with a knowing smile.

'Does it?' Kanu asked, wondering and taken aback a little. What about pain then? He did not feel well. He inhaled deeply a few times but still felt tightness in his chest. Was the air too thin? But they had not ascended to any great height. He moved his tongue a bit and felt that the pain was still there. Was it due to the cold air? That was funny; he smiled to himself. Forty years he had passed in Northern Europe and now he was afraid of the cold. This place was otherwise nice, but merely a frontier to a land that had effectively shut itself off from the outside mechanical world. The last and lone country in the world to keep even the television away. Probably, further north, deeper inside the mountains, would be the places to travel. Presently, it disturbed him that the senior monk had been all the way to Delhi, in search of a modern hospital for his health and the old script reader was painstakingly saving up for an operation in some foreign town that would enable him to see again.

They spent the evening prior to Nanu's departure in a hotel at the foothills of Darjeeling. It had rained two nights ago and there were reports about landslides. They did not venture further up in the mountains lest they were trapped and could not make it down to the airport in time for Nanu's flight to Delhi. Kanu sat on the bed with a blanket. Ved was writing his case notes on the hotel stationery in longhand. Nanu would carry that with him to New York for consultations. He would also carry a roll of film with pictures of his father. Not close-ups of his face but all of him, fully dressed with his old orange cap and Aviator sunglasses, firmly poised on a mountain slope. Ved wrote and from time to time asked Kanu to furnish a particular detail that he could not remember. Nanu talked about the Alps and compared them with the Himalayas. Kanu, for some reason, more than the snow on the Alps remembered a train ride to Chattels one cold but sunny afternoon.

Kanu prepared to sleep as Ved and Nanu got up. They would now go to the dining room below, for dinner, and perhaps a drink, and then would go back to their room for the night.

'Good night, Pa,' Nanu called as he switched off the light and pulled the door shut.

'Wait,' Kanu sat up and threw off the covers.

'What is it, Pa?' Nanu pushed open the door and came back into the room. Ved had already gone down the corridor.

Kanu smiled, ‘Meneer Nayan Mohan Chatterjee, do you know something? The ultimate science fiction is a journey through the world of the occult.’

Nanu stood still looking at Kanu. In the dim light of the room, Kanu could not perceive if Nanu was surprised or not.

‘I agree,’ Nanu said, ‘to some extent one can find an odyssey in either way. But you aren’t up to it.’ With that, he turned around and pulled the door shut behind him.

Twenty Six

The airport was small, and the terminal building looked like a country club. Only a few dangling loops of iron chains running between red coloured stakes and a line of white pots with green plants separated the plastic chairs in the open porch from the runway.

The plane began to taxi. A group of people who were waiting with Kanu and Ved stood up and waved frantically at the aircraft, which raced out of sight and Kanu could not see from where it took off. It reappeared a while later as a shining speck climbing up in the sky and then was lost in the clouds. It was better this way, Kanu thought. If he was to die now, Nanu would carry this memory of him, remember him as a man still capable of going out and experimenting with life. Like his pictures that he had made Nanu take.

Inside the small lounge, there was a coffee shop. Kanu ordered a drink of orange juice. An extreme sense of fatigue, which he could not attribute either to his illness or to his mental state, gripped him. 'Why is this?' he asked Ved.

'How have you been sleeping lately?' Ved asked. 'Probably we've travelled much more than we should've. I myself would have liked to sleep through the whole afternoon. Take a tranquiliser this evening, have a good meal, sleep through the night , and then see how you feel.'

Kanu quietly sipped his drink for a while. Then he said, 'No. It's not only that. For some time I've had this feeling, even before we got out for this short tour. When I wake up in the morning, my eyelids feel heavy and I've to fight to keep them open. My feet get swollen and I can hardly put on my slippers to go to the toilet. Late morning, when I can tend to my passion for reading, I fall asleep, sitting wherever I am.'

'And how are you eating?' Ved asked.

'I had been getting better taste and had even started enjoying some food. It has not been so for the past week. Swallowing is quite difficult.'

'It's your thyroid,' Ved put down his drink and said, 'We need to check on your thyroid.'

'Thyroid?' Kanu asked. He put his hand on his throat and felt there. He felt a little panic at this new thought and then relaxed as he saw Ved smiling

'Sorry,' Ved said. 'We should have checked on that earlier. The radiation you received probably knocked out your thyroid, made it non-functioning. It is known to happen often enough. This lethargy and swelling up could be due to that.'

Kanu would go back to Monabari in the afternoon by a local train. Ved would board the Calcutta Mail departing later in the evening. They had time to call on one of Ved's friends who could arrange for Kanu's tests and treatment. 'If you stay in these areas, it may be useful for you to know him; he is close to Shanti Babu,' Ved said.

Ved's friend appeared to be a jocular fellow. Unhurried, easy going. Accustomed to the money and fame of a successful practice in a smaller city, he had no stress to show. 'Ayurveda, Tibetan medicine…' he guffawed as he made a long list to Ved to describe his practice. 'To practise here, take history like a homeopath; examine the patient like a hakim, talk about esoteric practices like a lama, and then use your allopathy to cure the patient.' He told Ved, laughing and bobbing up and down in his chair.

'And what does that make you?' Ved asked. 'A doctor of medicine or a shaman?'

'They mean the same thing, don't you know?' Ved's friend quipped. 'Once a month I visit Shanti Babu's ashram, hold a clinic there for the poor disciples, widows, old people, people who have no one to look after them — particularly the widows. Every one of them is a storehouse of various sorts of maladies, real or imaginary. Can I practise modern medicine with them?' Ved's friend picked up a journal from his table and opened a page that had a picture of a newly introduced machine. 'Can I ask them to do this and do that? So what do I do? I teach them Ayurvedic concoctions, hakim's recipes, pranayams. I do exactly the opposite when I treat the managers and the sahibs from the tea gardens. I write for them a plethora of tests but seldom talk about how they should live their lives.'

'Shanti Babu wants him to stay in his ashram,' Ved said pointing towards Kanu. 'That way, he says, Mr Chatterjee can be nearer to you, in case of any need.'

Ved's friend looked sceptically at Ved for a moment and then straightened up in his chair. 'Welcome to the brotherhood,' he said extending his hand to Kanu.

Before Kanu could shake the hand offered to him, Ved cut in. 'However, I personally think that Monabari has suited him well. He gets there the kind of attention he needs for his food and other things.'

Kanu was surprised to hear Ved saying that seriously. True, he had promised Shanti Babu to buy an old van for his ashram but nobody had seriously discussed his staying there. The old preacher though had cautioned him against the possibility of being submerged into the quicksand of mawkish mellifluous life of Monabari, of his being stuck with the petty greeds and gripes of the place. He himself had already formed an idea that Ved had an interest in keeping him in Monabari. He needed some more time to decide about that. He would not like to join Shanti Babu's ashram as a crippled man either. Besides, Kalyani would be hurt if he did anything that was abrupt.

Ved's friend arranged for Kanu to stay back for the night, to take the tests early next morning.

Next day when he came back to Monabari, he did not tell anyone in the Ganguly household about his difficulties and the medical tests he had undergone in the town.

Sona, finding him home captured him. He was pleased to see that Kanu was able to use the household tools to fix his broken toys. Encouraged, Sona pulled out a broken wooden chariot that little boys pull at the time of the Chariot Festival.

Kanu examined the wooden contraption. The lower planks had come loose and the axle connecting the two wheels had separated. All he had to do was to drive in a few nails to hold the planks together and then attach the wheel rod below it.

'Hold it like this,' he said to Sona. There was no workbench so he managed to do the job by placing the toy at the edge of the verandah and sitting on his haunches.

'I put one nail here, one nail there, two more on this side and then we shall see how many more we need to put in.' He took the hammer and began to strike a nail. He struck thrice and his shoulder began to ache. He dropped the hammer.

Sona sensed his discomfort and called Badal. Badal came and with a few strong effortless swings hammered the nails in. Kanu sat aside rubbing his shoulder and gave instructions but he felt mortified.

He retired to his room feeling extremely tired. That day he could not eat his lunch well. Even the simple act of mixing the rice and the curry in his plate and then taking the food to his mouth tired him. After lunch, he had his windows closed, curtains drawn, and slept. He did not go out for his usual evening stroll.

The next few days he had to pass in bed. It was now obvious to everybody, more so to Kalyani, that he was not well and Kanu did not pretend otherwise. Deep had finally left Monabari, transferred to a hospital nearer his home. Kanu missed him. The young doctor was a minimalist and his penchant for making light of any situation often helped. Kalyani sent Badal to Siliguri to consult Ved's friend.

Badal returned in the afternoon. 'Your test results have come. The doctor has sent these medicines and this note about how you should take them.'

Kanu read the notes. His test results had confirmed what Ved and the other doctor suspected. He would now have to live on a supplementation of thyroxin for the rest of his life but it was no indication that his condition had worsened. All that it meant was that radiotherapy had knocked out his normal thyroid and that was a price, along with a few other ones, he would have to pay for the cure of his illness. The note from Ved's friend warned him that the new medicines could excite his heart. Kanu should keep a count of his pulse rate and report should he feel any palpitation in his chest.

Kalyani came. 'Would you like some tea now?' she asked Badal. 'Or you can go and have a wash; I've kept some snacks prepared for you. I will fry them as soon as you have washed. You can have your tea with that.'

Kanu told her the news about his test results. 'I will take it slow from now on,' he assured Kalyani.

'Tell me about your medicines so that I can remind you. And please don't fret about allowing Jugu to give you hot oil massages every day before your bath. Ma has asked him to take out your bedding and warm clothes and put them in the sun for a while.' She said and went back to her kitchen.

Badal on his way back had also collected a packet that Ved had sent by courier. It contained some pamphlets about the government rules and guidelines for voluntary societies, a facsimile of the project report of a reputed society, and a few photographs and newspaper cuttings showing award ceremonies and felicitation functions. In the photographs the recipients of the awards beamed and every one else smiled. There was also a book, written by an American author, titled, *Positive Mind: Beautiful Living - Ten sure ways to change your life*. Kanu smiled. Probably the book was new to the Indian market, and Ved had come across it recently, but these books were dime a dozen in the west and Kanu had seen many, perhaps some by this same author. All this, Kanu understood Ved had sent as props to his argument that Kanu should engage in certain activities. If only they knew that Kanu was not a rich man.

The after dinner brushing of teeth, washing his mouth, and gargling had become more than a simple ritual. In the bathroom mirror, his face looked puffy as he laboured massaging his teeth and gums slowly, methodically, savouring what little taste he got from the toothpaste. Suddenly the brush dropped from his hand and instinctively he bent down to pick it up. He felt a numbness spreading through his arm and a shooting pain passing through the lower part of his body. As he began to straighten up, he felt choked. It was even difficult to grasp the edge of the washbasin and stand up. This had not happened to him before. What was happening? Was he having a heart attack? What would happen now? Would the lights go out and then there would be darkness forever? Confusing thoughts ran through his head in rapid succession, tumbling over each other, as pebbles and rocks carried by a torrent suddenly let loose. Summoning all his strength, he took a long breath and then let out a muffled cry and moved his head side to side in a desperate attempt to break loose from the unseen hold that threatened to strangle him. He concentrated on his efforts and began to draw in long slow breaths, trying to develop a rhythm, all the time telling himself — not here, not now. Gradually the tension eased and he realised that he had not gone limp. On the contrary, his muscles were taut and his body tended to arch back. He was now sweating but that terrible sense of oppression was gone and he had no pain in his chest. Slowly the terror and the alarm of the past moments receded but when he tried to go back to the bed, it was like swimming under water, against a heavy current. Then he lost sense.

Consciousness came back to him a short while later; the choking sensation had lessened. He kept quiet, debating in his mind if he should alert Kalyani or Chapal but waited to see if that feeling would return. He gathered all his pillows together and half reclined on them with his head up, stretching out his limbs and making them as limp as possible, and tried to control his respiration. One, two, three, he counted as he breathed in the air, and then one, two, as he breathed out. One by one, the lights outside went out as the Ganguly household, retiring with the hope of a restful night, went to sleep and it became dark and quiet. Now more than the panic, the strangeness of the situation amazed him. Far from his own world, in a small room in some remote corner of some other world, unattended by anyone whom he could call a kin, all of a sudden death lurked to obliterate him forever, without a trace, like a mercenary in a far-off war or like a castaway.

He had expected his death to be different, in fact wanted it to be so. But so soon!

The night deepened. His tired body lumbered between sleep and wakefulness. At sometime during the night he became fully awake again, could hear the crickets sounding outside and a few jackals howling. Customarily, the village dogs began to bark. His mind was now clear enough to think. Since the operation, his right shoulder had been painful and often he used to get tingling sensations in his upper limbs. He had discussed some of these symptoms with Ved and his friend only the other day and knew that probably his spinal cord had received some degree of radiation and an important nerve to his shoulder might have been partially damaged during the operation. That might cause some symptoms like the tingling he used to get. Nevertheless, this numbness and the shooting pain were new, and so was this choking sensation. Neither Ved, nor his friend had mentioned anything about this choking sensation.

Kanu began to take stock of his own situation: dryness of mouth, shoulder pain, scar in the neck, inability to move his head freely, frequent sore throats, tiredness even after mild exercise. Swallowing was becoming more difficult. He had numbness with occasional tingling sensation in his limbs. He even got tiny jolts like an electric shock once or twice. While sleeping, he had to change sides frequently as his mouth became dry and he had difficulty breathing. Recently his tongue felt heavier and his speech had become more slurred, a development that he was trying not to be worried about. The good side was that there was no lump developing in his neck. He had no cough; his appetite was still good. There was no unbearable pain, no headache, nor burning sensation in the mouth. He was producing more saliva than before though it was very thick and that made swallowing difficult.

Kanu did not know when he fell asleep again; he woke up feeling better. Other than a slight pain and heaviness in the upper part of his throat, he had no discomfort. He poured some hot water from the thermos kept in his room, dissolved two aspirin tablets in it and gargled.

He wrapped himself with a shawl, covering his neck and lower face and pulled a chair in front of the east side window. As he opened the window, the cold fresh air rushed in along with the first light of the day.

'Dada, you did wake up early today!'

Kanu had not noticed when Kalyani had come. She stood there with a glass of health drink in her hand. He took the glass from her hand and turned towards the window again; words did not come to his mouth.

Kalyani waited for a minute more. Then she picked up the empty thermos from the table and as she was about to leave the room, she said, 'From tonight I'll ask Jugu to sleep outside your room.'

Rajen Babu and his wife, for the first time, spent some time in his room. Rajen Babu sent for the new doctor who had replaced Deep.

The doctor was not available immediately. He had gone to the district headquarters to attend to some administrative business. He came late at night. Dr Bose was a family man and had been in the rural health service for more than fifteen years. He knew all the ropes and within a short time had picked up the threads left by Deep to set up a good practice. So far posted at some subsidiary health center, which had no indoor beds, he considered this posting to a larger health center that had separate wards for male and female patients as a promotion.

Kanu let the doctor examine him and answered the few questions he asked. He had expected Deep to have alerted the new doctor about him but from the doctor's questions he understood that Deep had done no such thing.

Dr Bose did not want to spend much time with him; neither did he did settle down to know Kanu better. His examination was quick and his prescription was forthright. Though he did not ask for any tests, he was firmly convinced about what was good for Kanu and what medicines he must take. He administered one antibiotic injection, which would be repeated twice daily for three days. He prescribed a few drugs and a gargle to use three times daily, plus one more time before going to bed at night with tea liquor. If Kanu could take a concoction made from the leaves of a herb soaked in warm water mixed with sugar cubes, it would help him more.

'I know how to do it,' Kalyani assured Kanu and the doctor.

Dr Bose pocketed the one hundred-rupee note Kanu offered him. 'I don't have change right now with me but that fifty rupees can take care of my visit tomorrow.'

The medicines and the rest helped and Kanu got back some strength within the next couple of days. The antibiotics reduced the inflammation in his chest and throat and he could cough out the phlegm. His breathing became easier and he started his *pranayams* and other exercises but he could no longer adhere to his normal routine of long solitary excursions to the outskirts of Monabari.

He settled for small walks in the garden at the back and then parked himself on the roof of his room where the stairwell offered a shade for some hours in the morning. Rajen Babu made a seat for him there. On most days, some time later, Badal would join him there and tell him about his grandiose plans for business, which Rajen Babu always summarily dismissed as mere fancies of a scatterbrain. This morning he was particularly agitated. The previous day's newspaper had carried a story that a fresh business graduate from South India had received an offer of a salary of sixty lakh rupees a year.

'Why don't you try for this government loan?' Kanu asked Badal. He drew his attention to the full-page advertisement of a government-sponsored project named after a late prime minister. 'You at least should have no problem with providing the collaterals.'

'That one?' Badal looked peeved. 'The banks will give me a loan of one lakh rupees to start a small business. If I have to pay back that loan with interest in five years time, which means sixty monthly installments,

I pay the bank two thousand five hundred rupees per month. Consider the costs, my living included. I would need to earn at least seven to eight thousand rupees a month. Name a business that can give me that kind of earning from the very beginning?'

Badal, like everybody else, Kanu found out, was hopeful about the place he lived in but was disparaging about the people and the system that ran it. 'Even a small place like Jorabari has two agencies, one for fertilisers and one for motorcycles,' Badal lamented. 'What is Joarabari compared to Monabari? But people there aren't so wicked and have love for each other.'

It suited Kanu that Monabari had no business activity. No large saw mill, no rice mill, let alone a modern plant for food processing or a fishery. It had a market and traders like Gopal Sahoo but being away from any main north-south or east- west routes, situated too deep in the woodlands, it stood aside, unable to develop into a hub.

'Why don't we do something from what we've here? Like breeding fish? Prawns they tell me have a huge market, or set up a center to teach the local women to make hand woven things from jute…' Kanu stopped in mid sentence watching Badal becoming exceedingly animated and staring at him with wide eyes. In a moment he understood what had made Badal perk up. Unwittingly he had used the word *we*, making himself a partner in Badal's scheme of things and that had enthused the somewhat naive young man. He reframed his words, 'I mean you have so many possibilities to explore…'

Badal was too excited to notice the change. 'Of course we can do so many things, only you've to say yes. If I knew what money I shall have to handle, then I know the people who can advise us.' He stopped to listen to a gradually rising sound of 'Vroom, vroom.' He stood up from his chair and went to the edge of the roof to have a look.

A red motorcycle arrived and stopped at a little distance from the

Ganguly house. The rider got down and idly strolled into a house.

Badal was livid with rage. He caricatured, 'Vroom, vroom… whole day that rascal makes this noise. As if he is the only owner of a motorcycle in this world. But wait, a better make is going to hit the market soon. Did you see the advertisement in the newspapers?'

'Who was that?' Kanu asked Badal.

'That was Balaram Haldar. You've seen him before,' Badal said. He turned to Kanu and his face contorted into a smirk. 'With boys like Balaram around, you can certainly forget about your plan for breeding fish. They'll put folidol in the tanks at night.'

When Kanu got down from the roof, he found carpenters working in the unfinished room adjoining his. Three long benches, as found in primary schools, a chair, a table, and a blackboard crowded the verandah.

'What are these for?' Kanu was curious.

'Those are for the private students of my dear big brother. Every morning before the school starts, he goes out to give private lessons. Now he is going to have a regular coaching school here. Big money in it. Have twelve students in each batch, eight batches to rotate through the week, take fifty rupees from each student, and add that to your salary of a schoolmaster, and you earn more than the district commissioner himself.'

Kanu was concerned. A big crowd of students romping so near every morning and evening would make his stay impossible.

Badal took a step back and whispered, 'If you'd decided earlier, we could've made an office here for a dot com agency!'

Monabari, unknown to Kanu, interpreted his withdrawal in quite the opposite way. When he did not go out to Monabari, Monabari trooped into his small room. First came Umanath and Mahen, and then it was almost anybody whom Kanu had chanced to meet during his brief sojourn in this place. Even people like Jairam, and Bhola Pal, whom Umanath and others had expeditiously asked Kanu to avoid and whom the Gangulys abhorred, came to see him. Ajoy Pradhan sent his emissaries. They talked in different voices but all wanted to know what he would do in Monabari. They came and went at all hours of the day and talked so excitedly that Kanu agreed to meet an assembly of the local people on one Sunday afternoon.

Twenty Seven

A big banner adorned the wall at the back of the hall in the public library. *Monabari- Kadabari Anchalik Unnayan Samiti* - it read in Bengali and below that, in smaller letters in English – Monabari-Kadabari Regional Development Society, Government registered No 57357. The medium sized room was full of people who sat on the floor, some stood near the door, and a few enthusiastic ones crowded outside the open windows.

Kanu sat in one of the three chairs placed in front of the banner. Umanath and a gentleman Kanu had not seen before occupied the other two. *Sabhapati* or the president of the panchayat samiti, for some reason, was absent.

'Rarely a godsend opportunity like this knocks at our door, but we the foolish people, we squander them.' Umanath began to shout even before the crowd had settled down. 'There are people amongst us who even dare to doubt the goodwill of a kind man. Moreover, this gentleman, he is too gentle to let everyone know about his novel and generous gesture. But we have a duty to help him, help him to help us change our Monabari, which some crooked uncaring men have made miserable and sordid.' He said the last sentence after dramatically extending his arm in one direction as if to indicate where those uncaring men were.

Umanath paused to wipe his nose and clear his throat while a murmur rose and subsided. He resumed in a more strident voice, 'And now I want to ask the gathering one question, Yes or No — do we want to rebuff this gentleman in such a way that he ultimately decides to shift his project to some other place where other people will gladly welcome him? Shanti Babu will, I know.' Umanath stopped suddenly and sat down.

Another speaker rose, a middle-aged man who was a resident of Monabari but who now worked in another town. He began, 'I'm one of the unfortunate people who had not met Mr Chatterjee but ever since I've heard about his mission, I kept praying to God. I gather that he had already published his photographs about the plight of the poor people of Monabari in foreign magazines. People in London, in America, in Rome, in Bosnia, in Frankfurt know about Monabari now.' The speaker pointed his finger to different places on an imaginary invisible world map on the wall and pronounced the names of the far off places with sufficient pauses in between to let his audience visualise the people of those places waking up in morning and getting excited after reading about Monabari and seeing its photographs in their morning papers. 'We don't want to know if they pay for those photographs, it is none of our concern, but if Mr Chatterjee has made those people interested, funds should come.'

Speaker after speaker rose to say adulatory things about Kanu and to weave tales about an imaginary project. Kanu did not know what to say. He was angry with Umanath for not having cautioned him that the meeting would be so large and formal.

Jairam Haldar held up his hand. 'We've been hearing about this big project for the last few months. We still don't know if Kanu Babu really wants to do something. If he does, he must form a committee.'

Kanu at first declined to speak but he had to say something. He chose a middle ground to do some vague posturing. 'I must confess to you that I've been too busy attending to my own matters and I have not had time to think of something concrete — that I can tell you about right now. Besides,' he heard himself saying despite his self-imposed caution, 'the nonsensical talk I heard during the election had made me sad. I hope the good people of Monabari in future shall scotch all such idle talks. Nothing will be done without consulting them.' He stopped as he saw the crowd looking at him uncomfortably. Expressions of incomprehension, disappointment, and concern gradually clouded the faces in front of him. Kanu thought, at first, that the disappointment was because he did not come forth with a tangible plan but he soon understood that the reason was different. The gathering did not understand what he was telling them. His speech, which had become more slurred recently, was of no use for public oratory.

The other gentleman who occupied the third chair, and who Kanu by this time knew was the new block development officer, had to leave. He spoke a few final words, asked the villagers to support the government's literacy programme, and concluded the meeting. Kanu readily accepted his offer of a lift leaving behind a confused crowd but not before some of them had come up to him and expressed desires for 'private meetings'.

A mild breeze ruffled the placid water of Nandatalao. Flocks of ducks and geese sailed through the green surface, dragging after them long trails. The water level of Nandatalao had gone down and the water lilies looked taller. Kanu thought about the previous day's meeting as he keenly watched a frog leaping from a water plant to the shore but missing it. Its front legs strained to get a hold on the slippery mud and its hind legs frantically propelled in the air to find ground underneath them. After a few anxious moments, it finally got hold of itself, attaching its footpads to the mud, and then, after what seemed to be a very well calculated move, it jumped to a drier spot. Kanu turned his head and looked in the direction of Monabari. Monabari indeed did fancy him as a munificent son it did not have. The place was innocent enough to embrace him as its own progeny, giving him its trust and affection.

Buried within all the outside politics and squabbles, the foibles and duplicities of the Manik Babus, of the Bhola Pals, and the Gopal Sahoos, or of the village councils, there was a simple honest desire to get care. Monabari was looking up to him as the giver of that care, as its benefactor, as a god with a boon! The realisation mortified him. If only they knew that Kanu was not a rich man. What money he had would aid no commerce. Neither had he published the photographs he had taken in any foreign magazines. Why did the man have to make that up!

A cormorant perched on a tree trunk that curved upwards from the edge of the bank of the pond. It had the luxury of waiting patiently before it made a move. Kanu sighed. His own time had run out. Now either he would have to dig in here and build something or explain his situation and risk the humiliation of being called a pretender, a hollow man of no consequence. Alternatively, his stay in Monabari would have to end— his fate would once again make him rudderless.

'Babu, won't you go home?' someone called.

Kanu looked up to see a smiling but panting Jugu. Kalyani had sent him to look for him. He looked at his watch. It was almost twelve. When he got up, he suddenly felt a pain in his right calf. It was a different kind of pain. He sat back to look at his leg where it hurt. The calf of his left leg was swollen. It seemed to have assumed a dusky red colour and was painful to touch.

'Jugu, I think I've sprained my leg. Can you allow me to lean on you?'

Jugu had to do more than that. He almost carried Kanu back to the nearby road and then fetched a rickshaw for him.

Back in his room, Kanu had to lie down on the bed. The pain had intensified and he felt feverish.

Kalyani came soon after. 'Your face is red, were you in the sun for a longtime?' She touched Kanu's forehead, something she had never done before. She allowed her hand to rest on his forehead, unabashedly, and then said in an intimate tone, 'What odd things you do, you're worse than Sona.'

Immediately after lunch, Kanu suffered a chill. By afternoon he developed high fever. The calf of his leg swelled up further and it hurt. Dr Bose came and in his usual brisk manner prescribed some new drugs. He gave some ointment to be massaged on the leg and ordered absolute bed rest. This time he asked for some blood tests.

That confinement in bed made Kanu feel sicker. Dr Bose visited him daily. Badal shuttled between Siliguri and Monabari bringing in advice from Ved's friend. The fever continued for a few days but after that it began to come down, the pain in his calf lessened and his breathing became easier but he developed a persistent irritation. When he mentioned that, Dr Bose gave him a medicine that made him urinate more but miraculously it solved many of his problems, including his leg edema and throat congestion.

Over the next few days, there was no further worsening of his condition. The pain in the leg subsided though the calf muscle remained tender. Kanu moved very little out of his bed, except to sit in an armchair when he had visitors. He talked very little, mostly listening to other people's talk that hovered around politics and the Kamtapuri movement, and at times, cautiously, about his project. Monabari was still not ready to abandon all hopes about him. Rajen Babu and his wife made constant enquiries. Mahen, Kalyani, and Umanath held regular parleys, at times openly in front of Kanu, discussing his illness. They discussed his illness, his diet, his physicians, and inevitably, the talks at times turned to the mystics, the fakir in Naodanga, the priest in Jalpesh, a lama in Siliguri. Even an old physician in Lataguri, who was now crippled and could not walk, but was still swarmed by hundreds of patients daily, featured in the list. That physician had outgrown the science he practised to become a part of the local folklore. People went to him not for his medicine but out of habit, almost as a ritual in time of sickness.

On a Sunday morning a few days later, Kanu waited with others for the arrival of a famous *kaviraj*. He was the most venerable physician on this side of the Ganga and, at the age of eighty, an example to his patients of a life well led. He wanted to see Kanu exactly in the conditions he lived. The ground, the air, the radiance, the sky, everything that surrounded Kanu, he wanted to see for himself, because a proper diagnosis could be made only when all these had been considered. Umanath explained that to Kanu. They were the *panchabhuts*, the five elemental energies. Health or sickness depends on their being in harmony, on their being in accord with the functions of a body. When that harmony is lost, sickness develops. Kanu was further impressed when he came to know that the aged physician would require to start at the wee hours to complete a two-hour journey to reach Monabari at the first light.

The *kaviraj* had a great physique. He showed his large wrists to Kanu. 'Even today I can cut my trees,' he said. He spent a long time hearing the history of his illness. He was particularly interested to hear what effect the weather and the food in Netherlands had on Kanu. He spent some time examining his pulse but for a lesser time than Kanu had expected he would.

When he spoke his mind, he spoke with the solemnity of delivering a final judgement and his voice boomed. 'For years, alien and harsh conditions had polluted the elements of your body and agitated them. The phlegm and the wind are agitated, particularly the *Udana* wind that produces speech. I'll give you some drugs to purify those poisons but you must adhere to a very close schedule. The auspicious air that flowed from the river Ganga nurtured and ripened your young body. To get rid of these impurities accumulated inside you, you must return to your birthplace. In the scriptures it is written that to be able to live in one's birthplace is to be blessed.'

To Serampore then, ultimately, Kanu thought. Renting a house on the bank of the river Ganga would mean that Kanu might not have to vex the anxious inhabitants of his ancestral house. He would ask Rajat to find for him a dwelling on the river shore, at Maa Ganga's very bosom. He would ask him to search out his mother's portmanteau and bring it to him there. The thoughts and the new expectations stimulated him, made him ignore his physical ills, and he had all arrangements put in place sooner than anyone had expected. Until the time Rajat was able to locate a good house, he arranged to stay in a rented place near the hospital in Calcutta and get this present malaise sorted out. For once Kanu was pleased with his fate and did not object when the Ganguly family wanted to depute Badal to accompany him.

Thus, a couple of days later, when Kanu left Monabari for Calcutta, his feelings about a lost relationship were made less acute by this new dream about a river that flows from north to south, from west to east, from the hills to the sea and purifies the land that it flows through and the people who dip in it. Surely, that holy water there would remember him.

Twenty Eight

An arch made of bamboo slips covered by the thick foliage of a liana and a nice garden fronted the two-storied cottage that Ved rented and made ready for Kanu's stay. Originally designed to serve as a weekend retreat, just outside the city limits, it was not on any river but the great Bay of Bengal was merely fifty miles away. Whole day a steady cool breeze driven in by the sea wind and sucked inland from the sea blew over the cottage.

That southern breeze greeted him when Kanu went up to the terrace of the cottage and looked out at the open land punctuated by endless lines of coconut trees. On the left side, miles away, the land had extended further, transforming the coast into a maze of mangrove forests and shifting soil of mudflats outlined by numerous creeks and brooks and rivers so wide that boatmen would lose sight of shores on both sides. Straight down and towards the right, the sea was nearer and there, every year, on a particular winter day, pilgrims from all over India, whole villages at times, from the very young to the very old, converged to dip in the icy water at sunrise to attain salvation. 'One pilgrimage to Gangasagar is equal to all other pilgrimages done many times over,' Vikhuram had told Kanu often.

The terrace had a garden and an attic room made of glass and timber. Kanu lazed through the first day there, at times simply basking in the morning sun, at times retreating to a shadowy corner to read books. Next morning, Vikhuram brought with him his cousin Kenaram to do the household chores. Badal looked happy. He had been out to get a feel of the neighbourhood. Though a few houses existed in this area, and the city's public transport service stopped a good three kilometers away, an express bus service could take him downtown in less than an hour. There was even a video parlour nearby. The hospital itself was just thirty minutes' drive away.

Kanu tried to settle down to a routine that would allow him to finish some important tasks he had planned to finish before finally departing for Serampore , ignoring the constant niggling ache from the swelling in and around his mouth. He also tired easily. The doctors in the hospital changed the drugs he was having in Monabari. It appeared that the physician there had put him on a drug, which brought about a dramatic relief to his symptoms initially, but its effect had now reached a plateau and it had caused complications. His blood sugar had gone up and the little microbes that had always tried to invade his body but were held at bay by an alert defence system now infected him. The doctors had begun to withdraw that drug gradually, slowly adjusting its removal from the body but they took time to come up with an effective alternative that could lessen his distress. A week passed and still Kanu did not feel any better. The pain in his throat continued, along with that sense of exasperation, and occasionally he had difficulty in getting enough air into his lungs. The efforts of going to the banks and to the studio exhausted him.

Kanu put down the newspaper he was reading. An announcement that 'Calcutta' the British given name of the city would soon change to its Bengali name 'Kolkata' made major stories in the day's newspaper. The wise men of the city had put forward their views. Some had consented happily, a few had objected. The supplement, however, grabbed his attention more. It carried articles on the completion of hundred years of writing a book *Interpretation of Dreams.* One of the articles detailed personal accounts of the author himself. What he read there amazed him. He reclined back on his pillow and closed his eyes. The sweet heavy smell of burning tobacco entered his senses and he could easily visualise the famous psychologist described in the article working in his home in Vienna almost seventy years ago. The psychologist crouched behind the patient to whisper his questions and smoked continually his favorite Trabuco cigars. Spiralling tendrils of smoke covered both of them and the strong aroma of tobacco wafted through the rooms. For the psychologist, that act was more than the mere act of smoking a cigar. It was for him a mystical ritual, an important part of his life, without which he felt his existence to be incomplete. He paid a heavy price, developing ulcers of the mouth, which later turned cancerous. He suffered heavily, undergoing as many as sixteen operations for his oral ulcer that harassed him through his whole life, and yet he persisted with the habit almost with the zeal of a devotee. The scribe had speculated in the article why the shrink failed to untangle himself from his own vile obsession and did what he did. 'I know why,' Kanu cried out; he knew the answer instinctively. The shrink did not want to lose the control over his life to a disease, or to any other condition.

The smell grew stronger and Kanu realised that the smell was real. Someone, one of the servants or Badal, was smoking outside the window. Kanu had not smoked since his diagnosis. It now amazed him how easily he had given up a lifelong addiction. He took up the newspaper and began to read again. The last paragraph was almost a confirmation of his thought. Up until the very end of his life, even after migrating to England to escape the Nazis, the psychologist did not stop his work. When he realised that he could work no more he had his bed brought to his study in his new home in London, where his books and collection of antiquities were, and told his daughter to give him morphine. Even at the end, he remained the master of his own life and died perhaps with a smirk and a cigar in his mouth.

Badal came in. 'Did you call me, dada?' he asked.

'No, but what have you been up to?' Kanu smiled.

'Counting the birds, what else.' Badal made a face. Then his expression changed. 'When are you going to go upstairs? The roses and the dahlias are in bloom. They are nice plants, only needed a little watering.'

Kanu looked at Badal who seemed pleased. Flowers make everyone happy. Near their house in Serampore, they had a tree that bloomed in early autumn. The flowers unfurled at night and their scent spread through the night but when they would pass by the tree in the morning, the fragrance would be gone but the ground below it would be all white as if snow had fallen. Kanu could remember the smell but could not remember the name of the flower. He asked Badal.

'*Shiuli*, I think you are talking about *shiuli*,' Badal said.

'Yes, *shiuli* or *shefali*.' Kanu remembered. The night flowering jasmine, the flower of sadness, the flowers that drop off by themselves without waiting to be plucked.

'I have an idea that flowers that are white are the most fragrant and flowers that show many colours often have no smell at all. Is that true?' Kanu asked.

' Roses have scent, so do golden champaks,' Badal said at first in a matter-of-fact tone but then added with a little more spirit, 'then there is lotus, even some varieties of violets and lilies smell good.' He paused searching for a few more names and added with some uncertainty, 'Hyacinths also , the garden varieties. If you don't need me can I go out after lunch? I can buy the mobile phones today if you want.'

In the afternoon Rajat came and with him came Moli. This twenty-year-old niece of Kanu had become a regular visitor since Kanu came here and she had taken on herself to see that the windows put on drapes and that the dining table had a cloth on it. She saw to it that the floors were mopped and the furniture was dusted. The last one proved most onerous, as even the most vigorous dusting in the morning would find the furniture, by afternoon, covered with ash white layers, thick enough to scribble on with one's fingers.

Kanu showed her his photo albums, old ones, and told her about the windmills, about the old cities of Europe and their narrow gravelled paths and stone houses with projecting cornices, the medieval castles, and churches with their spires and the stained glass windows.

'Did you have carpets in all the rooms?' she would ask Kanu. She had seen English households on television but could not believe a friend of hers, recently married into a family settled in England, when she said that even her bathrooms had carpets. 'And malls as big as the Howrah station?' She looked agitated.

When Rajat and Moli left, it was already dark. Badal went out with them to escort them to the bus stand. He stood in the porch and saw them departing, smiling at the thought of Badal having a very uneven fight at hand against dreams about carpeted bathrooms. He switched off the lone light in the porch and sat there. A microphone blared at some distance and the wind easily carried the sounds to him. Kanu listened. It was an audio play interspersed by devotional songs.

Kenaram came and sprayed a mosquito repellant. He stood listening to the songs. 'Ramprasad, Kalisangeet. Aha! What devotion,' he said.

Kanu listened to the songs and the fervent implorations of the singer, who could not put his mind to any of his worldly obligations but only craved to see the goddess Kali in person. Instead of writing figures in the account books he was ordered to maintain, he wrote songs that spoke of his yearning. The wind changed direction and the lyrics became incomprehensible though the tunes were still audible. What would the devotee have done if the goddess had responded to his entreaties? The thought amused Kanu. What would anyone do if God were to appear before him or her in person? Ask Him to perform some miracles like a magician to prove His godliness?

Kanu felt the chill and shivering he had experienced frequently in the last few days seizing him again. This time it was stronger. By the time Badal came, Kanu was already in bed.

Ved came next morning and examined him. 'That's thrush you're developing, an opportunistic fungal infection, and probably a bacterial infection is also growing on top of it.' Ved arranged for more tests and wanted to engage professional nurses to take care of the intravenous channel required for administering antibiotics; his blood sugar needed monitoring.

When Ved came back late in the evening to check on his arrangements Kanu said, 'Do what you have to do, but I would expect that you won't forget the morphine.'

'Morphine? We've no morphine.'

Kanu felt exasperated—how could this doctor be so naïve at times! He had talked often with Ved for him to understand that he didn't mean only the drug morphine when he said 'morphine'. 'What I want is that, when I become hopelessly ill,' he said as clearly as possible, 'no one should make desperate attempts to add a few more days to my miseries. Least of all, I don't want to be hooked up to machines and then decompose slowly little by little. Be merciful and let me go. Help me to go in such an eventuality.'

'But we can't do that.'

'Why not?'

'For several reasons, good or bad,' Ved shook his head. 'Besides, our oath forbids it.' He rose and put his hand on his chest and, as if acting in a drama, recited, 'I will neither give a deadly drug to anybody if asked for it, nor will I make a suggestion to that effect.' Ved walked to the couch set against the wall and parked himself there. 'But why are you thinking about death right now?'

'Not death. That is there, waiting for me. Maybe in another two or three years or even before that. It's not death that I'm particularly worried about. It's about how I die.'

'Is that a particular worry with you? How you die? I would not care how I die, even if that makes a hero or a coward of me. Of any illness, or accident, I make no distinction,' Ved said. 'Suppose I have to die underneath a tall skyscraper crashing down, in full view of the world, with live telecast, or just by a minute insect sting in some remote jungle, unknown, unnoticed , what does it matter to me? When I'm not there, I'm not there.'

Kanu shook his head, 'You don't care because you are not threatened with that possibility right now or in near future.' His voice cracked as he strained to raise it to put emphasis on his words 'If in the first case, I've to die slowly under the rubble, bleeding and suffocating, enduring pains from my broken arms and legs, then certainly I would prefer the second one provided the insect had enough poison to kill me instantly.'

Kanu's grave tone, the strain in his voice, and repeated mentions of death seemed to make the room gloomy. 'You're worried about suffering then,' Ved said in a low voice. He got up from the couch and put a hand on Kanu's shoulder.

'Exactly. When I say the manner of my death, I talk about the suffering that'll go with it. Not whether people will write a requiem to remember me and hold a mass or forget me.'

Ved grinned and his eyes twinkled. Apparently, he wanted to remove the gloom in the room by drawing Kanu into a light-hearted banter but he himself seemed ready for a debate. He went back, sat down on the couch again, and spoke with a little perkiness, 'That doesn't make you a very religious person. The gates of heaven will not open unless you have done your quota of suffering! Are you not worried how your god will judge you?' he asked, settling deeper in the couch and pulling his legs up.

Kanu closed his eyes; he felt tired. This was no time for him to debate. He could tell the young doctor that it was not about spirituality alone. Many men who did not believe in God had smiles on their lips when they had been tortured to death, and men who did believe in God, mighty men who shaped destinies of nations, cried like children while facing execution. Ved was bringing up that stale debate about God existing or not existing or about the possibility of another life after this life and that bored Kanu. The old farmer or the wisest sage, no one had ever come back to add this final piece of information. Like everyone else, Kanu would know or would not know the answer to that question only when he would die. Right now, this debate to him was idle talk, to be indulged in by people who still had time to tend to their lands, their cattle, to build their monuments and who like Ved, or even like some patients in the cancer ward, imagined that death called only at other people's houses. For a sick person like him, whose life was gradually turning into a non-life, as Nanu would have put it, every new day was a miracle. The more important issue for him was to decide, when the time would come, if, lured by that miracle of one more new day, should he persist like a crippled beggar rolling in the dust clinging to his rags and yet pushing forward his begging bowl? He remembered Ved had asked him a question and he wanted to give him an answer.

'My god is a good man,' Kanu said opening his eyes. 'He will close no door against me.'

'You're not to have any stupid thoughts,' Ved said, 'it is against the law; you know it.'

'Beats me, why it's so,' Kanu said simply. He had never thought of committing suicide, not as a deliberate act. All he wanted was not to cower before Mr Death and beg to persist even when his life would not be worth living anymore. He opened his eyes and saw Ved watching him with anxious eyes. The night was cold and it seemed that there was not enough air in the room for two persons. The windows were all closed and Moli had covered them with heavy drapes with large prints of yellow flowers with many petals. Kanu pushed himself up from the bed and hobbled to a window. He put his left hand over a flower on the drape and mumbled, without caring if Ved could make out anything from his slur, because he had said this to him many a times before. 'I want to die in an open field, with the sun on my head and sunflowers around me at high noon; never in the dark or at night. Do not abandon me to machines.'

Kanu felt a shadow approaching from behind and then he felt two strong arms propping him up and guiding him back to the bed. The floor under his feet rocked sideways and the bed seemed to be floating in the air.

When he opened his eyes again he saw Ved sitting on the bed and looking at him. This time Kanu's vision was clear and he could read his watch that showed it was 9 pm. 'You'll be late for your dinner!' Kanu said mildly to Ved but when Ved stood up to leave, he asked him to wait.

When Ved left with the two large folio bags in which Kanu had carefully stacked the photographs he had taken, he noticed that unlike the other nights, this night Ved did not say when he was coming to see him again. He felt disturbed. All through his illness, this one option, this idea of enlisting a doctor's help or using drugs to elude pain and mortification at the end, was always present at the back of his mind. Now without that assurance from Ved he felt unprotected. He had not considered that what was a common practice for the doctors in Amsterdam would be a taboo for the doctors here. Kanu closed his eyes and tried to sleep. As he closed his eyes, he saw the image of the goddess Kali with a slashed abdomen floating under his eyelids and then that image dissolved and a new image of a pigeon hacked through its neck and blood spluttering from its severed body filled in. Startled, Kanu opened his eyes. He wished that the spectral powers were true and he could direct them to manipulate the tides in his favour.

Ved came early in the morning. 'Rajen Babu died last night, a stroke, in his sleep,' he said without much preamble. 'Badal has to go.'

Badal looked in disbelief and appeared numb but he began to move quicker when Kanu offered to buy him a ticket for the morning flight to Siliguri. By hiring a car from the airport at Bagdogra, Badal would be home by noon. That possibility put some colour back in his face. Barring Ajoy-da, no one known to Badal in Monabari had ever taken a plane ride, not even Jairam or his brother Balaram.

Rajat came in the afternoon and appeared cheerful. Kanu could not discern any deceit when he told Kanu that he had located a good house. He asked Rajat to arrange for his shifting to that house as soon as possible. He hoped that the doctors in the hospital would be able to come up with a plan that would make it possible.

Twenty Nine

A sudden downpour, unexpected at this time of the year, made the night cold. Just after midnight, Kenaram called Ved from a nearby house. Chatterjee saab was having difficulty in breathing. The desperation in his voice alarmed Ved.

When they received Kanu Chatterjee in the intensive care unit, he was still in high spirits. 'Sorry for the bother but this is so upsetting,' Ved heard him saying through the wheezes.

He did not look at all well. He was visibly panting and was running a fever. He could eat very little of his dinner and then could not sleep because the pain in his throat intensified and now he was feeling out of breath. The resident on duty ran thorough the routine checkups. Blood pressure was normal, he reported, but Kanu had a rapid heart rate, and the chest, on both sides, was full of crackling sounds.

Kanu had his eyes closed and he lay still in a head up position propped up by the folding bed. An oxygen mask covered the lower portion of his face and a bluish white bed sheet covered the rest of his body from shoulders to the feet. His arms and legs lay still, as if lifeless. Only his chest and abdomen moved, and they moved with what seemed like a purposeful rhythm as if they had an aspiration to fulfill. Ved stood at Kanu's bedside and watched oxygen flowing into his air-starved lungs. Gradually the ashen blue hue on Kanu's face faded and the normal ruddy glow of a healthy skin began to return.

A few minutes later Kanu opened his eyes and his lips moved. 'Thanks, I feel better,' he seemed to be saying through the mask.

As the doctors waited for the emergency X-ray films and initial blood tests, the nurses made coffee and passed around pieces of cake. Ved noticed a few Happy New Year stickers still stuck at places on the fashionable cupboards and the nicely painted walls. The X-ray showed considerable whitening of normal black lung shadows but there was no collection of fluid that required drainage. The windpipes would need some cleaning; the phlegm blocking the windpipes should be sucked out. 'How good is his oxygen saturation?' he asked the resident.

The resident looked at the console, watched it for a couple of seconds and then said, 'It is holding between ninety and ninety- one. Much better than when he came in.'

That figure, if held, should be acceptable, Ved thought. An oxygen saturation index of around ninety per cent was not the ideal figure for a healthy person, in fact it was low, but should be acceptable as a figure to start with for a patient with diseased lungs in intensive care settings. Besides, clinically Kanu already looked better. Ved was about to tell that to the resident when the telephone on the nurses' table began to ring.

Even before the staff nurse picked up the telephone and began to speak another young doctor came running. 'Three zero seven is bleeding from his mouth,' he paused for a few seconds to regain his breath, 'we telephoned Dr Ghosh. He has asked to shift the patient to ICU.'

'Where are the relatives?' the resident on duty at the intensive care unit asked.

'They have gone to the blood bank. He is pouring blood like an open tap,' the young doctor was distraught with excitement.

'Will you sign the order for shifting the patient?' the resident asked Ved.

'Why not, if you want me to?' Ved said. A nurse brought the case file. He took it from the nurse's hand and leafed through the thick file. This was a fifty-year-old man, stricken by an obstinate ulcer that had kept eating through the left side of his gullet, infiltrating through the tissues in the neck despite radiation and chemotherapy to the limits of his tolerance. This was his eleventh admission in this hospital. During his last admission, he had his left external carotid artery, the blood vessel that carried blood to the tissues in his neck and face, tied to mitigate the possibility of such a cataclysmic bleeding but evidently, even that had not worked for him.

A minute later, the patient was wheeled into the ICU with a nurse holding a bottle of fluid and another one holding a large pack to his mouth to soak up a steady trickle of blood. As he was put to bed, the patient gurgled out another mouthful of blood. Slowly and methodically the residents began the drill they had been tutored to do in such conditions: suck out the blood from the mouth and throat to keep the airway clean, set the patient for a tracheostomy, infuse colloids to restore fluid volume in the body, inject drugs that help the blood to coagulate.

As soon as the tube was put in the trachea to create a direct passage so that air could now go into the lungs without being obstructed by the large clots of blood in the throat, and the inflated cuff of a balloon around the tube blocked passage of blood into his lungs, the gurgling respiration of the patient became easier. The bleeding lessened but it was probably more due to a low blood pressure or because the patient had no more blood to lose. The resident began to pack the throat with a roll of ribbon like gauge. 'It's a big one, easily taking two finger tips,' he said and lifted up his blood stained gloved fingers to show the size of the ulcer. With airway established further down in the throat, now he could pack it without any danger. With an ulcer as big as that, with a low platelet count, with a superadded infection, with so much blood already in his lungs, with vitals beaten and withered, Ved knew, the residents knew, the nurses knew, even the ward staff knew, that the patient stood very little chance to make it through.

The efforts however continued, as they must continue. Blood was transfused; antibiotics were administered. The residents discussed and argued over the correct drugs and dosages to restore the balance of electrolytes. The patient convulsed a few times, only half heartedly, throwing the upper part of his body into a few chaotic spasms and then the monitor began to register a drop in the heart rate. It dropped down to sixty, then fifty-four, forty-two, thirty-five. The ward attendant watching the monitor quickly retrieved the CPR trolley from the other end of the ward and pushed it to the patient's bedside and plugged the defibrillator to an electric socket in the wall. The resident put one knee on the patient's bed and crouched over the limp form there. With his hands outstretched over the patient's chest and his palms extended and placed one above the other, ready to coax the failing heart to begin beating again, he looked like a possessed man wanting to stall the progress of time.

Someone drew the curtain around the bed. The nurses did not wait for a final signal from the resident, who, before he pronounced 'dead', would have to go through some motions that are often unimportant but mandatory: a step by step checkup that the respiration has stopped, that there is no heart beat audible even after one has listened very carefully for five minutes, that the eyes do not blink when teased with a cotton swab, that the pupils have become widely dilated. Once people even used to hold mirrors in front of the nose of the patient to see if it would get foggy from the breath of life or waited to see if the body would get stiff from rigor mortis. All that had become unnecessary with machines that could register each and every sign of life. Most of the times, though, the quiet and the hue of death are so authoritative that a look at the patient is enough.

On his bed, Kanu lay still, inert to all communications, his face hidden behind a hissing oxygen mask. Only the chest heaved to draw in some air.

Ved stepped out to the open terrace between the intensive unit and the male ward from where the patient had just been wheeled in. Outside it was all cold and silent; the sky was dark. If it was true, he thought, that a man's soul could survive the worn out body and was able to find a new one again, then the soul of the man who had just died might be in a wandering flight somewhere through that dark night sky at this moment. Kanu Chatterjee had always wanted to die in an open space, at high noon. All through the last few months, he had often talked about death, not his own but of other people about whom he used to read a great deal. He talked a lot about van Gogh and people like him who died when it was not glorious for them to die. Ved had always presumed that van Gogh died amongst sunflowers, in an open field, at the shore of a blue sea, under a particularly yellow sun that he loved to paint. Ved quizzed him about that and he told him one day the real story how the painter had died.

'The painter used to get seizures every three months when he would go out of his mind for a few days and would wander about doing crazy things. For the last three months of his life, he lived in a place called Auverse for the air and the light. On a hot July noon, he walked to the cornfield where he used to go daily to paint the colours he loved to paint and shot himself with the sun in his eyes. He did not die there, though.

He died two days later in the company of his beloved brother Theo, in the house of the local physician who looked after him.'

'He died out of desperation then!' Ved had wondered when he heard the story.

'Out of desperation or out of a magnificent sense of satisfaction that only a creator knows — I don't know, which one is true.' Mr Chatterjee had said. 'Maybe he could do no more for himself. As a painter, he had filled all the spaces that he wanted to fill with his colours. And he had no other life for himself to drag on.'

'Was it then an act of lunacy or the clever ploy of a failed man?' Mr Chatterjee had argued his own theories. How much effort did the painter make to end his own life? Why did he not do it in the privacy of his own room? Was he afraid that others might hear the sound of the gun? Moreover, if it was a sudden lunatic act, why did he carry a gun with him to the field? Was it usual in those days in Europe for people like him to carry firearms with them?'

Kanu had felt it was an important question. How did the painter come into possession of a gun? A poor painter like him, who could not buy even the pastels he wanted to paint or the colours he wanted to spread! If the painter had pursued a well thought out plan to commit suicide and acquired a gun to do that, then his shooting himself could not have been an impetuous act of lunacy.

Looking at the sky and thinking about all that, Ved now wanted to know what made Kanu Chatterjee think of people who had drifted in life, either by choice or through fate.

A man was trying to suppress a retching nearby. He turned around to see a person inclined over the balustrade guarding the terrace. He could not see his features but he knew who it was. The man had a bottle of water in his hand. He took a few swigs from the bottle and gargled. Ved approached him and asked gently, 'Are you all right?'

The man nodded slowly, wiped his face with a hand towel he was carrying, and then said, 'He was next to my bed. Till this evening he talked to me.' His tone was accusing, as if Ved had something to answer for. He watched the man hobbling towards him, supporting and dragging his right leg with his right arm.

'Why are you not sleeping?' Ved asked in a soft voice as he came nearer.

'I can't, most nights.' The man turned to face Ved. In the white light diffused through the glass windows of the ward, Ved could see his eyes were red and misty. Then he turned his face away and stood watching the sky as if something spectacular was happening there. 'From next morning I'm going to have one more course of radiotherapy,' he said almost to himself. 'I hope this time it works.'

Ved was familiar with this man's ordeal. This man, Naren, had a rather rare kind of tumour, a nerve tissue tumour to be precise, a type that grows slowly and does not kill quickly. He was young, in his late twenties, an expert in high precision welding who had lost four jobs in the last three years as his disease dragged him repeatedly to this hospital. His posture had stooped and when he walked, he dragged his right lower limb pitifully, supporting it with his right arm. Apart from that, he was in good shape till now. Somewhere inside his body, some runaway wicked cells were conspiring against him, travelling through his body in search of soil where they would set up more colonies and lay a siege. If his disease could not be arrested, it would be a painful end for him.

Ved came back into the ICU. On his bed, Kanu seemed to be asleep, his face still hidden behind the hissing oxygen mask. Only the chest heaved.

On the table at the nurses' station, two plastic bags of blood lay discarded. They had arrived too late to be of any use. The resident doctor came back from the other end of the hall closing the door against the sounds of muffled cries. He indicated the paper he was holding in his hand. 'Putting the time at 1.30,' he said.

The patient had died at least fifteen minutes earlier. But the time was unimportant, since it would not mark any new beginning. Only the family pundit would use it to decide if the man had died at an inauspicious moment and if rites should be performed to free his soul. Ved told the resident that he was going back to his quarters. It was 1.45. A new dawn would soon arrive and tomorrow morning he would have to decide if he should shift Mr Chatterjee to some other hospital in the city that provided specialised care for lung diseases. It occurred to him that though he had heard about the new machines brought in other hospitals, he had a very vague idea about the physicians there.

***

It was Naren Ved kept thinking about as he changed to go to bed. A paper dropped from his shirt pocket. He picked it up; it was a fax from Nanu he had received last evening when he returned after visiting Kanu. Ved put it under the telephone on the bedside table. Nanu had written about a wonder drug that he was trying to procure for Kanu. Ved shook his head. It was too late but at the end, everyone seems to believe in miracles.

Thirty

Just when the dissonant rings of his bedside telephone jarred the quiet of the night and broke through Ved's sleep, he was slipping into a dream. A cheerless posse of men and women crossed a field covered with hard cakes of mud latticed by thick serpentine roots of enormous tree trunks and the trees rose so high that their tops could not be seen. The light was faint and all objects looked shadowy. Ved watched as the first group hobbled past, supporting themselves on crutches and sticks. A particularly strong and well-built man came next, with empty sockets where his eyes should have been. He had a begging bowl in his hand and, though he had no eyes to stare with, he had an animal ferocity in his face. The man alternately raised his other free hand, made a fist, and threw punches around him. He dropped the hand and hid it behind his cloak and his body twisted with pain. A child ran by. She had a grotesque head and ill-formed limbs. A few women lumbered by, their garments blood soaked and torn at places revealing charred flesh. A young man stood silently leaning against a tree. An easel stood nearby but there was no canvas on it. He began to climb the tree, heaving himself up by hooking his hands on the branches. He looked down and shouted, 'What does it matter if it is one day or one year, or a whole lifetime! There is no light here, and no flowers, not even a small bush. How would I know what colours I must paint? I want sunlight; up there, there would be light.'

Before Ved could answer, a woman appeared. She motioned to the young man climbing the tree and gestured to him to come down. Ved recognised the young man. It was Naren; he was pointing towards the easel. The woman smiled and stepped back to stand beside the easel and now there was a picture on it. In the shadows under the large trees, the painting was not visible but everyone knew that in it danced two bottle green cypresses, and tobacco and orange coloured chestnuts and a petite yew tree with a violet trunk and pale lemon leaves. From the background, some noise gradually pitched up. Then there was a distinct yelp, arising in the distance but coming nearer, like the voice of a master calling back his runaway dogs.

The scream pitched higher and higher. The dream disappeared. The yelp was actually the familiar ringing of the telephone on Ved's bedside table. In the quietness of a sleeping world, it transmitted a sense of urgency and apprehension. The call was from the on-duty resident of the intensive care unit and he spoke with urgency, 'Mr Chatterjee needs to be ventilated, we have to intubate him.'

The resident's tone conveyed a sense of finality and he needed an answer or a quick assent to his proposed line of action, immediately. Mr Chatterjee's instructions were clear about what Ved must say when such a call would come. A firm 'No'. But the call had come before Ved had expected it. The awkwardness of the timing and the manner in which the whole thing had precipitated made him angry.

'Sir?' the resident now sounded diffident, his voice toned down, but he persisted, '336 is in distress. Saturation is dropping, even with full flow of oxygen. He needs assisted ventilation.'

'Did you get the report of his blood count?' Ved asked.

'Yes sir, it's way high, he is developing sepsis.'

'Change the antibiotic; give him steroids, inotropes, do whatever you want to do but keep him away from the ventilator. Is he getting insulin?'

'Yes. But he has passed only about ten cc of urine since admission.' The resident's tone changed, bordering on hysteria, 'He is desaturating, it's eighty-six now, pressure ninety over forty, and heart rate one hundred and twenty-two.' Obviously, the resident was talking with his eyes on the monitor. He was going crazy at the prospect of losing two patients in quick succession. 'I am calling in Dr Roy.'

'Good boy, do that,' Ved said. The call was over but he could feel the resident hesitating to hang up. He toned down his voice and said as softly as possible, 'Forget about the ventilator; will you? The patient will not agree to that.' As he put down the receiver, the white paper pressed under the telephone caught his eye. It was the fax from Nanu informing him about the new drug that had received approval for day-to-day clinical practice. They had found the drug to be so good that ongoing clinical trials to test its efficacy had been prematurely closed. This now presented a new dilemma. Should efforts be renewed to make Kanu live to try this new one?

Dr Roy called sooner than Ved had expected. The intensive unit was a new addition and everyone connected with it was serious that it did not acquire a bad name.

'It's better to intubate him now,' Dr Roy said. 'It's always better to do it early, rather than trying an emergency one when he has gone into a failure.'

'I don't think the patient will agree. You've to ask him, don't you?'

'That is one problem, since he has no relative around. I talked to him. I've explained to him that he has got pneumonia and the illness is affecting his other organs. He was a long time smoker so his lungs can't on their own cope with this emergency demand. But if required, I told him that, only if absolutely required, and only as a matter of precaution, we might assist his breathing for a few hours with a ventilator.' Dr Mohan Roy spoke in an unhurried but precise manner.

'Is he fully conscious?' Ved asked.

'I would say he is conscious enough to understand. Till now, but the way he is going, he will not remain conscious for long.'

'He never wanted to be on a ventilator; you'll not have his consent to hook him to one.'

'He has said 'yes' to what I have told him. Would you like to come over?'

Ved closed his eyes and pressed the receiver tight against his ears. He wanted to make sure that what he heard was correct. For a moment, he debated if he should get up and rush to the ICU but then decided against it. Dr Mohan Roy and his team had a world of their own, a chemical world, so to speak. As Dr Roy would say, 'It's all in the chemistry. In the physicochemical equations. After all, it was a chance chemical reaction that began the story. Why one rules and the other gets ruled, why one man worries about morality and another does not, all that can now be explained by numbers , in a better way than by any philosophy. Numbers that show if the blood has turned alkaline or acidic, if it is depleted of potassium or has an excess of sodium, and in what ratio the gases are present in the minutest capillaries all through the body—in the heart, in the brain or in the kidneys. If those numbers become incorrect, we correct them. So what is this big fuss about ventilators?'

'All right, go ahead. You're the boss,' Ved said and put down the receiver and looked at his watch: 3.30 am. Ved calculated rapidly. Nanu must be informed but that would have to wait till tomorrow morning when he would be able to send an e-mail to Nanu from his cousin's office, which had internet connection. Before that he had nothing else to do other than to go back to sleep. He formulated the words he would write to Nanu. 'On coramin' – once people used to say that to hint at imminent death. That was what Ved's mother had asked him to say when years ago she had sent him to deliver the latest news about her ailing father to her uncle's place a few houses down the street, for his first unescorted foray. As soon as he repeated those words, the women in the house began to cry. He wondered if 'On Ventilator' would purport the same meaning to Nanu. Or, perhaps, by then, it would be time to send the final message.

He settled back in the bed but as he turned to switch off the bedside lamp, two fat bags silently sitting on his table caught his eye. Kanu had given him those bags to hand them over to Kabir da as soon as possible. For a possible publication. The light from his bedside lamp shone on the black leather of the bags and they seemed to have come alive, demanding to make a communication. Ved rose again, switched on the lights, and brought the folio bags to his bed. Inside were four photo albums, neatly stacked. A small book accompanied them, with some numbers written serially, each with a caption and a short description. Some entries had technical data, giving details of readings from light meters, exposures, filters used.

Ved pulled out the photographs, a good number of which were black and white prints. He began to look at them one by one, consulting the notes in the little book and matching them with the numbers pencilled at the back. Even his untrained eyes could catalogue them into two distinct categories; one was of close up portraits of people, showing only the face or at times even a small part of it. The other group was made of photographs of people engaged in activities of everyday life. Every picture had captured a particular happy instant in someone's life, as if it vied to keep that fleeting moment permanent by freezing it into an image. The colour photographs were remarkable in their lack of colour, as if someone had blotted out some of the colours of the spectrum from them. Besides the albums, there were two thick well-stuffed envelopes and in them were prints that had been enlarged. Gripping pictures of nameless men and women. With a strange trepidation, Ved made a foray through the pile. An old woman smiled at him from one of those photographs, which showed only her toothless face, with creases as deep as furrows, and she had two large earrings. In another photograph, an old man lazed on his side on the porch of a mud hut with his back pressed against the wall. The angle of the camera had shortened his body and lower limbs, which looked dwarfed and shrivelled but showed his smiling face looking up from an extended neck and his eyes were wide with a joyful expectation. An elderly woman was evidently caught unawares surfacing from a dip into the water of a pond. She sported a broad coy smile but had squeezed her eyes shut in order to hide her embarrassment.

There were many more and he sifted through— a face ardently held between two palms, as if one was adoring oneself; a peasant bending down with a sickle in his hand, turning a beaming face to someone outside the frame, the verdant background somehow blurred below a dull sky. These were all black and white photographs, but they seemed to have a colour of their own, and in them were frozen smiling elderly faces, each captured during a happy moment, unencumbered by any anticipation about a future misery or by any grief from a past mishap. The eyes looked lively, sparkling from an inner joy, the wrinkled coarse skin alive with an unearthly shine.

Only two photographs in this group were in colour. One showed an old bearded man with his head leaning proudly against a thick wooden column that had lost its paint and was chipped at places. The other one had caught a much younger woman, in full frontal view, animated and coming forward, her head inclined regally to one side. These two, Ved could recognise immediately. They were Rahamat, the old khansama in Monabari and Keka Burman, Mahen's wife. There was also a brown envelope with a letter and a few signed but blank cheques. The letter was an official instruction to a particular bank manager on how to disburse an account. Ved looked at the letter and at the men and women in the photographs.

'Only seven people were present during his last journey. In a signal act of respect and love they hung on the walls around the painter's lifeless body all the paintings van Gogh had done in Auverse, took off their hats and stood there till the hearse came to carry the body away.' Mr Chatterjee had narrated the last journey of Vincent van Gogh from *Lust for Life*, a chronicle of a man's savage passion to touch life through art, passions so severe as to make their contentment impossible in the world he lived.

Ved picked up the loose large prints of the images created by Kanu Chatterjee, the images that he wanted to be as pure and faithful as sunflowers and then lined them up against the walls one after another, holding them in place with his books. He switched on all the lights of his room before going to bed.

***

When he woke up next morning, it was already ten past nine. With a cup of tea, he stood on the balcony of his quarters and watched the hospital gradually coming alive. Till a few years ago the road passing by this hospital, at this time of the day, would be as quiet as a backstreet in a small city. Buses from a lone route serviced this place only once in an hour. Few people living in the houses around here then had cars. Now there was a profusion of them. The old cycle rickshaws that carried people from the main bus routes, however, still existed and so did the families that would come with their torn old baggage and beddings prepared to make a temporary dwelling under any of the large trees at the back of the hospital and wait in fascination for their turn to enter the new cool stylish buildings.

Ved went back to his room, retrieved Nanu's two-page fax from the bedside table and came back to the verandah to read it carefully again.

The new drug was a gift from nature. The wise men of the past were right. There are always enough elixirs around us, in the water and in the soil, in the small bushes and in the large trees, in their fruits and leaves and flowers, even in the wind that carries their fragrance. Only people had lost touch with them. Nature was generous enough to keep this drug not only in the barks of the yew trees but in their leaves too. Every year as the trees would burgeon with new leaves, people would have new sources of medicine. The trees need not be cut; the forests can be preserved.

Ved stood and watched the morning growing older around him. Just in front and below where he stood, the open ground and the brick red path were now full of people as they crisscrossed between the buildings like busy ants. On his right side, the coconut and palm trees guarded the older part of the hospital. On his left, the new additions hovered against each other with their stylish facades. There, windows with glass panes set in black cast iron frames formed long lines of rectangular boxes. At the topmost level, at the extreme left, and above the tall Debdaru trees, a panel of panes, distinct from the others, jutted out. They had white steel frames around smoky gray glasses. Ved's gaze became fixed on one of those opaque panes protecting a cool interior from the sun and wind of the outside world.

There, behind that window, reposing between clean white sheets and surrounded by machines that churned out graphs and charts, a man was sailing through the twilight of an unknown world. Nobody around him knew that man. Nobody knew if he had thoughts of his own. Nobody knew for sure at present, while a machine forced the breath of life into him, whether he was on a journey to this or that side of the world. Nobody knew if he was at that moment decaying little by little, becoming more dead than alive with every passing moment, and if his soul had already separated from his body and was meeting his God, the God, he hoped would be a good man to him. Nobody knew either if there would still be a tomorrow for the renewal of his travel.

Or, there would be, merely, a few more days for him to hang on in a dark corner, away from sunlit yellow fields. Which, for that matter, was never important. In the first place.